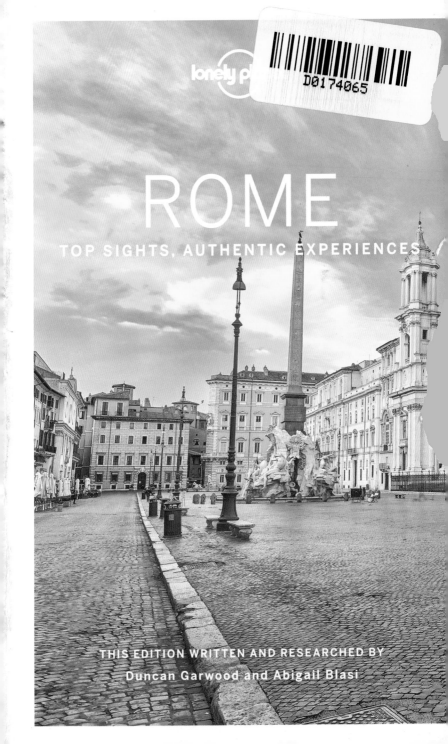

lonely pl

ROME

TOP SIGHTS, AUTHENTIC EXPERIENCES

THIS EDITION WRITTEN AND RESEARCHED BY
Duncan Garwood and Abigail Blasi

Lonely Planet's
Rome

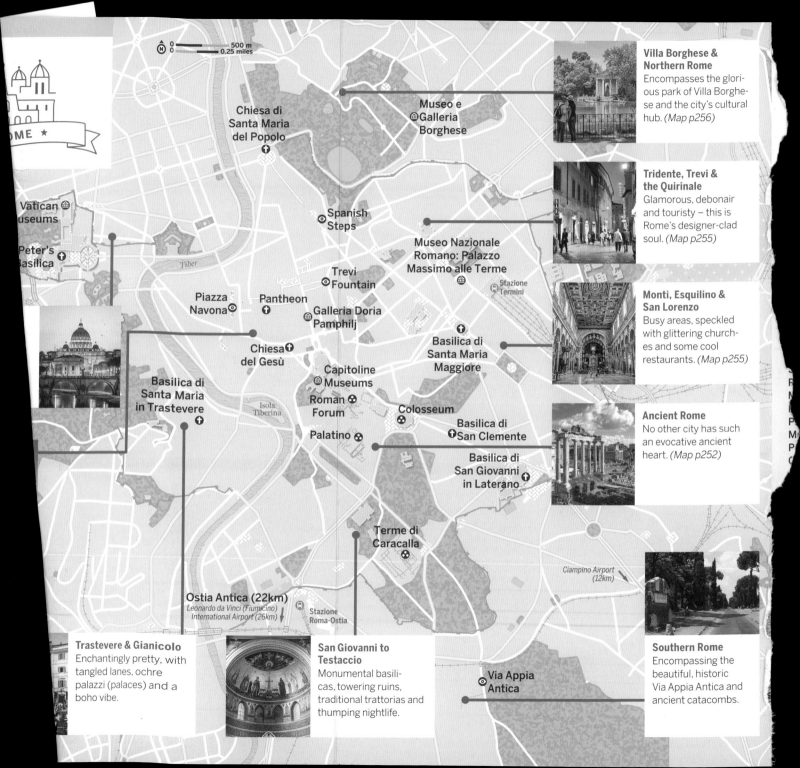

ROME ★

Villa Borghese & Northern Rome
Encompasses the glorious park of Villa Borghese and the city's cultural hub. (Map p256)

Tridente, Trevi & the Quirinale
Glamorous, debonair and touristy – this is Rome's designer-clad soul. (Map p255)

Monti, Esquilino & San Lorenzo
Busy areas, speckled with glittering churches and some cool restaurants. (Map p255)

Ancient Rome
No other city has such an evocative ancient heart. (Map p252)

Southern Rome
Encompassing the beautiful, historic Via Appia Antica and ancient catacombs.

San Giovanni to Testaccio
Monumental basilicas, towering ruins, traditional trattorias and thumping nightlife.

Trastevere & Gianicolo
Enchantingly pretty, with tangled lanes, ochre palazzi (palaces) and a boho vibe.

Chiesa di Santa Maria del Popolo

Museo e Galleria Borghese

Vatican Museums

Peter's Basilica

Spanish Steps

Museo Nazionale Romano: Palazzo Massimo alle Terme

Stazione Termini

Trevi Fountain

Piazza Navona

Pantheon

Galleria Doria Pamphilj

Tiber

Chiesa del Gesù

Basilica di Santa Maria Maggiore

Basilica di Santa Maria in Trastevere

Capitoline Museums

Roman Forum

Isola Tiberina

Colosseum

Basilica di San Clemente

Palatino

Basilica di San Giovanni in Laterano

Terme di Caracalla

Ciampino Airport (12km)

Ostia Antica (22km)
Leonardo da Vinci (Fiumicino) International Airport (26km)

Stazione Roma-Ostia

Via Appia Antica

500 m
0.25 miles

*An ancie
metropo
of haunt
awe-ins
made fo
piazza
memori*

Rome
over th
artisti
icons
Pantl
(cap
and
role
les
ce
ar
s
t

Vatican City, Borgo & Prati
Home to a stunning wealth of artistic treasures.

Centro Storico
The city's tangled historic centre is packed with incredible sights. *(Map p250)*

FROM LEFT: WEERAKARN SATITNIRAMAI, PHILIP GAME, GREG ELMS, WIN-
INITIATIVE, DIGITALER LUMPENSAMMLER, DE AGOSTINI/G. NIMATALLAH,
EURASIA/ROBERTHARDING, MARCO BOTTIGELLI, PENNAPAZZA /GETTY IMAGES ©

Plan Your Trip
This Year in Rome

2017

Rome

Rome's calendar bursts with events, ranging from traditional neighbourhood shindigs and saints' days to shopping bonanzas, catwalk parades and major cultural festivals.

Above: Natale di Roma (p9)

Top Festivals & Events

Carnevale – 26 Feb (p7)
Natale di Roma – 21 Apr (p9)
Lungo il Tevere – Summer (p11)
Romaeuropa – Late Sep to Dec (p14)

Plan Your Trip
This Year in Rome

January

As New Year celebrations fade, the winter cold digs in. It's a quiet time of year but the winter sales are a welcome diversion.

6 January
✿ Epiphany
A witch known as La Befana delivers gifts to Italian kids for Epiphany, the last day of the Christmas holidays. To mark the occasion, a costumed procession makes its way down Via Concilizione to St Peter's Square.

17 January
✿ Festa di Sant'Antonio Abate
Animal-lovers take their pets to be blessed at the Chiesa di Sant'Eusabio on Piazza Vittorio Emanuele in honour of the patron saint of animals.

Late January
☆ Alta Roma
Fashionistas descend on town for the winter outing of Rome's top fashion event. Catwalk shows, held in venues across town, provide sneak previews of seasonal collections by local and international designers.

PAOLO CIPRIANI/ GETTY IMAGES ©

7 January
🛍 Shopping Sales
The first Saturday of the month sees bargain hunters descend on the city's shops for the winter sales. Until mid-February stores offer savings of between 20% and 50%.

February

Rome's winter quiet is shattered by high-spirited carnival celebrations, which signal that spring is on the way.

5 February

☆ Six Nations Rugby

The Azzurri kick off the Six Nations rugby tournament against Wales at the Stadio Olimpico. Further home matches follow on 11 February (against Ireland) and 11 March (against France).

14 February

☆ Valentine's Day

Romance breaks out across town. Some museums and galleries offer two-for-one ticket discounts while restaurants prepare special St Valentine Day's menus. Book early.

Mid-February

☆ Equilibrio Festival della Danza Nuova

The Auditorium Parco della Musica stages emerging talents and affirmed international choreographers at this festival of contemporary dance.

26 February

☆ Carnevale

In the days leading up to Carnevale, Rome really goes to town with leaping horse shows on Piazza del Popolo, costumed parades down Via del Corso, street performers on Piazza Navona, and crowds of kids in fancy dress.

Carnevale parade

LUIGI DE POMPEIS / ALAMY STOCK PHOTO ©

Plan Your Trip
This Year in Rome

March

The onset of spring brings blooming flowers, rising temperatures and unpredictable rainfall. Unless Easter falls in late March, the city is fairly subdued and low-season prices still apply.

15 March

☉ Re-Enactment of Caesar's Death

Romans remember the assassination of Caesar on the Ides of March, 44 BC. To get everyone in the mood, costumed performers re-enact the stabbing on the very spot it happened, in the ruins of Largo di Torre Argentina.

19 March

🎉 Festa di San Giuseppe

The Feast of St Joseph is celebrated in the Trionfale neighbourhood. Little stalls are set up to serve *fritelle* (fried pastries) and there's usually a market near the church of San Giuseppe.

Around 18 & 19 March

☉ Giornate FAI di Primavera

Palazzi, churches and archaeological sites that are generally closed to the public open their doors for a weekend of special openings, courtesy of Italy's main conservation body, the Fondo Ambiente Italiano.

Late March

🏃 Maratona di Roma

Sightseeing becomes sport at Rome's annual marathon (www.maratonadiroma.it). The 42km route starts and finishes near the Colosseum, taking in many of the city's big attractions.

Maratona di Roma

PACIFIC PRESS/CONTRIBUTOR/GETTY IMAGES ©

April

April is a great month, with lovely, sunny weather, fervent Easter celebrations, azaleas on the Spanish Steps and Rome's birthday festivities. Expect high-season prices.

14–17 April

☘ Easter

On Good Friday the pope leads a candlelit procession around the Colosseum, and there are other smaller parades around the city. At noon on Easter Sunday (16 April) the Pope blesses the crowds in St Peter's Square.

Mid-April

◉ Mostra delle Azalee

From mid-April to early May the Spanish Steps are decorated with 600 vases of blooming, brightly coloured azaleas.

21 April

☘ Natale di Roma

Rome celebrates its birthday with music, historical re-creations and fireworks. Events are staged throughout the city but the focus is Campidoglio and Circo Massimo.

25 April

☘ Festa della Liberazione

Schools, shops and offices shut as Rome commemorates the liberation of Italy by Allied troops and resistance forces in 1945.

From left: Azaleas on the Spanish Steps; Natale di Roma
STEFANO PATERNA/ROBERT HARDING ©; EMIPRESS/SHUTTERSTOCK ©

Plan Your Trip
This Year in Rome

May

May is a busy, high-season month. The weather's perfect – usually warm enough to eat outside – and the city is looking gorgeous with blue skies and spring flowers.

1 May

☆ Primo Maggio
Thousands of fans troop to Piazza di San Giovanni in Laterano for Rome's free May Day rock concert. It's a mostly Italian affair with big-name local performers, but you might catch the occasional foreign guest star.

15 May

☆ Italian Open Tennis Tournament
The world's top tennis stars bash it out on the clay courts of the Foro Italico at the Internazionali BNL d'Italia, one of Europe's major tournaments.

Late May

☆ Coppa Italia Final
Football fans fill the Stadio Olimpico for the final of Italy's main football cup. Neither of Rome's two sides have won since Lazio raised the trophy in 2013.

Late May

☆ Show Jumping
Villa Borghese sets the attractive stage for Rome's annual horse-jumping event, known officially as the Concorso Ippico Internazionale di Piazza di Siena.

From left: Primo Maggio; Show jumping

June

Summer has arrived and with it hot weather and the Italian school holidays.

2 June

✿ Festa della Repubblica

A big military parade along Via dei Fori Imperiali is the highlight of ceremonial events held to commemorate the birth of the Italian Republic in 1946. Presiding is the President of the Republic and other assorted worthies.

Mid-June

☆ Isola del Cinema

The Isola Tiberina provides the picturesque backdrop for this open-air film festival (www.isoladelcinema.com), which screens a range of Italian and international films with a focus on independent productions.

23 June

✿ Festa di San Giovanni

The feast day of St John the Baptist is commemorated around the Basilica di San Giovanni in Laterano. Traditionally, stewed snails and *porchetta* (herbed suckling pig) are served.

29 June

✿ Festa dei Santi Pietro e Paolo

Rome celebrates its two patron saints, Peter and Paul, with a mass at St Peter's Basilica and a street fair on Via Ostiense near the Basilica di San Paolo Fuori-le-Mura.

Late June

☆ Roma Incontro Il Mondo

Villa Ada (www.villaada.org) is transformed into a colourful multiethnic village for this popular annual event. There's a laid-back party vibe and an excellent program of concerts ranging from Roman rap to jazz and world music.

GARI WYN WILLIAMS / ALAMY STOCK PHOTO ©/ARTWORK BY ALBA GONZALES

Summer

✿ Lungo il Tevere

Nightly crowds converge on the river Tiber for this popular summer-long event. Stalls, clubs, bars, restaurants and dance floors line the river bank as Rome's nightlife goes al fresco.

Plan Your Trip
This Year in Rome

July

Hot summer temperatures make sightseeing a physical endeavour, but come the cool of evening, the city's streets burst into life as locals come out to enjoy summer festivities.

June–July

☆ Rock in Roma

Dust down the denims for Rome's big rock fest. Headline acts from recent editions have included Iron Maiden, Bruce Springsteen and Primal Scream.

July–Early August

☆ Opera at the Terme di Caracalla

The hulking ruins of a vast 2nd-century baths complex provide the spectacular setting for the Teatro dell'Opera di Roma's summer season. Also ballet and the occasional rock concert.

July

☆ Luglio Suona Bene

From Sting to Santana, music legends take to the outdoor stage at the Auditorium Parco della Musica for a month-long series of concerts held as part of the Luglio Suona Bene (July Sounds Good) festival.

Mid-July

☆ Invito alla Danza

Rome's oldest dance festival provides a showcase for traditional and experimental dance. Top international performers take to the stage at the Teatro Villa Pamphilj.

Late July

❀ Festa de' Noantri

Trastevere celebrates its roots with a raucous street party in the last two weeks of the month. Centred on Piazza Santa Maria, events kick off with a religious procession and continue with much eating, drinking, dancing and praying.

BIGPILESTOCK / ALAMY STOCK PHOTO ©

June–October

❀ Estate Romana

Rome's big summer festival (www.estateromana.comune.roma.it) involves everything from concerts and dance performances to book fairs, puppet shows and late-night museum openings.

August

08

Rome melts in the heat as locals flee the city for their summer holidays. Many businesses shut down but hoteliers offer discounts and there are loads of summer events to enjoy.

June–September

✿ Gay Village

The big annual event in Rome's gay calendar is held between June and September, usually at the Parco del Ninfeo in EUR. Expect huge crowds, DJs, dance music, film screenings, cabarets and theatrical performances.

5 August

✿ Festa della Madonna della Neve

On 5 August rose petals are showered on celebrants in the Basilica di Santa Maria Maggiore to commemorate a miraculous 4th-century snowfall.

15 August

✿ Ferragosto

The Festival of the Assumption is celebrated with almost total shutdown, as what seems like Rome's entire population decamps to the sea.

20 August

☆ Football Season Starts

While the rest of Italy basks in the summer sun, the nation's footballers return to work. The Serie A season kicks off around 20 August and the city's ardent fans can finally get their weekly fix.

A S Roma fans watching football at the Stadio Olimpico (p198)

Plan Your Trip
This Year in Rome

September

Life returns to the city after the August torpor. The kids go back to school and locals return to work but there's still a relaxed summer vibe and the weather's perfect.

June–September

◉ Night Visits
A lot of Rome's headline sights offer night visits over the summer and through September. In past years, these have included the Colosseum and Vatican Museums.

Mid-September

✗ Taste of Rome
Foodies flock to the Auditorium Parco della Musica to revel in world food. Join Rome's top chefs for tastings, performances and three days of food-related events. Check www.tasteofroma.it.

Late September

♟ Clubbing
Late September is a good time for party-goers as the city's main clubs return to town after their summer exodus. Curtain-raiser events are a guarantee of big nights and sweaty dance floors.

Late September– Early December

☆ Romaeuropa
Established international performers join emerging stars at Rome's premier dance and drama festival (www.romaeuropa.net). Events range from avant-garde dance performances to installations and readings.

From left: Roman cuisine; Orchestra dell'Accademia Nazionale di Santa Cecilia, Auditorium Parco della Musica (p192)
CARLO A/GETTY IMAGES ©; B O'KANE / ALAMY STOCK PHOTO ©

10
October

Autumn is a good time to visit – the warm weather is holding, Romaeuropa ensures plenty of cultural action and, with the schools back, there are far fewer tourists around.

Early October

☆ Start of Santa Cecilia Symphony Season

Rome's premier orchestra, the Orchestra dell'Accademia Nazionale di Santa Cecilia, returns to its home stage at the Auditorium Parco della Musica for the start of the symphonic season. For concert details see www.santacecilia.it.

Early October–January

✦ Fotografia Festival

Photographs covering a range of styles and subjects are juxtaposed against the contemporary architecture of the MACRO modern art museum at Rome's premier photographic festival (www.fotografia festival.it).

Late October– Mid-December

☆ Chamber Music Concerts

Designed by baroque genius Francesco Borromini, the Chiesa di Sant'Agnese in Agone on Piazza Navona hosts a series of chamber music concerts.

B O'KANE / ALAMY STOCK PHOTO ©

Mid-October

✦ Festa del Cinema di Roma

Held at the Auditorium Parco della Musica in mid-October, Rome's film festival rolls out the red carpet for Hollywood hotshots and bigwigs from Italian cinema. Consult the program at www.romacinemafest.it.

Plan Your Trip
This Year in Rome

November

Although the wettest month, November has its compensations – low-season prices, excellent jazz concerts and no queues outside the big sights. Autumn is also great for foodies.

1 November

✿ Ognissanti

Celebrated as a national holiday, All Saints' Day commemorates the Saint Martyrs, while All Souls' Day, on 2 November, is set aside to honour the deceased. Many Romans leave flowers on tombs at the Cimitero di Campo Verano.

Mid-November

☆ Festival Internazionale di Musica e Arte Sacra

Over several days in mid-November, the Vienna Philharmonic Orchestra and other top ensembles perform a series of classical concerts in Rome's four papal basilicas and other churches. Check the program at www.festivalmusicaeartesacra.net.

Late November

☆ Start of Opera Season

Towards the end of November the opera season gets underway at the Teatro dell'Opera di Roma, the city's opera house. The theatre is also home to Rome's principal ballet corps with the dance season starting in December.

VINZO/ GETTY IMAGES ©

Mid-November

☆ Rome Jazz Festival

For jazz fans, the Auditorium Parco della Musica is the place to be in mid-November, as performers from around the world play to appreciative audiences during the three-week Roma Jazz Festival (www.romajazz festival.it).

December

The build-up to Christmas feels festive, as the city twinkles in anticipation. Every church has a presepe (nativity scene) displayed, from intricate small tableaux to life-sized extravaganzas.

6 December

🏠 Piazza Navona Christmas Fair

Rome's most beautiful baroque square becomes a big, brash marketplace as brightly lit market stalls set up shop, selling everything from nativity scenes to stuffed toys and teeth-cracking *torrone* (nougat).

8 December

✿ Immaculate Conception

Tradition dictates that the Pope, in his capacity as the Bishop of Rome, celebrates the Immaculate Conception in Piazza di Spagna. Earlier in the day Rome's fire brigade place a garland of flowers atop the Colonna dell'Immaculata in adjacent Piazza Mignanelli.

Early December

☉ Christmas Lights

Crowds fill Via del Corso for the annual switching on of the Christmas lights early in December. Over the river in the Vatican, a huge Christmas tree and life-sized nativity scene adorn St Peter's Square.

31 December

✿ Capodanno

Rome is a noisy place to be on New Year's Eve as big firework displays usher in the new year and outdoor concerts are held across town, most notably on Piazzas del Quirinale and del Popolo.

RICHARD I'ANSON/GETTY IMAGES ©

Piazza Navona Christmas Fair

Plan Your Trip
Need to Know

Daily Costs

Budget
Less than €100

- Dorm bed: €15–€30
- Double room in a budget hotel: €50–€110
- Pizza or pasta: €6–€12

Midrange
€100–250

- Double room in a hotel: €110–€200
- Lunch and dinner in local restaurants: €25–€45
- Museum admission: €4–€15
- Roma Pass, a three-day card covering museum entry and public transport: €36

Top End
More than €250

- Double room in a four- or five-star hotel: €200–€450
- Top restaurant dinner: over €45
- Opera ticket: €40–€200
- City-centre taxi ride: €10–€15
- Auditorium concert ticket: €25–€90

Advance Planning

- **Two months before** Book high-season accommodation.
- **Three to four weeks before** Check for concerts at www.auditorium.com and www.operaroma.it.
- **One to two weeks before** Reserve tables at A-list restaurants. Sort out tickets to the pope's weekly audience at St Peter's.
- **Few days before** Book for the Museo e Galleria Borghese (compulsory) and for the Vatican Museums (advisable to avoid queues).

Useful Websites

- **Lonely Planet** (www.lonelyplanet.com/rome) Destination low-down, hotel bookings and traveller forum.
- **060608** (www.060608.it) Rome's official tourist website.
- **Coopculture** (www.coopculture.it) Information and ticket booking for Rome's monuments.
- **Vatican Museums** (www.vatican.va) Book tickets and avoid the queues.
- **Auditorium** (www.auditorium.com) Check concert listings.

Currency

Euro (€)

Language

Italian

Visas

Not required by EU citizens. Not required by nationals of Australia, Canada, New Zealand and the USA for stays of up to 90 days.

Money

ATMs are widespread. Major credit cards are widely accepted but some smaller shops, trattorias and *pensioni* (small hotels or guesthouses) might not take them.

Mobile Phones

Local SIM cards can be used in European, Australian and unlocked US phones. Other phones must be set to roaming.

Time

Western European Time (GMT/UTC plus one hour)

For more, see the **Survival Guide** (p233)

When to Go

In spring and early autumn there's good weather and many festivals and outdoor events. It's also busy and peak rates apply.

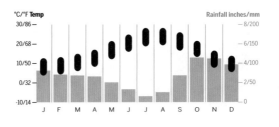

°C/°F Temp — Rainfall inches/mm

J F M A M J J A S O N D

Arriving in Rome

○ Leonardo da Vinci (Fiumicino) Airport
Direct trains to Stazione Termini run from 6.23am to 11.23pm, €14; slower trains run to Trastevere, Ostiense and Tiburtina stations from 5.57am to 10.42pm, €8; buses to Stazione Termini from 5.35am to midnight, €4 to €9; private transfers cost from €13 per person; taxis cost €48 (fixed fare to within the Aurelian walls).

○ Ciampino Airport Buses to Stazione Termini run from 7.45am to 11.59pm, €4; private transfers cost from €13 per person; taxis cost €30 (fixed fare to within the Aurelian walls).

○ Stazione Termini Airport buses and trains as well as international trains arrive at Stazione Termini. From here, continue by bus, metro or taxi.

Getting Around

Rome's main public-transport hub is Stazione Termini, the only point at which the city's two main metro lines cross. The metro is quicker than surface transport but the network is limited and the bus is often a better bet. Children under 10 travel free.

○ Metro The main lines are: A (orange; 5.30am to 9.30pm Thursday to Sunday, replacement bus MA1–MA2 to 11.30pm, to 1.30am Saturday) and B (blue; 5.30am to 11.30pm Monday to Thursday, to 1.30am Friday and Saturday).

○ Buses Most routes pass through Stazione Termini. Buses run 5.30am to midnight, with limited services throughout the night.

Sleeping

Rome is expensive and with the city busy year-round, you'll want to book as far ahead as you can to secure the best deal and the place you want.

Accommodation options range from palatial five-star hotels to hostels, B&Bs, convents, *pensioni* (small hotels or guesthouses) and a good range of Airbnb options. Hostels are the cheapest, offering dorm beds and private rooms. B&Bs range from simple homestyle set-ups to chic boutique outfits with prices to match, while religious institutions provide basic, value-for-money accommodation but may insist on a curfew. Hotels are plentiful and there are many budget, family-run *pensioni* in the Termini area.

Plan Your Trip
Top Days in Rome

JULIAN ELLIOTT PHOTOGRAPHY / GETTY IMAGES ©

Ancient Rome

The Colosseum is an appropriate high on which to start your odyssey in Rome. Next, head to the nearby crumbling scenic ruins of the Palatino, followed by the Roman Forum. After lunch enjoy 360-degree views from Il Vittoriano and classical art at the Capitoline Museums.

❶ Colosseum (p36)

More than any other monument, it's the Colosseum that symbolises the power and glory of ancient Rome. Visit its broken interior and imagine the roar of the 50,000-strong crowd as the gladiators fought for their entertainment.

⭕ Colosseum to Palatino

🚶 Walk south down the Via di San Gregorio to the Palatino.

❷ Palatino (p60)

The gardens and ruins of the Palatino (included with the Colosseum ticket) are an atmospheric place to explore, with great views across Circo Massimo and the Roman Forum. The Palatino was the most exclusive part of ancient Rome, home of the imperial palace, and is still today a hauntingly beautiful site.

⭕ Palatino to Roman Forum

🚶 Still in the Palatino, follow the path down past the Vigna Barberino to enter the Roman Forum near the Arco di Tito.

Day
01

MAREMAGNUM/GETTY IMAGES ©

3 Roman Forum (p80)

Sprawled beneath the Palatino, the Forum was the empire's nerve centre, a teeming hive of law courts, temples, piazzas and shops. See where the vestal virgins lived and the Curia, where senators debated matters of state.

➲ Roman Forum to Terre e Domus

🥾 Exit the Forum onto Via dei Fori Imperiali and head up Via Alessandrina through the Imperial Forums to Terre e Domus near Trajan's Column.

4 Lunch at Terre e Domus (p124)

Lunch on earthy Lazio food and wine at this bright modern restaurant just off Piazza Venezia.

➲ Terre e Domus to Il Vittoriano

🥾 Return to Piazza Venezia and follow up to the mountainous monument Il Vittoriano.

5 Il Vittoriano (p75)

Il Vittoriano is an ostentatious, overpowering mountain of white marble. Love it or hate it,

it's an impressive sight, but for an even more mind-blowing view, take the glass lift to the top and you'll be rewarded with 360-degree views across the whole of Rome.

➲ Il Vittoriano to Campidoglio & Capitoline Museums

🥾 Descend from Il Vittoriano and head left to the sweeping staircase, La Cordonata. Climb the stairs to reach Piazza del Campidoglio and the Capitoline Museums.

6 Campidoglio & Capitoline Museums (p72)

With wonderful views over the Forum, the piazza atop the Capitoline hill (Campidoglio) was designed by Michelangelo and is flanked by the world's oldest national museums. The Capitoline Museums harbour some of Rome's most spectacular ancient art, including the iconic depiction of Romulus and Remus sat under a wolf, the *Lupa capitolina*.

From left: Tempio di Saturno (p82), Roman Forum; Il Vittoriano (p75)

Plan Your Trip
Top Days in Rome

NIKADA/GETTY IMAGES ©

Vatican City & Centro Storico

On day two, hit the Vatican. Blow your mind at the Sistine Chapel and Vatican Museums, then complete your tour at St Peter's Basilica. Dedicate the afternoon to sniffing around the historic centre, including Piazza Navona and the Pantheon.

❶ Vatican Museums (p40)

With more than 7km of exhibits, it'd be hard to see it all in a morning, but make a beeline for the Pinacoteca, the Museo Pio-Clementino, Galleria delle Carte Geografiche, Stanze di Raffaello (Raphael Rooms) and the Sistine Chapel.

◑ Vatican Museums to Fa-Bio

🀰 From the Vatican Museums entrance, turn downhill and follow the walls towards Piazza del Risorgimento. Take a left down Via Vespasiano and then the first right to Via Germanico and Fa-Bio.

❷ Lunch at Fa-Bìo (p132)

Grab a light lunch bite at this tiny takeaway. It's very popular so you'll need to squeeze through to the counter to order your *panino* (sandwich), salad or smoothie, all made with quality organic products.

◑ Fa-Bio to St Peter's Basilica

🀰 From the takeaway, double back to Piazza del Risorgimento, then follow the crowds to reach St Peter's Basilica.

Day

02

ARTIE PHOTOGRAPHY (ARTIE NG)/GETTY IMAGES ©

❸ St Peter's Basilica (p46)

Approaching St Peter's Square from the side, you'll see it as Bernini intended: a surprise. Visit this beautiful public square and the church itself, home to Michelangelo's *Pietà* and a breathtaking dome – it's worth climbing the latter for astounding views.

◗ St Peter's Basilica to Castel Sant'Angelo

🕴 From near St Peter's Square, walk along the Borgo Sant'Angelo to reach Castel Sant'Angelo.

❹ Castel Sant'Angelo (p49)

If you're not feeling overwhelmed by sightseeing, visit the interior of this ancient Roman tomb that became a fortress.

◗ Castel Sant'Angelo to Piazza Navona

🕴 Cross the river via the pedestrianised Ponte Sant'Angelo, then follow the river eastwards for around 300m before turning right inland at the next bridge, following Via G Zanardelli to reach Piazza Navona.

❺ Piazza Navona (p64)

This vast baroque square is a showpiece of the *centro storico,* and full of vibrant life.

The lozenge-shaped space is an echo of its ancient origins as the site of a stadium.

◗ Piazza Navona to Pantheon

🕴 It's a short walk eastwards from Piazza Navona to Piazza della Rotonda, where you'll find the Pantheon.

❻ Pantheon (p50)

This 2000-year-old temple, now a church, is an extraordinary building, the innovative design of which has served to inspire generations of architects and engineers.

◗ Pantheon to Armando al Pantheon

🕴 There are plenty of excellent restaurants around the Pantheon, and Armando al Pantheon, within sight of the temple, is one of Rome's best local restaurants.

❼ Dinner at Armando al Pantheon (p127)

Go for a taste of authentic Roman cuisine at long-time favourite Armando al Pantheon.

From left: St Peter's Square (p49); Castel Sant'Angelo (p49)

Plan Your Trip
Top Days in Rome

RACHEL LEWIS/GETTY IMAGES ©

Villa Borghese, Tridente & Trevi

Start your day at the brilliant Museo e Galleria Borghese, before rambling around the shady avenues of the surrounding park of Villa Borghese. Next, explore the Tridente neighbourhood, including the Spanish Steps and Via dei Condotti, before heading to the Trevi Fountain.

❶ Museo e Galleria Borghese (p54)

Book ahead and start your day at the Museo e Galleria Borghese, one of Rome's best art museums. The highlight is a series of astonishing sculptures by baroque genius Gian Lorenzo Bernini.

➲ Museo e Galleria Borghese to Villa Borghese

🏃 Work your way through the leafy paths of Villa Borghese towards the Pincio.

❷ Villa Borghese (p57)

Meander through the lovely, rambling park of Villa Borghese, formerly the playground of the mighty Borghese family. En route you'll pass the Piazza di Siena and walk along tree-shaded lanes to reach the Pincio, a panoramic terrace offering great views across Rome.

➲ Villa Borghese to the Spanish Steps

🏃 From the Pincio, exit along Viale Gabriele D'Annunzio and follow on to the top of the Spanish Steps.

Day

03

RICHARD CUMMINS/GETTY IMAGES ©

❸ Spanish Steps (p100)

The Spanish Steps are a glorious flight of ornamental rococo steps, with views over the glittering, designer-store-packed streets of the Tridente district and Piazza di Spagna.

↻ The Spanish Steps to Via dei Condotti

🚶 Walk down the Spanish Steps to Via dei Condotti.

❹ Via dei Condotti (p151)

Via dei Condotti is Rome's most exclusive shopping street, lined by big-name designers and jewellers such as Prada, Bulgari, Fendi and Salvatore Ferragamo. Even if you haven't got cash to splash, it's well worth a wander to window-shop and people-watch.

↻ Via dei Condotti to Enoteca Regionale Palatium

🚶 From Via Condotti, turn south along Via Belsiana to reach the Enoteca Regionale Palatium.

❺ Lunch at Enoteca Regionale Palatium (p130)

Specialising in produce from Lazio, this sleek wine bar is a great place to try local wines and delicacies, such as Frascati white wine and *porchetta* (pork roasted with herbs).

↻ Enoteca Regionale Palatium to Piazza Del Popolo

🚶 Returning along Via Belsiana, turn right at Via Vittoria, then left at Via del Babuino, to reach Piazza del Popolo.

❻ Piazza del Popolo (p89)

The huge, oval Piazza del Popolo dates from the 16th century and is overlooked by Chiesa di Santa Maria del Popolo, which contains a remarkable array of masterpieces.

↻ Piazza del Popolo to Trevi Fountain

🚶 Walk back along Via del Corso, then turn left up Via Sabini to reach the Trevi Fountain.

❼ Trevi Fountain (p86)

End your day at this foaming, fantastical baroque fountain designed by Nicola Salvi, where you can toss in a coin to ensure a return visit to Rome.

From left: View from Pincio Hill Gardens (p58); Spanish Steps (p100) and Chiesa della Trinità dei Monti (p101)

Plan Your Trip
Top Days in Rome

VITO ARCOMANO/ALAMY STOCK PHOTO ©

Southern Rome, Monti & Trastevere

On your fourth day, venture out to Via Appia Antica and the catacombs. Start the afternoon by visiting the Museo Nazionale Romano: Palazzo Massimo alle Terme, then drop by the Basilica di Santa Maria Maggiore. Finish with an evening in Trastevere.

Day

04

❶ Catacombe di San Sebastiano (p78)

Start your day underground, by taking a tour of one of the three networks of catacombs that are open to the public. It's a fascinating and chilling experience to see the tunnels where early Christians buried their dead.

○ Catacombe di San Sebastiano to Villa di Massenzio

🏃 Walk around 100m south along Via Appia and you'll see Villa di Massenzio on your left.

❷ Villa di Massenzio (p79)

The best preserved part of Maxentius' 4th-century ruined palace is the Circo di Massenzio, which was once a racetrack with the capacity for 10,000 people.

○ Villa di Massenzio to Mausoleo di Cecilia Metella

🏃 Walk 50m or so onwards along Via Appia to the Mausoleo di Cecilia Metella.

❸ Mausoleo di Cecilia Metella (p79)

With travertine walls and an interior decorated with a sculpted frieze bearing Gaelic

BORIS-B/SHUTTERSTOCK ©

shields, ox skulls and festoons, this great, rotund tomb is an imposing sight.

🔵 Mausoleo di Cecilia to Qui Non se More Mai

🚶 From the tomb, continue up the road for a few metres to Qui Non se More Mai.

④ Lunch at Qui Non se More Mai (p143)

Fortify yourself for the afternoon ahead with a lunch of hearty Roman pasta and expertly grilled meat at this rustic restaurant (closed Sunday and Monday).

🔵 Qui Non se More Mai to Palazzo Massimo alle Terme

🚌 After lunch, hop on a bus to Termini station to visit the Palazzo Massimo alle Terme.

⑤ Museo Nazionale Romano: Palazzo Massimo alle Terme (p68)

This light-filled museum holds part of the Museo Nazionale Romano collection, with a splendid array of classical carving and an unparalleled selection of ancient Roman frescoes.

🔵 Palazzo Massimo alle Terme to Basilica di Santa Maria Maggiore

🚶 Walk about 200m southwest along Via Massimo d'Azeglio to reach Basilica di Santa Maria Maggiore.

⑥ Basilica di Santa Maria Maggiore (p104)

One of Rome's four patriarchal basilicas, this monumental church stands on the summit of the Esquilino hill, on the spot where snow is said to have miraculously fallen in the summer of AD 358.

🔵 Basilica di Santa Maria Maggiore to Trastevere

🚌 From Termini station, which is a short walk from the basilica, you can take a bus to Trastevere.

⑦ Trastevere (p138)

Spend the evening wandering the charismatic streets of Trastevere. This district is as popular with locals as it is with tourists, and is a beguiling place for an evening stroll before settling on a place for dinner.

From left: Villa di Massenzio (p79); people dining on a cobbled street

Plan Your Trip
Hotspots For...

CULTURE VULTURES

⊙ **Museo e Galleria Borghese** Houses the best baroque sculpture in town and some seriously good Old Masters. (p54)

☆ **Auditorium Parco della Musica** (pictured below) Rome's contemporary arts hub occupies a striking Renzo Piano–designed complex. (p192)

✕ **Glass Hostaria** Creative modern food in the heart of atmospheric Trastevere. (p139)

☆ **Alexanderplatz** Get into the swing at Rome's most celebrated jazz club. (p189)

🍷 **Il Tiaso** Modish Pigneto bar with indie art, a chilled vibe and live music. (p173)

⊙ **Trevi Fountain** Throw a coin into the fountain where Anita Ekberg cavorted in *La dolce vita*. (p86)

⊙ **Spanish Steps** (pictured above) Grab a perch and enjoy the parade of people on the piazza below. (p100)

🍷 **Stravinskij Bar** The swank Hotel de Russie provides the setting for stylish cocktails. (p172)

🍷 **Salotto 42** Join the beautiful people for an *aperitivo* at this hip bar. (p172)

🛍 **Fendi** Top up your wardrobe at the flagship store of the Fendi fashion house. (p157)

SPIRITUAL

👁 **St Peter's Basilica** A monument to architectural genius and papal ambition, this is the greatest church in the Catholic world. (p46)

👁 **Vatican Museums** Go face to face with Michelangelo's celebrated frescoes in the Sistine Chapel. (p40)

🏃 **Stadio Olimpico** For football fans a trip to Rome's Olympic stadium is a spiritual experience. (p198)

🍷 **Caffè Sant'Eustachio** The coffee at this busy bar is nothing short of heavenly. (p170)

🍴 **Aroma** Colosseum views and Michelin-starred food are the perfect marriage. (p141)

UNDERGROUND

👁 **Basilica di San Clemente** (pictured above) Duck under this multi-layered basilica to discover a pagan temple and 1st-century house. (p96)

👁 **Via Appia Antica** The Appian Way is home to Rome's most famous catacombs. (p76)

🍴 **Flavio al Velavevodetto** A classic Roman trattoria set in a hill made out of smashed vases. (p140)

🍷 **Lanificio 159** A great factory venue for gigs, club nights, markets and exhibitions. (p182)

🍷 **Locanda Atlantide** Get down and dirty at this basement club. (p176)

HISTORY BUFFS

👁 **Colosseum** Rome's breathtaking arena encapsulates all the drama of ancient Rome. (p36)

👁 **Palatino** According to legend, this is where Romulus and Remus founded Rome. (p60)

🍴 **Armando al Pantheon** A family-run restaurant near the Pantheon, famed for its authentic Roman food. (p127)

🍴 **Chiostro del Bramante Caffè** Enjoy a coffee in the historic confines of a Renaissance cloister. (p125)

⭐ **Terme di Caracalla** (pictured above) Towering Roman ruins set the stage for summer opera. (p98)

Plan Your Trip
What's New

Co.So

Join hipsters, mixologists and aficionados at Co.So (p174), one of the city's new breed of cocktail bars in the bohemian Pigneto district.

Enoteca La Torre

After years of success in Viterbo, chef Danilo Ciavattino has transferred his fine-dining restaurant Enoteca La Torre (p135) to the romantic riverside environs of Villa Laetitia.

Pasticceria De Bellis

Pastry making becomes fine art at Pasticceria De Bellis (p125), a designer pastry shop selling a range of edible mini-masterpieces in the historic centre.

Temakinho

The vibrant Monti neighbourhood sets the stage for sushi, sake and cocktails at the popular Brazilian-Japanese Temakinho (p136).

La Ciambella

A laid-back eatery serving everything from breakfast to pizzas and cocktails, La Ciambella (p126) sits over an ancient baths complex near the Pantheon.

Spot

Refined mid-century furnishings, glassware and objets d'art take centre stage at Spot (p159), a fascinating shop in Monti.

Plan Your Trip
For Free

Need to Know

○ **Transport** Holders of the Roma Pass are entitled to free public transport.

○ **Wi-Fi** Free wi-fi is available in many hostels, hotels, bars and cafes.

○ **Tours** To take a free tour check out www. newromefreetour.com.

Art

Feast on fine art in Rome's churches. They're all free and many contain priceless treasures by big-name artists such as Michelangelo, Raphael, Bernini and Caravaggio. Major art churches include St Peter's Basilica (p46), the Basilica di San Pietro in Vincoli (p105), Chiesa di San Luigi dei Francesi (p67), and Chiesa di Santa Maria del Popolo (p88).

All state-run museums are free on the first Sunday of the month, including the Museo Carlo Bilotti (p59). The Vatican Museums (p40) are free on the last Sunday of the month.

Monuments

Some of Rome's best known sites are free.

A pagan temple turned church, the Pantheon (p50) is a staggering work of architecture with its record-breaking dome and echoing interior.

You don't have to spend a penny to admire the Trevi Fountain (p86), although most people throw a coin in to ensure their return to Rome.

According to legend, if you tell a lie with your hand in the Bocca della Verità (Mouth of Truth; p75), it'll bite your hand off.

Piazzas & Parks

People-watching on Rome's piazzas is a signature city experience. Top spots include Piazza Navona (p64), Campo de' Fiori (p67) and Piazza di Spagna (p101).

It doesn't cost a thing to enjoy Rome's most famous park, Villa Borghese (p57). Greenery can also be found at Villa Celimontana (p99) and Gianicolo.

Above: Piazza Navona (p64)

Plan Your Trip
Family Travel

DOUG OGDEN/DESIGN PICS/GETTY IMAGES ©

Despite a reputation as a highbrow cultural destination, Rome has a lot to offer kids. Child-specific sights might be thin on the ground but if you know where to go there's plenty to keep the little ones occupied and parents happy.

Need to Know

○ **Getting Around** Cobbled streets make getting around with a pram difficult.

○ **Eating Out** In a restaurant ask for a *mezza porzione* (child's portion) and *seggiolone* (highchair).

○ **Supplies** Buy baby formula and sterilising solutions at pharmacies. Disposable nappies (diapers; *pannolini*) are available from supermarkets and pharmacies.

○ **Transport** Under 10s travel free on all public transport.

History for Kids

Everyone wants to see the Colosseum (p36) and it doesn't disappoint, especially if accompanied by tales of bloodthirsty gladiators and hungry lions. For maximum effect prep your kids beforehand with a Rome-based film.

Spook your teens with a trip to the catacombs on Via Appia Antica (p76). These pitch-black tunnels, full of tombs and ancient burial chambers, are fascinating, but not suitable for children under about seven.

Hands-On Activities

Kids love throwing things, so they'll enjoy flinging a coin into the Trevi Fountain (p86). And if they ask, you can tell them that about €3000 is thrown in on an average day.

Another favourite is putting your hand in the Bocca della Verità (p75), the Mouth of Truth. Just don't tell a fib, otherwise the mouth will bite it off.

ILPO MUSTO / ALAMY STOCK PHOTO ©

Food for Kids

Pizza al taglio (by the slice) is a godsend for parents. It's cheap (about €1 buys two slices of *pizza bianca* – with rosemary, salt and olive oil), easy to get hold of (there are hundreds of takeaways around town), and works wonders on flagging spirits.

Ice cream is another manna from heaven, served in *coppette* (tubs) or *coni* (cones). Child-friendly flavours include *fragola* (strawberry), *cioccolato* (chocolate) and *bacio* (with hazelnuts).

Run in the Park

When the time comes to let the kids off the leash, head to Villa Borghese (p57), the most central of Rome's main parks. There's plenty of space to run around in – though it's not absolutely car-free – and you can hire family bikes.

A Family Day Out

Many of Rome's ancient ruins can be boring for children – they just look like piles of

Best Food Stops

Forno Roscioli (p124)
Fatamorgana (p138)
Gelateria del Teatro (p125)
Forno di Campo de' Fiori (p125)
Trapizzino (p140)

old stones – but Ostia Antica (p94) is different. Here your kids can run along the ancient town's streets, among shops, and up the tiers of its impressive amphitheatre. A trip to Ostia also means a quick ride on a train. However, note that there's little shade on the site so bring water and hats, and take all the usual precautions.

From left: Colosseum (p36); Forno Roscioli (p124)

TOP EXPERIENCES

The very best to see and do

Colosseum

A monument to raw, merciless power, the Colosseum (Colosseo) is the most thrilling of Rome's ancient sights. It was here that gladiators met in mortal combat and condemned prisoners fought off wild beasts in front of baying, bloodthirsty crowds. Two thousand years on and it's Italy's top tourist attraction, drawing more than five million visitors a year.

Great For...

ℹ Need to Know

Map p252; ☏06 3996 7700; www.coop culture.it; Piazza del Colosseo; adult/reduced incl Roman Forum & Palatino €12/7.50; ⊘8.30am-1hr before sunset; ⓜColosseo

★ **Top Tip**

Beat the queues by getting your ticket at the Palatino (Via di San Gregorio 30).

Built by Vespasian (r AD 69–79) in the grounds of Nero's vast Domus Aurea complex, it was inaugurated in AD 80, eight years after it had been commissioned. To mark the occasion, Vespasian's son and successor Titus (r 79–81) staged games that lasted 100 days and nights, during which 5000 animals were slaughtered. Trajan (r 98–117) later topped this, holding a marathon 117-day killing spree involving 9000 gladiators and 10,000 animals.

The 50,000-seat arena was originally known as the Flavian Amphitheatre, and although it was Rome's most fearsome arena it wasn't the biggest – the Circo Massimo could hold up to 250,000 people. The name Colosseum, when introduced in medieval times, was not a reference to its size but to the Colosso di Nerone, a giant statue of Nero that stood nearby.

With the fall of the Roman Empire in the 5th century, the Colosseum was abandoned and gradually became overgrown. In the Middle Ages it served as a fortress for two of the city's warrior families, the Frangipani and the Annibaldi. Later, during the Renaissance and baroque periods, it was plundered of its precious travertine, and marble stripped from it was used to make huge palaces such as Palazzo Venezia, Palazzo Barberini and Palazzo Cancelleria.

More recently, pollution and vibrations caused by traffic and the metro have taken their toll. It has recently undergone a €25-million clean-up, the first in its 2000-year history.

Exterior

The outer walls have three levels of arches, framed by Ionic, Doric and Corinthian

Interior of the Colosseum

columns. These were originally covered in travertine, and marble statues filled the niches on the 2nd and 3rd storeys. The upper level, punctuated with windows and slender Corinthian pilasters, had supports for 240 masts that held up a huge canvas awning over the arena, shielding the spectators from sun and rain. The 80 entrance arches, known as vomitoria, allowed the spectators to enter and be seated in a matter of minutes.

☑ Don't Miss

The hypogeum, a network of dank tunnels that extended beneath the main arena. Visits require advance booking and cost €9 on top of the normal Colosseum ticket.

DEVASHAYAM CHANDRA DHAS/GETTY IMAGES ©

Arena

The arena originally had a wooden floor covered in sand to prevent the combatants from slipping and to soak up the blood. It could also be flooded for mock sea battles. Trapdoors led down to the hypogeum, a subterranean complex of corridors, cages and lifts beneath the arena floor.

Stands

The *cavea,* for spectator seating, was divided into three tiers: magistrates and senior officials sat in the lowest tier, wealthy citizens in the middle, and the plebs in the highest tier. Women (except for vestal virgins) were relegated to the cheapest sections at the top. And as in modern stadiums, tickets were numbered and spectators were assigned a precise seat in a specific sector – in 2015 restorers uncovered traces of red numerals on the arches, indicating how the sectors were numbered. The podium, a broad terrace in front of the tiers of seats, was reserved for the emperor, senators and VIPs.

Hypogeum

The hypogeum served as the stadium's backstage area. Sets for the various battle scenes were prepared here and hoisted up to the arena by a complicated system of pulleys. Caged animals were kept here and gladiators would gather here before show time, having come in through an underground corridor from the nearby Ludus Magnus (Gladiator School).

The hypogeum, and top tier, are open to the public by guided tour only.

✕ Take a Break

Head up to Cavour 313 (p170) for a postarena break. The highlight here is its wine offerings, but you can also snack on cheese and cured-meat platters.

Vatican Museums hallway

IZZET KERIBAR/GETTY IMAGES ©

Vatican Museums

Founded in the 16th century, the Vatican Museums boast one of the world's greatest art collections. Highlights include spectacular classical statuary, rooms frescoed by Raphael, and the Michelangelo-decorated Sistine Chapel.

Great For...

☑ **Don't Miss**

The *Laocoön* and other magnificent sculptures in the Museo Pio-Clementino.

Housing the museums are the lavishly decorated halls and galleries of the Palazzo Apostolico Vaticano. This vast 5.5-hectare complex consists of two palaces – the Vatican palace (nearer to St Peter's) and the Belvedere Palace – joined by two long galleries. Inside are three courtyards: the Cortile della Pigna, the Cortile della Biblioteca and, to the south, the Cortile del Belvedere. You'll never cover it all in one day, so it pays to be selective.

Pinacoteca

Often overlooked by visitors, the papal picture gallery contains Raphael's last work, *La Trasfigurazione* (Transfiguration; 1517–20), and paintings by Giotto, Fra Angelico, Filippo Lippi, Perugino, Titian, Guido Reni, Guercino, Pietro da Cortona, Caravaggio and Leonardo da Vinci, whose haunting *San*

Spiral staircase

WIBOWO RUSLI/GETTY IMAGES ©

ℹ Need to Know

Musei Vaticani; ☏06 6988 4676; http://
mv.vatican.va; Viale Vaticano; adult/reduced
€16/8, last Sun of month free; ⏱9am-4pm
Mon-Sat, 9am-12.30pm last Sun of month;
Ⓜ Ottaviano-San Pietro

✗ Take a Break

Search out Pizzarium (p132) for some
of Rome's best sliced pizza.

★ Top Tip

Avoid queues by booking tickets online (http://biglietteriamusei.vatican.
va/musei/tickets/do); the booking fee
costs €4.

Gerolamo (St Jerome; c 1480) was never
finished.

Museo Chiaramonti & Braccio Nuovo

The Museo Chiaramonti is effectively the
long corridor that runs down the eastern
side of the Belvedere Palace. Its walls are
lined with thousands of statues and busts
representing everything from immortal
gods to playful cherubs and ugly Roman
patricians. Near the end of the hall, off to
the right, is the Braccio Nuovo (New Wing;
currently closed for restoration), which
contains a famous statue of the Nile as a
reclining god covered by 16 babies.

Museo Pio-Clementino

This stunning museum contains some
of the Vatican Museums' finest classical
statuary, including the peerless *Apollo Belvedere* and the 1st-century *Laocoön,* both
in the **Cortile Ottagono** (Octagonal Courtyard). Before you go into the courtyard
take a moment to admire the 1st-century
Apoxyomenos, one of the earliest-known
sculptures to depict a figure with a raised
arm.

To the left as you enter the courtyard, the
Apollo Belvedere is a 2nd-century Roman
copy of a 4th-century-BC Greek bronze.
A beautifully proportioned representation
of the sun god Apollo, it's considered one
of the great masterpieces of classical
sculpture. Nearby, the **Laocoön** depicts a
muscular Trojan priest and his two sons in
mortal struggle with two sea serpents.

Back inside, the **Sala degli Animali** is
filled with sculpted creatures and some
magnificent 4th-century mosaics. Contin-
uing on, you come to the **Sala delle Muse**,
centred on the *Torso Belvedere*, another of
the museum's must-sees. A fragment of a

muscular 1st-century-BC Greek sculpture, this was found in Campo de' Fiori and used by Michelangelo as a model for his *ignudi* (male nudes) in the Sistine Chapel. It's currently undergoing restoration.

The next room, the **Sala Rotonda**, contains a number of colossal statues, including a gilded-bronze *Ercole* (Hercules) and an exquisite floor mosaic. The enormous basin in the centre of the room was found at Nero's Domus Aurea and is made out of a single piece of red porphyry stone.

Museo Gregoriano Egizio

Founded by Gregory XVI in 1839, this museum contains pieces taken from Egypt in Roman times. The collection is small, but there are fascinating exhibits, including the *Trono di Ramses II* (part of a statue of the seated king), vividly painted sarcophagi

dating from around 1000 BC, and some macabre mummies.

Museo Gregoriano Etrusco

At the top of the 18th-century Simonetti staircase, the Museo Gregoriano Etrusco contains artefacts unearthed in the Etruscan tombs of northern Lazio, as well as a superb collection of vases and Roman antiquities. Of particular interest is the *Marte di Todi* (Mars of Todi), a black bronze of a warrior dating to the late 5th century BC.

Galleria delle Carte Geografiche & Sala Sobieski

The last of three galleries – the other two are the **Galleria dei Candelabri** (Gallery of the Candelabra) and the **Galleria degli Arazzi** (Tapestry Gallery) – this 120m-long corridor is hung with 40 huge topograph-

Ceiling in the Galleria della Carte Geographiche

ical maps. These were created between 1580 and 1583 for Pope Gregory XIII based on drafts by Ignazio Danti, one of the leading cartographers of his day.

Beyond the gallery, the **Sala Sobieski** is named after an enormous 19th-century painting depicting the victory of the Polish King John III Sobieski over the Turks in 1683.

Stanze di Raffaello

These four frescoed chambers, currently undergoing partial restoration, were part of Pope Julius II's private apartments. Raphael himself painted the Stanza della Segnatura (1508–11) and the Stanza d'Eliodoro (1512–14), while the Stanza dell'Incendio di Borgo (1514–17) and Sala di Costantino (1517–24) were decorated by students following his designs.

The first room you come to is the **Sala di Costantino**, which features a huge fresco depicting Constantine's defeat of Maxentius at the battle of Milvian Bridge.

The **Stanza d'Eliodoro**, which was used for private audiences, takes its name from the *Cacciata d'Eliodoro* (Expulsion of Heliodorus from the Temple), an allegorical work reflecting Pope Julius II's policy of forcing foreign powers off Church lands. To its right, the *Messa di Bolsena* (Mass of Bolsena) shows Julius paying homage to the relic of a 13th-century miracle at the lakeside town of Bolsena. Next is the *Incontro di Leone Magno con Attila* (Encounter of Leo the Great with Attila) by Raphael and his school, and, on the fourth wall, the *Liberazione di San Pietro* (Liberation of St Peter), a brilliant work illustrating Raphael's masterful ability to depict light.

The **Stanza della Segnatura**, Julius' study and library, was the first room that Raphael painted, and it's here that you'll find his great masterpiece, *La Scuola di Atene* (The School of Athens), featuring philosophers and scholars gathered around Plato and Aristotle. The seated figure in front of the steps is believed to be Michelangelo, while the figure of Plato is said to be a portrait of Leonardo da Vinci, and Euclide (the bald man bending over) is Bramante. Raphael also included a self-portrait in the lower right corner – he's the second figure from the right.

The most famous work in the **Stanza dell'Incendio di Borgo** is the *Incendio di*

☑ Best Time to Visit

Tuesday and Thursday are quietest; Wednesday mornings are good while everyone is at the pope's weekly audience; and generally afternoon is better than the morning. Avoid Monday when many other museums are shut.

GONZALO AZUMENDI/GETTY IMAGES ©

☑ Audioguides

On the whole, exhibits are not well labelled, so consider hiring an audioguide (€7) or buying the excellent *Guide to the Vatican Museums and City* (€14).

Borgo (Fire in the Borgo), which depicts Pope Leo IV extinguishing a fire by making the sign of the cross. The ceiling was painted by Raphael's master, Perugino.

Sistine Chapel

The jewel in the Vatican's crown, the Sistine Chapel (Cappella Sistina) is home to two of the world's most famous works of art: Michelangelo's ceiling frescoes and his *Giudizio Universale* (Last Judgment).

The chapel was originally built for Pope Sixtus IV, after whom it's named, and consecrated on 15 August 1483. However, apart from the wall frescoes and floor, little remains of the original decor, which was sacrificed to make way for Michelangelo's two masterpieces. The first, the ceiling, was commissioned by Pope Julius II and painted between 1508 and 1512; the second, the spectacular *Giudizio Universale,* was painted between 1535 and 1541.

Michelangelo's ceiling design, which is best viewed from the chapel's main entrance in the far east wall, covers the entire 800-sq-metre surface. With painted architectural features and a cast of colourful biblical characters, it's centred on nine panels depicting scenes from the Creation, the story of Adam and Eve, the Fall, and the plight of Noah.

As you look up from the east wall, the first panel is the *Drunkenness of Noah,* followed by *The Flood* and the *Sacrifice of Noah.* Next, *Original Sin and Banishment from the Garden of Eden* famously depicts Adam and Eve being sent packing after accepting the forbidden fruit from Satan, represented by a snake with the body of a woman coiled around a tree. The *Creation of Eve* is then followed by the *Creation of Adam.* This, one of the most famous images in Western art, shows a bearded God pointing his finger at Adam, thus bringing him to life. Completing the sequence are the *Separation of Land from Sea;* the *Creation of the Sun, Moon and Plants;* and the *Separation of Light from Darkness,* featuring a fearsome God reaching out to touch the sun. Set around the central panels are 20 athletic male nudes, known as *ignudi.*

Opposite, on the west wall, is Michelangelo's mesmeric *Giudizio Universale,* showing Christ – in the centre near the top – passing sentence over the souls of the dead as they are torn from their graves to face him. The saved get to stay up in heaven (in the upper right), the damned are sent down to face the demons in hell (in the bottom right).

Near the bottom, on the right, you'll see a man with donkey ears and a snake wrapped around him. This is Biagio de Cesena, the papal master of ceremonies, who was a fierce critic of Michelangelo's composition. Another famous figure is St Bartholomew, just beneath Christ, holding his own flayed skin. The face in the skin is

God the Father with Angels on the ceiling of the Stanza dell'Incendio di Borgo (p43)

said to be a self-portrait of Michelangelo, its anguished look reflecting the artist's tormented faith.

The chapel's walls also boast superb frescoes. Painted between 1481 and 82 by a crack team of Renaissance artists, including Botticelli, Ghirlandaio, Pinturicchio, Perugino and Luca Signorelli, they represent events in the lives of Moses (to the left looking at the *Giudizio Universale*) and Christ (to the right). Highlights include Botticelli's *Temptations of Christ* and Perugino's *Handing over of the Keys*.

As well as providing a showcase for priceless art, the Sistine Chapel also serves an important religious function as the place where the conclave meets to elect a new pope.

★ Sistine Chapel Myth One

It's often said Michelangelo worked alone. He didn't. Throughout the job, he employed a steady stream of assistants to help with the plasterwork.

★ Sistine Chapel Myth Two

A popular myth is that Michelangelo painted the ceilings lying down. In fact, he designed a curved scaffolding that allowed him to work standing up.

FINE ART IMAGES/HERITAGE IMAGES/GETTY IMAGES/GETTY IMAGES ©

St Peter's Basilica and St Peter's Square

HANS-PETER MERTEN/GETTY IMAGES ©

St Peter's Basilica

In this city of outstanding churches, none can hold a candle to St Peter's Basilica, Italy's largest, richest and most spectacular basilica.

Great For...

☑ **Don't Miss**

The *Pietà*, Michelangelo's hauntingly sad depiction of a youthful Mary cradling the body of Jesus.

The original church was commissioned by the emperor Constantine and built around 349 on the site where St Peter is said to have been buried between AD 64 and 67. But like many medieval churches, it eventually fell into disrepair and it wasn't until the mid-15th century that efforts were made to restore it, first by Pope Nicholas V and then, rather more successfully, by Julius II.

In 1506 construction began on a design by Bramante, but when the architect died in 1514, building ground to a halt. In 1547 Michelangelo took the project on. He simplified Bramante's plans and drew up designs for what was to become his greatest architectural achievement, the dome. He never lived to see it built, though, and it was left to Giacomo della Porta, Domenico Fontana and Carlo Maderno to complete

Interior of St Peter's Basilica

ℹ Need to Know

Basilica di San Pietro; www.vatican.va; St Peter's Sq; ⏱7am-7pm summer, to 6.30pm winter; ⓂOttaviano-San Pietro; FREE

✕ Take a Break

Search out Fa-Bìo (p132) for a freshly made sandwich or a healthy lunchtime salad.

★ Top Tip

Strict dress codes are enforced, so no shorts, miniskirts or bare shoulders.

the basilica, which was finally consecrated in 1626.

Facade

Built between 1608 and 1612, Maderno's immense facade is 48m high and 118.6m wide. Eight 27m-high columns support the upper attic, on which 13 statues stand representing Christ the Redeemer, St John the Baptist and the 11 apostles. The central balcony, the **Loggia della Benedizione**, is where the pope stands to deliver his Urbi et Orbi blessing at Christmas and Easter.

Interior

At the beginning of the right aisle is Michelangelo's hauntingly beautiful **Pietà**. Sculpted when the artist was 25 (in 1499), it's the only work he ever signed – his signature is etched into the sash across the Madonna's breast.

On a pillar just beyond the *Pietà,* Carlo Fontana's gilt and bronze **monument to Queen Christina of Sweden** commemorates the far-from-holy Swedish monarch who converted to Catholicism in 1655.

Moving on, you'll come to the **Cappella di San Sebastiano**, home of Pope John Paul II's tomb, and the **Cappella del Santissimo Sacramento**, a sumptuously decorated baroque chapel.

Dominating the centre of the basilica is Bernini's 29m-high **baldachin**. Supported by four spiral columns and made with bronze taken from the Pantheon, it stands over the **high altar**, which itself sits on the site of St Peter's grave.

Above the baldachin, Michelangelo's **dome** soars to a height of 119m. Based on Brunelleschi's cupola in Florence, it's supported by four massive stone **piers** named after the saints whose statues adorn the Bernini-designed niches – Longinus, Helena, Veronica and Andrew.

At the base of the **Pier of St Longinus** is Arnolfo di Cambio's much-loved

13th-century bronze **statue of St Peter**, whose right foot has been worn down by centuries of caresses.

Dominating the tribune behind the altar is Bernini's extraordinary **Cattedra di San Pietro**, centred on a wooden seat that was once thought to have been St Peter's but in fact dates to the 9th century.

To the right of the throne, Bernini's **monument to Urban VIII** depicts the pope flanked by the figures of Charity and Justice.

Near the head of the left aisle are the so-called **Stuart monuments**. On the right is the monument to Clementina Sobieska, wife of James Stuart, by Filippo Barigioni, and on the left is Canova's vaguely erotic monument to the last three members of the Stuart clan, the pretenders to the English throne who died in exile in Rome.

Dome

From the **dome** (with/without lift €7/5; ⊘8am-5.45pm summer, to 4.45pm winter; Ⓜ Ottaviano-San Pietro) entrance on the right of the basilica's main portico, you can walk the 551 steps to the top or take a small lift halfway and then follow on foot for the last 320 steps. Either way, it's a long, steep climb. But make it to the top, and you're rewarded with stunning views.

Museo Storico Artistico

Accessed from the left nave, the **Museo Storico Artistico** (Tesoro; adult/reduced €7/5; ⊘9am-6.15pm summer, to 5.15pm winter; Ⓜ Ottaviano-San Pietro) sparkles with sacred relics. Highlights include a tabernacle by Donatello and the 6th-century *Crux Vaticana* (Vatican Cross).

St Peter's Square

Vatican Grottoes

Extending beneath the basilica, the **Vatican Grottoes** (⊙9am-6pm summer, to 5pm winter; ⓂOttaviano-San Pietro) `FREE` contain the tombs and sarcophagi of numerous popes, as well as several columns from the original 4th-century basilica. The entrance is in the Pier of St Andrew.

St Peter's Tomb

Excavations beneath the basilica have uncovered part of the original church and what archaeologists believe is the **Tomb of**

> ### ★ The World's Largest Church
> Contrary to popular opinion, St Peter's Basilica is not the world's largest church – the Basilica of Our Lady of Peace in Yamoussoukro on the Ivory Coast is bigger.

USABIN/GETTY IMAGES ©

St Peter (06 6988 5318; admission €13, over 15s only; ⓂOttaviano-San Pietro).

The excavations can only be visited by guided tour. To book a spot, email the Ufficio Scavi (scavi@fsp.va) as early as possible.

What's Nearby?

St Peter's Square
Piazza

(Piazza San Pietro; ⓂOttaviano-San Pietro)
Overlooked by St Peter's Basilica, the Vatican's central square was laid out between 1656 and 1667 to a design by Gian Lorenzo Bernini. Seen from above, it resembles a giant keyhole with two semicircular colonnades, each consisting of four rows of Doric columns, encircling a giant ellipse that straightens out to funnel believers into the basilica. The effect was deliberate – Bernini described the colonnades as representing 'the motherly arms of the church'.

Castel Sant'Angelo
Museum, Castle

(☎06 681 91 11; www.castelsantangelo.benicul-turali.it; Lungotevere Castello 50; adult/reduced €7/3.50; ⊙9am-7.30pm Tue-Sun; 🚌Piazza Pia)
With its chunky round keep, this castle is an instantly recognisable landmark. Built as a mausoleum for the emperor Hadrian, it was converted into a papal fortress in the 6th century and named after an angelic vision that Pope Gregory the Great had in 590. Nowadays, it houses the **Museo Nazionale di Castel Sant'Angelo** and its eclectic collection of paintings, sculpture, military memorabilia and medieval firearms.

> ### ★ Crowning Glory
> Near the main entrance, a red floor disk marks the spot where Charlemagne and later Holy Roman Emperors were crowned by the pope.

Pantheon

A striking 2000-year-old temple, now a church, the Pantheon is Rome's best-preserved ancient monument and one of the most influential buildings in the Western world. Its greying, pock-marked exterior might look its age, but inside it's a different story, and it's a unique and exhilarating experience to pass through its vast bronze doors and gaze up at the largest unreinforced concrete dome ever built.

Great For...

ℹ Need to Know

Map p250; www.pantheonroma.com; Piazza della Rotonda; ⊙8.30am-7.30pm Mon-Sat, 9am-6pm Sun; 🚊Largo di Torre Argentina) FREE

★ **Top Tip**
Mass is celebrated at the Pantheon at 5pm on Saturday and 10.30am on Sunday.

In its current form the Pantheon dates to around AD 125. The original temple, built by Marcus Agrippa in 27 BC, burnt down in AD 80, and although it was rebuilt by Domitian, it was struck by lightning and destroyed for a second time in AD 110. The emperor Hadrian had it reconstructed between AD 118 and 125, and it's this version that you see today.

Hadrian's temple was dedicated to the classical gods – hence the name Pantheon, a derivation of the Greek words *pan* (all) and *theos* (god) – but in 608 it was consecrated as a Christian church and it's now officially known as the Basilica di Santa Maria ad Martyres.

Thanks to this consecration, it was spared the worst of the medieval plundering that reduced many of Rome's ancient buildings to near dereliction. But it didn't escape entirely unscathed – its gilded-bronze roof tiles were removed and bronze from the portico was used by Bernini for the baldachino at St Peter's Basilica.

Exterior

The dark-grey pitted exterior faces onto busy, cafe-lined Piazza della Rotonda. And while its facade is somewhat the worse for wear, it's still an imposing sight. The monumental entrance **portico** consists of 16 Corinthian columns, each 13m high and each made of Egyptian granite, supporting a triangular **pediment**. Behind the columns, two 20-tonne **bronze doors** – 16th-century restorations of the original portal – give onto the central rotunda.

Rivets and holes in the brickwork indicate where marble-veneer panels were originally placed.

Interior of the Pantheon

The Inscription

For centuries the inscription under the pediment – 'M:AGRIPPA.L.F.COS.TERTIUM. FECIT' (Marcus Agrippa, son of Lucius, consul for the third time built this) – led scholars to think that the current building was Agrippa's original temple. However, 19th-century excavations revealed traces of an earlier temple and historians realised that Hadrian had simply kept Agrippa's original inscription.

Interior

Although impressive from outside, it's only when you get inside that you can really appreciate the Pantheon's full size. With light streaming in through the **oculus** (the 8.7m-diameter hole in the centre of the dome), the cylindrical marble-clad interior seems vast.

Opposite the entrance is the church's main **altar**, over which hangs a 7th-century icon of the *Madonna col Bambino* (Madonna and Child). To the left are the tombs of the artist Raphael, King Umberto I and Margherita of Savoy. Over on the opposite side of the rotunda is the tomb of King Vittorio Emanuele II.

Dome

The Pantheon's dome, considered the Romans' most important architectural achievement, was the largest dome in the world until Brunelleschi beat it with his Florentine cupola. Its harmonious appearance is due to a precisely calibrated symmetry – its diameter is exactly equal to the building's interior height of 43.3m. At its centre, the oculus, which symbolically connected the temple with the gods, plays a vital structural role by absorbing and redistributing the dome's huge tensile forces.

What's Nearby?

Basilica di Santa Maria Sopra Minerva   Basilica

(Map p250; www.santamariasopraminerva.it; Piazza della Minerva 42; ⏱6.45am-7pm Mon-Fri, 6.45am-12.30pm & 3.30-7pm Sat, 8am-12.30pm & 3.30-7pm Sun; 🚌Largo di Torre Argentina) Built on the site of three pagan temples, including one to the goddess Minerva, the Dominican Basilica di Santa Maria Sopra Minerva is Rome's only Gothic church. However, little remains of the original 13th-century structure and these days the main drawcard is a minor Michelangelo sculpture and the colourful, art-rich interior.

> ☑ **Don't Miss**
> The entrance doors – these 7m-high bronze portals provide a suitably grand entrance.

TTSTUDIO/SHUTTERSTOCK ©

> ✕ **Take a Break**
> For an uplifting drink head to La Casa del Caffè Tazza d'Oro (p171), a busy cafe serving some of the best coffee in town.

Museo e Galleria Borghese

Housing what's often referred to as the 'queen of all private art collections', this spectacular gallery boasts some of the city's finest art treasures, including a series of sensational sculptures by Gian Lorenzo Bernini and important paintings by the likes of Caravaggio, Titian, Raphael and Rubens.

Sale IV (p57) with the *Ratto di Proserpina*

Great For...

Need to Know

Map p256; ☎06 3 28 10; www.galleriaborghese.it; Piazzale del Museo Borghese 5; adult/reduced €11/6.50; 9am-7pm Tue-Sun; Via Pinciana

★ **Top Tip**

Remember to prebook your ticket, and take ID when you pick it up.

The museum's collection was formed by Cardinal Scipione Borghese (1579–1633), the most knowledgeable and ruthless art collector of his day. It was originally housed in his residence near St Peter's, but in the 1620s he had it transferred to his new villa just outside Porta Pinciana. And it's here, in the villa's central building, the Casino Borghese, that you'll see it today.

Over the centuries the villa has undergone several overhauls, most notably in the late 1700s when Prince Marcantonio Borghese added much of the lavish neoclassical decor.

The villa is divided into two parts: the ground-floor museum and the upstairs picture gallery.

Entrance & Ground Floor

The **entrance hall** features 4th-century floor mosaics of fighting gladiators and a 2nd-century *Satiro Combattente* (Fighting Satyr). High on the wall is a gravity-defying bas-relief of a horse and rider falling into the void by Pietro Bernini (Gian Lorenzo's father).

Sala I is centred on Antonio Canova's daring depiction of Napoleon's sister, Paolina Bonaparte Borghese, reclining topless as **Venere Vincitrice** (Venus Victrix; 1805–08). Its suggestive pose and technical virtuosity is typical of Canova's elegant, mildly erotic neoclassical style.

But it's Gian Lorenzo Bernini's spectacular sculptures – flamboyant depictions of pagan myths – that really steal the show. Just look at Daphne's hands morphing into

Villa Borghese

leaves in the swirling *Apollo e Dafne* (1622–25) in **Sala III**, or Pluto's hand pressing into the seemingly soft flesh of Persephone's thigh in the *Ratto di Proserpina* (Rape of Proserpina; 1621–22) in **Sala IV**.

Caravaggio, one of Cardinal Scipione's favourite artists, dominates **Sala VIII**. You'll see a dissipated *Bacchino malato* (Young Sick Bacchus; 1593–94), the strangely beautiful *La Madonna dei Palafrenieri* (Madonna of the Palafrenieri; 1605–06) and *San Giovanni Battista* (St John the Baptist; 1609–10), probably his last work. There's also the much-loved *Ragazzo col Canestro di Frutta* (Boy with a Basket of Fruit; 1593–95) and dramatic *Davide con la Testa di Golia* (David with the Head of Goliath; 1609–10) – Goliath's head is said to be a self-portrait.

Picture Gallery

With works representing the best of the Tuscan, Venetian, Umbrian and northern European schools, the upstairs picture gallery offers a wonderful snapshot of Renaissance art.

In **Sala IX** don't miss Raphael's extraordinary *La Deposizione di Cristo* (The Deposition; 1507) and his charming *Dama con Liocorno* (Lady with a Unicorn; 1506). In the same room you'll find Fra Bartolomeo's superb *Adorazione del Bambino* (Adoration of the Christ Child; 1499) and Perugino's *Madonna col Bambino* (Madonna and Child; early 16th century).

Next door, Correggio's *Danäe* (1530–31) shares wall space with a willowy Venus, as portrayed by Cranach in his *Venere e Amore che Reca Il Favo do Miele* (Venus and Cupid with Honeycomb; 1531).

Moving on, **Sala XIV** boasts two self-portraits by Bernini, and **Sala XVIII** contains two significant works by Rubens: *Compianto su Cristo morto* (The Deposition; 1603) and *Susanna e I Vecchioni* (Susanna and the Elders; 1605–07).

To finish off, Titian's early masterpiece *Amor Sacro e Amor Profano* (Sacred and Profane Love; 1514) in **Sala XX** is one of the collection's most prized works.

What's Nearby?

Villa Borghese
Park

(Map p256; entrances at Piazzale San Paolo del Brasile, Piazzale Flaminio, Via Pinciana, Via Raimondo, Largo Pablo Picasso; ☉dawn-dusk; 🚇Porta Pinciana) Locals, lovers, tourists, joggers – no one can resist the lure of Rome's most

---

☑ **Don't Miss**

Canova's *Venere Vincitrice,* his sensual portrayal of Paolina Bonaparte Borghese.

PHANT/GETTY IMAGES ©

✕ **Take a Break**

There's a bar in the basement entrance area, but for a more memorable meal head across the park to the Caffè delle Arti (p142).

celebrated park. Originally the 17th-century estate of Cardinal Scipione Borghese, it covers about 80 hectares of wooded glades, gardens and grassy banks. Among its attractions are several excellent museums, the landscaped **Giardino del Lago** (Map p256; boat hire per person €3 for 20 minutes; ⊙7am-9pm), and **Piazza di Siena** (Map p256; ▣Porta Pinciana), a dusty arena used for Rome's top equestrian event in May.

Museo Nazionale Etrusco di Villa Giulia   Museum
(Map p256; www.villagiulia.beniculturali.it; Piazzale di Villa Giulia; adult/reduced €8/4; ⊙8.30am-7.30pm Tue-Sun; ▣Via delle Belle Arti) Pope Julius III's 16th-century villa provides the charming setting for Italy's finest collection of Etruscan and pre-Roman treasures. Exhibits, many of which came from burial tombs in the surrounding Lazio region, range from bronze figurines and black *bucchero* tableware to temple decorations, terracotta vases and a dazzling display of sophisticated jewellery.

Must-sees include a polychrome terracotta statue of Apollo, the 6th-century-BC *Sarcofago degli Sposi* (Sarcophagus of the Betrothed) and the *Euphronios Krater,* a celebrated Greek vase.

Further finds relating to the Umbri and Latin peoples are on show in the nearby **Villa Poniatowski** (Map p256; 🕾06 321 96 98; www.villagiulia.beniculturali.it; Piazzale di Villa Giulia; incl Museo Nazional Etrusco di Villa Giulia adult/reduced €8/4; ⊙9am-1.30pm Tue-Sat, booking necessary; ▣Via delle Belle Arti). You'll need to book to enter here, with Sunday visits restricted to guided tours run by the Coop Arteingioco. Call 🕾06 4423 9949 for details.

Galleria Nazionale d'Arte Moderna e Contemporanea   Gallery
(Map p256; 🕾06 3229 8221; www.gnam. beniculturali.it; Viale delle Belle Arti 131, disabled entrance Via Gramsci 73; adult/reduced €8/4; ⊙8.30am-7.30pm Tue-Sun; ▣Piazza Thorvald-sen) Housed in a vast belle époque palace, this oft-overlooked gallery is an unsung

gem. Its superlative collection runs the gamut from neoclassical sculpture to abstract expressionism, with works by many of the most important exponents of 19th- and 20th-century art.

There are canvases by the *macchiaioli* (Italian Impressionists) and futurists Boccioni and Balla, as well as sculptures by Canova and major works by Modigliani, De Chirico and Guttuso. International artists represented include Van Gogh, Cézanne, Monet, Klimt, and Alberto Giacometti, whose trademark stick-figures share a room with a Jackson Pollock canvas, a curvaceous Henry Moore sculpture and a hanging mobile by Alexander Calder.

Pincio Hill Gardens   Gardens
(Map p256; Ⓜ Flaminio) Overlooking Piazza del Popolo, the 19th-century Pincio Hill is

Classical fountain, Villa Borghese

named after the Pinci family, who owned this part of Rome in the 4th century. It's quite a climb up from the piazza, but at the top you're rewarded with lovely views over to St Peter's and the Gianicolo Hill. Alternatively, you can approach from the top of the Spanish Steps. From the gardens you can strike out to explore Villa Borghese, the Villa dei Medici, or the Chiesa della Trinità dei Monti at the top of the Spanish Steps.

Museo Carlo Bilotti   Gallery
(Map p256; ☎06 06 08; www.museocarlobilotti. it; Viale Fiorello La Guardia; ⊗10am-4pm Tue-Fri winter, 1-7pm Tue-Fri summer, 10am-7pm Sat & Sun year-round; ☐Porta Pinciana) FREE The Orangery of Villa Borghese provides the handsome setting for the art collection of billionaire cosmetics magnate Carlo Bilotti. The main focus are 18 works by Giorgio

de Chirico (1888–1978), one of Italy's foremost modern artists, but also of note is a Warhol portrait of Bilotti's wife and daughter.

☑ **Best Views**

For unforgettable views over Rome's rooftops and domes, make your way to the Pincio Hill Gardens in the southwest of Villa Borghese.

★ **Top Tip**

Monday is not a good time for exploring Villa Borghese. Sure, you can walk in the park, but its museums and galleries are all shut – they are only open Tuesday through Sunday.

Stadio (p62)

Palatino

Rising above the Roman Forum, the Palatino (Palatine Hill) is an atmospheric area of towering pine trees, majestic ruins and memorable views. According to legend, this is where Romulus and Remus were saved by a wolf and where Romulus founded Rome in 753 BC. Archaeological evidence can't prove the myth, but it has dated human habitation here to the 8th century BC.

Great For...

ⓘ Need to Know

Palatine Hill; Map p252; ☏06 3996 7700; www.coopculture.it; Via di San Gregorio 30 & Via Sacra; adult/reduced incl Colosseum & Roman Forum €12/7.50; ⊙8.30am-1hr before sunset; ⓂColosseo

★ **Top Tip**

The best spot for a picnic is the grassy Vigna Barberini near the Orti Farnesiani.

The Palatino was ancient Rome's most exclusive neighbourhood. The emperor Augustus lived here all his life and successive emperors built increasingly opulent palaces. But after Rome's fall, it fell into disrepair and in the Middle Ages churches and castles were built over the ruins. Later, wealthy Renaissance families established gardens on the hill.

Most of the Palatino as it appears today is covered by the ruins of the emperor Domitian's 1st-century complex, which served as the main imperial palace for 300 years.

Stadio

On entering the Palatino from Via di San Gregorio, head uphill until you come to the first recognisable construction, the **stadio**. This sunken area, which was part of the

main imperial palace, was used by the emperor for private games. To the southeast of the stadium are the remains of a complex built by Septimius Severus, comprising baths (**Terme di Settimio Severo**) and a palace (**Domus Severiana**) where, if they're open, you can visit the **Arcate Severiane** (Severian Arches; Map p252; ☎06 3996 7700; www.coopculture.it; admission incl in Palatino ticket; ☻8.30am-1hr before sunset Tue & Fri; Ⓜ Colosseo), a series of arches built to facilitate further development.

Domus Augustana & Domu Flavia

Next to the *stadio* are the ruins of the **Domus Augustana** (Emperor's Residence), the emperor's private quarters in the imperial palace. Over two levels, rooms lead off a *peristilio* (porticoed courtyard) on each floor. You can't get to the lower level,

Domus Augustana

but from above you can see the basin of a fountain.

Over on the other side of the Museo Palatino is the **Domus Flavia**, the public part of the palace. The Domus was centred on a grand columned peristyle – the grassy area with the base of an octagonal fountain – off which the main halls led.

Museo Palatino

The **Museo Palatino** (admission incl in Palatino ticket; ⊙8.30am-1hr before sunset; ⓂColosseo) houses a small collection of finds from the Palatino. The downstairs section illustrates the history of the hill

---

☑ **Don't Miss**

The sight of the Roman Forum laid out beneath you from the viewing balcony on the Orti Farnesiani.

MARCPO/GETTY IMAGES ©

from its origins to the Republican age, while upstairs you'll find artefacts from the Imperial age, including a beautiful 1st-century bronze, the *Erma di Canefora*.

Casa di Livia & Casa di Augusto

Among the best-preserved buildings on the Palatino is the **Casa di Livia** (Map p252; ☑06 3996 7700; www.coopculture.it; incl Casa di Augusto €4; ⊙guided tour 1pm daily, prebooking necessary; ⓂColosseo), northwest of the Domus Flavia. Home to Augustus' wife Livia, it was built around an atrium leading onto what were once frescoed reception rooms. Nearby, the **Casa di Augusto** (Map p252; ☑06 3996 7700; www.coopculture.it; incl Casa di Livia €4; ⊙guided tour 1pm daily, prebooking necessary; ⓂColosseo), Augustus' separate residence, contains superb frescoes in vivid reds, yellows and blues.

Criptoportico

Reached from near the Orti Farnesiani, the **criptoportico** is a 128m tunnel where Caligula is said to have been murdered, and which Nero used to connect his Domus Aurea with the Palatino. It is now used for temporary exhibitions.

Orti Farnesiani

Covering the Domus Tiberiana (Tiberius' Palace) in the northwest of the Palatino, the **Orti Farnesiani** is one of Europe's earliest botanical gardens. Named after Cardinal Alessandro Farnese, who had it laid out in the mid-16th century, it commands breathtaking views over the Roman Forum.

✗ **Take a Break**

There are no great options in the immediate vicinity so hotfoot it to Terre e Domus (p124) for some rousing regional fare.

Fontana del Moro (p66)

Piazza Navona

With its ornate fountains, exuberant baroque palazzi (mansions) and pavement cafes, Piazza Navona is central Rome's elegant showcase square. Long a hub of local life, it hosted Rome's main market for close on 300 years, and today attracts a colourful daily circus of street performers, hawkers, artists, tourists, fortune-tellers and pigeons.

Great For...

ⓘ Need to Know

Map p250; 🚌 Corso del Rinascimento

★ **Top Tip**
Each December the piazza hosts a traditional Christmas market.

Stadio di Domiziano

Like many of Rome's landmarks, the piazza sits over an ancient monument. The 30,000-seat **Stadio di Domiziano** (Domitian's Stadium; Map p250; ☎06 4568 6100; www.stadiodomiziano.com; Via di Tor Sanguigna 3; adult/reduced €8/6; ⏰10am-7pm Sun-Fri, to 8pm Sat; ☒Corso del Rinascimento), the subterranean remains of which can be accessed from Via di Tor Sanguigna, used to host athletic meets – hence the name Navona, a corruption of the Greek word *agon*, meaning 'public games'.

Fountains

The piazza's grand centrepiece is Bernini's **Fontana dei Quattro Fiumi** (Fountain of the Four Rivers; Map p250), a showy fountain featuring four muscular personifications of the rivers Nile, Ganges, Danube and Plate.

The **Fontana del Moro** (Map p250), at the southern end of the square, was designed by Giacomo della Porta in 1576.

At the northern end of the piazza, the 19th-century **Fontana del Nettuno** (Map p250) depicts Neptune fighting with a sea monster, surrounded by sea nymphs.

Main Buildings

Overlooking Bernini's Fontana dei Quattro Fiumi is the **Chiesa di Sant'Agnese in Agone** (Map p250; www.santagneseinagone.org; concerts €13; ⏰9.30am-12.30pm & 3.30-7pm Mon-Sat, 10am-1pm & 4-8pm Sun), an elaborate baroque church designed by Francesco Borromini.

Further down, the 17th-century **Palazzo Pamphilj** (Map p250) was built for Pope Innocent X and now houses the Brazilian Embassy.

Piazza Navona

What's Nearby?

Chiesa di San Luigi
dei Francesi   Church

(Map p250; Piazza di San Luigi dei Francesi 5;
⊙10am-12.30pm & 3-7pm, closed Thu afternoon;
🚌Corso del Rinascimento) Church to Rome's
French community since 1589, this opulent
baroque *chiesa* (church) is home to a
celebrated trio of Caravaggio paintings: the
Vocazione di San Matteo (The Calling of
Saint Matthew), the *Martirio di San Matteo*
(The Martyrdom of Saint Matthew) and
San Matteo e l'angelo (Saint Matthew and
the Angel), known collectively as the St
Matthew cycle.

☑ Don't Miss

Bernini's Fontana dei Quattro Fiumi,
the piazza's high-camp central
fountain.

CHANCLOS/SHUTTERSTOCK ©

Museo Nazionale Romano:
Palazzo Altemps   Museum

(Map p250; 📞06 3996 7700; www.coopculture.
it; Piazza Sant'Apollinare 44; adult/reduced
€7/3.50; ⊙9am-7.45pm Tue-Sun; 🚌Corso
del Rinascimento) Just north of Piazza
Navona, Palazzo Altemps is a beautiful
late-15th-century *palazzo,* housing the best
of the Museo Nazionale Romano's formidable collection of classical sculpture. Many
pieces come from the celebrated Ludovisi
collection, amassed by Cardinal Ludovico
Ludovisi in the 17th century.

Campo de' Fiori   Piazza

(Map p250; 🚌Corso Vittorio Emanuele II) Noisy,
colourful 'Il Campo' is a major focus of Roman life: by day it hosts one of Rome's best-
known markets, while at night it morphs
into a raucous open-air pub. For centuries
the square was the site of public execu-
tions, and it was here that the philosopher
Giordano Bruno was burned at the stake
for heresy in 1600. The spot is marked by a
sinister statue of the hooded monk, created
by Ettore Ferrari and unveiled in 1889.

Palazzo Farnese   Historic Building

(Map p250; www.inventerrome.com; Piazza
Farnese; admission €5; ⊙guided tours 3pm,
4pm & 5pm Mon, Wed & Fri; 🚌Corso Vittorio
Emanuele II) Home of the French embassy,
this formidable Renaissance *palazzo,* one
of Rome's finest, was started in 1514 by
Antonio da Sangallo the Younger, continued
by Michelangelo and finished by Giacomo
della Porta. Inside, it boasts a series of
frescoes by Annibale Carracci that are
said by some to rival Michelangelo's in
the Sistine Chapel. The highlight, painted
between 1597 and 1608, is the monumental
ceiling fresco *Amori degli Dei* (The Loves of
the Gods) in the recently restored Galleria
dei Carracci.

✕ Take a Break

Grab a bite in a Renaissance cloister at
the Chiostro del Bramante Caffè (p125).

Ancient Roman mosaic (p70)

Museo Nazionale Romano: Palazzo Massimo alle Terme

Every day, thousands of tourists, commuters and passers-by hurry past this towering neo-Renaissance palazzo without giving it a second glance. They don't know what they're missing. This is one of Rome's great museums, an oft-overlooked treasure trove of classical art. The sculpture is truly impressive but what really takes the breath away is the collection of vibrantly coloured frescoes and mosaics.

Great For...

ℹ️ **Need to Know**

Map p255; 📞 06 3996 7700; www.coopcul ture.it; Largo di Villa Peretti 1; adult/reduced €7/3.50; 🕙 9am-7.45pm Tue-Sun; Ⓜ Termini

Sculpture

The ground and 1st floors are devoted to sculpture, examining imperial portraiture as propaganda and including some breath-taking works of art.

Ground-floor showstoppers include the 5th-century-BC *Niobide morente* (Dying Niobid) and two 2nd-century-BC Greek bronzes – the *Pugile* (Boxer) and the *Principe ellenistico* (Hellenistic Prince). Upstairs, look out for *Il discobolo* (Discus Thrower), a muscular 2nd-century-AD copy of an ancient Greek work. Another admirable body belongs to the graceful *Ermafrodite dormiente* (Sleeping Hermaphrodite).

Also fascinating are the elaborate bronze fittings that belonged to Caligula's ceremonial ships.

Frescoes & Mosaics

On the 2nd floor you'll find the museum's thrilling exhibition of ancient mosaics and frescoes. These vibrantly coloured panels were originally used as interior decor and provide a more complete picture of the inside of a grand ancient Roman villa than you'll see anywhere else in the world. There are intimate *cubicula* (bedroom) frescoes focusing on nature, mythology, domestic and sensual life, and delicate landscape paintings from the winter *triclinium* (dining room).

The museum's crowning glory is a room of frescoes from Villa Livia, one of the homes of Augustus' wife Livia Drusilla. The frescoes depict a paradisiacal garden full of a wild tangle of roses, violets, pomegranates, irises and camomile under a deep-blue sky. These decorated a summer triclinium, a large living and dining area

Third-century marble sarcophagus, Museo Nazionale Romano: Terme di Diocleziano

built half underground to provide protection from the heat. The lighting mimics the modulation of daylight and highlights the richness of the millennia-old colours.

Basement

The basement contains a coin collection that's far more absorbing than you might expect, tracing the Roman Empire's use of coins for propaganda purposes. There's also jewellery dating back several millennia that looks as good as new, and the disturbing remains of a mummified eight-year-old girl, the only known example of mummification dating from the Roman Empire.

☑ Don't Miss

Il discobolo; the athletic pose of the discuss thrower is a homage to the male physique.

GONZALO AZUMENDI/GETTY IMAGES ©

What's Nearby?

Museo Nazionale Romano: Terme di Diocleziano   Museum

(Map p255; ☎06 3996 7700; www.coopculture.it; Viale Enrico de Nicola 78; adult/reduced €7/3.50; ☉9am-7.30pm Tue-Sun; Ⓜ Termini) The Terme di Diocleziano was ancient Rome's largest bath complex, covering about 13 hectares and with a capacity for 3000 people. This branch of the Museo Nazionale Romano supplies a fascinating insight into Roman life through memorial inscriptions and other artefacts. Outside, the vast, elegant cloister was constructed from drawings by Michelangelo.

Chiesa di Santa Maria della Vittoria   Church

(Map p255; Via XX Settembre 17; ☉8.30am-noon & 3.30-6pm; Ⓜ Repubblica) This modest church is an unlikely setting for an extraordinary work of art – Bernini's extravagant and sexually charged *Santa Teresa trafitta dall'amore di Dio* (Ecstasy of St Teresa). This daring sculpture depicts Teresa, engulfed in the folds of a flowing cloak, floating in ecstasy on a cloud while a teasing angel pierces her repeatedly with a golden arrow.

Galleria Nazionale d'Arte Antica: Palazzo Barberini   Gallery

(Map p255; ☎06 3 28 10; www.galleriabarberini. beniculturali.it; Via delle Quattro Fontane 13; adult/reduced €7/3.50, incl Palazzo Corsini, valid 3 days €9/4.50; ☉8.30am-7pm Tue-Sun; Ⓜ Barberini) Commissioned to celebrate the Barberini family's rise to papal power, Palazzo Barberini is a sumptuous baroque palace that impresses even before you go inside and start on the breathtaking art. Many high-profile architects worked on it, including rivals Bernini and Borromini: the former contributed a large squared staircase, the latter a helicoidal one.

✕ Take a Break

Drop into Panella L'Arte del Pane (p135) for a coffee and gourmet snack.

Palazzo dei Conservatori (p74)

Capitoline Museums

Dating to 1471, the Capitoline Museums are the world's oldest public museums. Their collection of classical sculpture is one of Italy's finest, including crowd-pleasers such as the iconic Lupa capitolina (Capitoline Wolf), but there's also a formidable picture gallery with masterpieces by the likes of Titian, Tintoretto, Rubens and Caravaggio.

Great For...

❶ Need to Know

Musei Capitolini; Map p252; ☎06 06 08; www.museicapitolini.org; Piazza del Campidoglio 1; adult/reduced €11.50/9.50; ☉9.30am-7.30pm, last admission 6.30pm; ☒Piazza Venezia

★ Top Tip

In a tunnel between the two *palazzi*, the Tabularium commands inspiring views over the Roman Forum.

The museums occupy two stately palazzi on **Piazza del Campidoglio** (Map p252). The entrance is in **Palazzo dei Conservatori** (Map p252), where you'll find the original core of the sculptural collection and the Pinacoteca (picture gallery).

Palazzo dei Conservatori: 1st Floor

Before you start on the sculpture collection proper, check out the marble body parts littered around the ground-floor **courtyard**. The mammoth head, hand and feet all belonged to a 12m-high statue of Constantine that stood in the Basilica di Massenzio in the Roman Forum.

Of the sculpture on the 1st floor, the Etruscan *Lupa capitolina* (Capitoline Wolf) is the most famous. Dating to the 5th century BC, the bronze wolf stands over her

suckling wards, Romulus and Remus, who were added in 1471.

Other crowd-pleasers include the *Spinario,* a delicate 1st-century-BC bronze of a boy removing a thorn from his foot, and Gian Lorenzo Bernini's *Medusa* bust.

Also on this floor, in the modern **Esedra di Marco Aurelio**, is the original of the equestrian statue that stands outside in Piazza del Campidoglio.

Palazzo dei Conservatori: 2nd Floor

The 2nd floor is given over to the **Pinacoteca**, the museum's picture gallery.

Each room harbours masterpieces but two stand out: the **Sala Pietro da Cortona**, which features Pietro da Cortona's famous depiction of the *Ratto delle sabine* (Rape of the Sabine Women; 1630), and the **Sala di**

Sculptures in the Palazzo Nuovo

Santa Petronilla, named after Guercino's huge canvas *Seppellimento di Santa Petronilla* (The Burial of St Petronilla; 1621–23). This airy hall also boasts two works by Caravaggio: *La Buona Ventura* (The Fortune Teller; 1595) and *San Giovanni Battista* (John the Baptist; 1602).

Tabularium

A tunnel links Palazzo dei Conservatori to Palazzo Nuovo via the **Tabularium**, ancient Rome's central archive.

Palazzo Nuovo

Palazzo Nuovo (Map p252) contains some unforgettable show-stoppers. Chief among

---

☑ Don't Miss

The *Galata Morente* (Dying Gaul) in the Sala del Gladiatore in Palazzo Nuovo.

VIACHESLAV LOPATIN/SHUTTERSTOCK ©

---

them is the **Galata Morente** (Dying Gaul), a Roman copy of a 3rd-century-BC Greek original that movingly depicts the anguish of a dying Gaul warrior.

Another superb figurative piece is the the *Venere Capitolina* (Capitoline Venus), a sensual yet demure portrayal of the nude goddess.

What's Nearby?

Il Vittoriano   Monument

(Map p252; Piazza Venezia; ⊗9.30am-5.30pm summer, to 4.30pm winter; ⊒Piazza Venezia) FREE Love it or loathe it, as most locals do, you can't ignore Il Vittoriano (aka the Altare della Patria; Altar of the Fatherland), the massive mountain of white marble that towers over Piazza Venezia. Begun in 1885 to honour Italy's first king, Victor Emmanuel II, it incorporates the **Museo Centrale del Risorgimento** (Map p252; www.risorgimento.it; adult/reduced €5/2.50; ⊗9.30am-6.30pm, closed 1st Mon of month), a small museum documenting Italian unification, and the **Tomb of the Unknown Soldier**.

For Rome's best 360-degree views, take the **Roma dal Cielo** (Map p252; adult/reduced €7/3.50; ⊗9.30am-6.30pm Mon-Thu, to 7.30pm Fri-Sun) lift to the top.

Bocca della Verità   Monument

(Mouth of Truth; Piazza Bocca della Verità 18; donation €0.50; ⊗9.30am-5.50pm summer, to 4.50pm winter; ⊒Piazza Bocca della Verità) A bearded face carved into a giant marble disc, the *Bocca della Verità* is one of Rome's most popular curiosities. Legend has it that if you put your hand in the mouth and tell a lie, the Bocca will slam shut and bite your hand off.

The mouth, which was originally part of a fountain, or possibly an ancient manhole cover, now lives in the portico of the **Chiesa di Santa Maria in Cosmedin**, a handsome medieval church.

✕ Take a Break

Head up to the 2nd floor of Palazzo dei Conservatori for a bite at the panoramic Caffè Capitolino (p124).

Via Appia Antica

Ancient Rome's regina viarum (queen of roads) is now one of Rome's most exclusive addresses, a beautiful cobbled thoroughfare flanked by grassy fields, ancient ruins and towering pine trees. But it has a dark history – it was here that Spartacus and 6000 of his slave rebels were crucified, and the early Christians buried their dead in the underground catacombs.

Great For...

ⓘ Need to Know

Appian Way; ☏06 513 53 16; www.parco appiaantica.it; bike hire hour/day €3/15; ⊘Info Point 9.30am-1pm & 2-5.30pm Mon-Fri, 9.30am-6.30pm Sat & Sun, to 5pm winter; ⌨Via Appia Antica

★ **Top Tip**
The stretch near the Basilica di San Sebastiano is traffic-free on Sunday.

Heading southeast from Porta San Sebastiano, Via Appia Antica was named after Appius Claudius Caecus, who laid the first 90km section in 312 BC. It was later extended in 190 BC to reach Brindisi, some 540km away on the southern Adriatic coast.

Catacombe di San Sebastiano

The **Catacombe di San Sebastiano** (⏏06 785 03 50; www.catacombe.org; Via Appia Antica 136; adult/reduced €8/5; ⏱10am-5pm Mon-Sat, closed Dec; ⏹Via Appia Antica) were the first burial chambers to be called catacombs, the name deriving from the Greek *kata* (near) and *kymbas* (cavity), because they were located near a cave. During the persecutory reign of Vespasian from AD 258, they are said to have provided a safe haven for the remains of Saints Peter and Paul.

The 1st level is now almost completely destroyed, but frescoes, stucco work and epigraphs can be seen on the 2nd level. There are also three perfectly preserved mausoleums and a plastered wall with hundreds of invocations to Peter and Paul, engraved by worshippers in the 3rd and 4th centuries.

Above the catacombs, the **Basilica di San Sebastiano** preserves one of the arrows allegedly used to kill St Sebastian, and the column to which he was tied.

Catacombe di San Callisto

Founded at the end of the 2nd century and named after Pope Calixtus I, the **Catacombe di San Callisto** (⏏06 513 01 51; www.catacombe.roma.it; Via Appia Antica 110 & 126; adult/reduced €8/5; ⏱9am-noon & 2-5pm, closed Wed & Feb; ⏹Via Appia Antica)

Ruins along Via Appia Antica

became the official cemetery of the newly established Roman Church. In the 20km of tunnels explored to date, archaeologists have found the tombs of 500,000 people and seven popes who were martyred in the 3rd century.

The patron saint of music, St Cecilia, was also buried here, though her body was later removed to the Basilica di Santa Cecilia in Trastevere. When her body was exhumed in 1599, it was apparently perfectly preserved.

Catacombe di Santa Domitilla

Among Rome's largest and oldest, the **Catacombe di Santa Domitilla** (☑06 511 03 42; www.domitilla.info; Via delle Sette Chiese 283; adult/reduced €8/5; ☺9am-noon & 2-5pm Wed-Mon, closed Jan; ☐Via Appia Antica) were established on the private burial ground of Flavia Domitilla, niece of the emperor Domitian. They contain Christian wall paintings and the haunting underground Chiesa di SS Nereus e Achilleus, a 4th-century church dedicated to two Roman soldiers martyred by Diocletian.

What's Nearby?

Mausoleo di Cecilia Metella   Ruin

(☑06 3996 7700; www.coopculture.it; Via Appia Antica 161; adult/reduced incl Terme di Caracalla & Villa dei Quintili €7/4; ☺9am-1hr before sunset Tue-Sun; ☐Via Appia Antica) Dating to the 1st century BC, this great drum of a mausoleum encloses a burial chamber, now roofless. In the 14th century it was converted into a fort by the Caetani family, who were related to Pope Boniface VIII, and used to frighten passing traffic into paying a toll.

Villa di Massenzio   Ruin

(☑06 780 13 24; www.villadimassenzio.it; Via Appia Antica 153; ☺9am-1pm Tue-Sat; ☐Via Appia Antica) The outstanding feature of Maxentius' enormous 4th-century palace complex is the **Circo di Massenzio** (Via Appia Antica 153; ☐Via Appia Antica), Rome's best-preserved ancient racetrack – you can still make out the starting stalls used for chariot races. The 10,000-seat arena was built by Maxentius around 309, but he died before ever seeing a race here.

> ☑ **Don't Miss**
>
> The ruins of Villa di Massenzio, littering the green fields by the side of the cobbled Via.

DAVID SOANES PHOTOGRAPHY/GETTY IMAGES ©

> ✕ **Take a Break**
>
> Just south of the Mausoleo di Cecilia Metellia, Qui Non se More Mai (p143) is good for grilled meats and authentic Roman pastas.

Tempio di Saturno (p82)

Roman Forum

The Roman Forum was ancient Rome's showpiece centre, a grandiose district of temples, basilicas and vibrant public spaces. Nowadays, it's a collection of impressive, if badly labelled, ruins that can leave you drained and confused. But if you can get your imagination going, there's something wonderfully compelling about walking in the footsteps of Julius Caesar and other legendary figures of Roman history.

Great For...

ℹ Need to Know

Foro Romano; Map p252; ☑06 3996 7700; www.coopculture.it; Largo della Salara Vecchia & Via Sacra; adult/reduced incl Colosseum & Palatino €12/7.50; ⊗8.30am-1hr before sunset; 🚇Via dei Fori Imperiali

★ **Top Tip**
Exit near the Arco di Settimuio Severo to continue up to Campidoglio and the Capitoline Museums.

Originally an Etruscan burial ground, the Forum was first developed in the 7th century BC, growing over time to become the social, political and commercial hub of the Roman Empire. In the Middle Ages it was reduced to pasture land and extensively plundered for its marble. The area was systematically excavated in the 18th and 19th centuries and work continues to this day.

Via Sacra to Campidoglio

Entering the Forum from Largo della Salara Vecchia, you'll see the **Tempio di Antonino e Faustina** (Map p252) ahead to your left. Erected in AD 141, this was transformed into a church in the 8th century, the **Chiesa di San Lorenzo in Miranda** (Map p252). To your right is the 179 BC **Basilica Fulvia Aemilia** (Map p252).

At the end of the path, you'll come to **Via Sacra** (Map p252), the Forum's main thoroughfare, and the **Tempio di Giulio Cesare** (Tempio del Divo Giulio; Map p252), which stands on the spot where Julius Caesar was cremated.

Heading right brings you to the **Curia** (Map p252), the original seat of the Roman Senate, though what you see today is a reconstruction of how it looked in the reign of Diocletian (r 284–305).

At the end of Via Sacra, the **Arco di Settimio Severo** (Arch of Septimius Severus; Map p252) is dedicated to the eponymous emperor and his sons, Caracalla and Geta. Close by, the **Colonna di Foca** (Column of Phocus; Map p252) rises above what was once the Forum's main square, **Piazza del Foro**.

The eight granite columns that rise behind the Colonna are all that survive of the

Tempio di Antonino e Faustina

Tempio di Saturno (Temple of Saturn; Map p252), an important temple that doubled as the state treasury.

Tempio di Castore e Polluce & Casa delle Vestali

From the path that runs parallel to Via Sacra, you'll pass the stubby ruins of the **Basilica Giulia** (Map p252). At the end of the basilica, three columns remain from the 5th-century-BC **Tempio di Castore e Polluce** (Temple of Castor and Pollux; Map p252). Nearby, the 6th-century **Chiesa di Santa Maria Antiqua** (Map p252) is the oldest Christian church in the Forum.

☑ Don't Miss

The Basilca di Massenzio, to get some idea of the scale of ancient Rome's mammoth buildings.

Back towards Via Sacra is the **Casa delle Vestali** (House of the Vestal Virgins; Map p252), home of the virgins who tended the flame in the adjoining **Tempio di Vesta** (Map p252).

Via Sacra towards the Colosseum

Heading up Via Sacra past the **Tempio di Romolo** (Temple of Romulus; Map p252), you'll come to the **Basilica di Massenzio** (Basilica di Costantino; Map p252), the largest building in the Forum.

Beyond the basilica, the **Arco di Tito** (Arch of Titus; Map p252) was built in AD 81 to celebrate Vespasian and Titus' victories against rebels in Jerusalem.

What's Nearby?

Imperial Forums Archaeological Site
(Fori Imperiali; Map p252; Via dei Fori Imperiali; 🚇Via dei Fori Imperiali) The forums of Trajan, Augustus, Nerva and Caesar are known collectively as the Imperial Forums. These were largely buried when Mussolini bulldozed Via dei Fori Imperiali through the area in 1933, but excavations have since unearthed much of them. The standout sights are the Mercati di Traiano (Trajan's Markets), accessible through the Museo dei Fori Imperiali, and the landmark **Colonna di Traiano** (Trajan's Column; Map p252).

Mercati di Traiano Museo dei Fori Imperiali   Museum

(Map p252; 📞06 06 08; www.mercatiditraiano.it; Via IV Novembre 94; adult/reduced €11.50/9.50; ⏰9.30am-7.30pm, last admission 6.30pm; 🚇Via IV Novembre) This striking museum brings to life the **Mercati di Traiano**, emperor Trajan's great 2nd-century market complex, while also providing a fascinating introduction to the Imperial Forums with multimedia displays, explanatory panels and a smattering of archaeological artefacts.

✕ Take a Break

Continue up to the Capitoline Museums to enjoy inspiring views and coffee at the Caffè Capitolino (p124).

Roman Forum

In ancient times, a forum was a market place, civic centre and religious complex all rolled into one, and the greatest of all was the Roman Forum (Foro Romano). Situated between the Palatino (Palatine Hill), ancient Rome's most exclusive neighbourhood, and the Campidoglio (Capitoline Hill), it was the city's busy, bustling centre. On any given day it teemed with activity. Senators debated affairs of state in the **Curia ❶**, shoppers thronged the squares and traffic-free streets and crowds gathered under the **Colonna di Foca ❷** to listen to politicians holding forth from the **Rostrum ❷**. Elsewhere, lawyers worked the courts in basilicas including the **Basilica di Massenzio ❸**, while the Vestal Virgins quietly went about their business in the **Casa delle Vestali ❹**.

Special occasions were also celebrated in the Forum: religious holidays were marked with ceremonies at temples such as **Tempio di Saturno ❺** and **Tempio di Castore e Polluce ❻**, and military victories were honoured with dramatic processions up Via Sacra and the building of monumental arches like **Arco di Settimio Severo ❼** and **Arco di Tito ❽**.

The ruins you see today are impressive but they can be confusing without a clear picture of what the Forum once looked like. This spread shows the Forum in its heyday, complete with temples, civic buildings and towering monuments to heroes of the Roman Empire.

TOP TIPS

» Get grandstand views of the Forum from the Palatino and Campidoglio.

» Visit first thing in the morning or late afternoon; crowds are worst between 11am and 2pm.

» In summer it gets hot in the Forum and there's little shade, so take a hat and plenty of water.

Colonna di Foca & Rostrum
The free-standing, 13.5m-high Column of Phocus is the Forum's youngest monument, dating to AD 608. Behind it, the Rostrum provided a suitably grandiose platform for pontificating public speakers.

Campidoglio (Capitoline Hill)

ADMISSION

Although valid for two days, admission tickets only allow for one entry into the Forum, Colosseum and Palatino.

Tempio di Saturno
Ancient Rome's Fort Knox, the Temple of Saturn was the city treasury. In Caesar's day it housed 13 tonnes of gold, 114 tonnes of silver and 30 million sestertii worth of silver coins.

JONATHAN SMITH/GETTY IMAGES ©

LONELY PLANET/GETTY IMAGES ©

Tempio di Castore e Polluce
Only three columns of the Temple of Castor and Pollux remain. The temple was dedicated to the Heavenly Twins after they supposedly led the Romans to victory over the Latin League in 496 BC.

Arco di Settimio Severo

One of the Forum's signature monuments, this imposing triumphal arch commemorates the military victories of Septimius Severus. Relief panels depict his campaigns against the Parthians.

Curia

This big barn-like building was the official seat of the Roman Senate. Most of what you see is a reconstruction, but the interior marble floor dates to the 3rd-century reign of Diocletian.

Basilica di Massenzio

Marvel at the scale of this vast 4th-century basilica. In its original form the central hall was divided into enormous naves; now only part of the northern nave survives.

JULIUS CAESAR

Julius Caesar was cremated on the site where the Tempio di Giulio Cesare now stands.

Via Sacra

Tempio di Giulio Cesare

Casa delle Vestali

White statues line the grassy atrium of what was once the luxurious 50-room home of the Vestal Virgins. The virgins played an important role in Roman religion, serving the goddess Vesta.

Arco di Tito

Said to be the inspiration for the Arc de Triomphe in Paris, the well-preserved Arch of Titus was built by the emperor Domitian to honour his elder brother Titus.

ANDREA IZZOTTI/SHUTTERSTOCK/GETTY IMAGES ©

Trevi Fountain

The recently restored Fontana di Trevi is Rome's largest and most celebrated fountain. A foaming ensemble of mythical figures, wild horses and cascading rock falls, it takes up the entire side of the 17th-century Palazzo Poli.

Great For...

☑ Don't Miss

The contrasting seahorses, or moods of the sea.

Immortalised by Anita Ekberg's dip in Federico Fellini's film *La dolce vita* – apparently she wore waders under her iconic black ballgown – the Trevi Fountain is one of Rome's great must-see sights. It was completed in 1762 and named Trevi in reference to the *tre vie* (three roads) that converge on it.

The water still comes from the Aqua Virgo, an underground aqueduct that was built by General Agrippa during the reign of Augustus some 2000 years ago. Then, as now, the water flows in from the Salone springs around 19km away.

The Design

The fountain's design, conceived by Nicola Salvi in 1732, depicts Neptune, the god of the sea, in a shell-shaped chariot being led by Tritons and two seahorses, one wild,

❶ Need to Know

Fontana di Trevi; Map p255; Piazza di Trevi; Ⓜ Barberini)

✕ Take a Break

For a hearty meal make for Colline Emiliane (p130), up towards Piazza Barberini.

★ Top Tip

The fountain's dazzling white stone photographs best in the soft late-afternoon light.

one docile, representing the moods of the sea. In the niche to the left of Neptune, a statue represents Abundance; to the right is Salubrity.

On the eastern side is a strange conical urn. Known as the *Assso di coppe* (Ace of Cups), this was supposedly placed by Nicola Salvi to block the view of a busybody barber who had been a vocal critc of Salvi's design during the fountain's construction.

Throw Your Money In

The famous tradition (since the 1954 film *Three Coins in the Fountain*) is to toss a coin into the water and thus ensure you'll one day return to Rome. About €3000 is thrown in on an average day. For years much of this was scooped up by local thieves but in 2012 the city authorities clamped down, making it illegal to remove coins from the water. The money is now collected daily and handed over to the Catholic charity Caritas.

What's Nearby?

Palazzo del Quirinale   Palace

(Map p255; ☏06 4 69 91; www.quirinale.it; Piazza del Quirinale; admission €10, ½hr tour €1.50, 2½hr tour €10; ⊙9.30am-4pm Tue, Wed & Fri-Sun, closed Aug; Ⓜ Barberini) Overlooking Piazza del Quirinale, this immense palace is the official residence of Italy's head of state, the Presidente della Repubblica. For almost three centuries it was the pope's summer residence, but in 1870 Pope Pius IX begrudgingly handed the keys over to Italy's new king. Later, in 1948, it was given to the Italian state.

MARIA GOLOVIANKO/SHUTTERSTOCK ©

Chiesa di Santa Maria del Popolo

A magnificent repository of art, this is one of Rome's earliest and richest Renaissance churches, with lavish chapels decorated by artists such as Caravaggio, Bernini, Raphael and Pinturicchio.

Great For...

☑ **Don't Miss**

Pinturicchio's wonderful frescoes.

The first chapel was built here in 1099 to exorcise the ghost of Nero, who was secretly buried on this spot and whose ghost was thought to haunt the area. It had since been overhauled, but the church's most important makeover came when Bramante renovated the presbytery and choir in the early 16th century and Pinturicchio added a series of frescoes. Bernini further reworked the church in the 17th century.

Cerasi Chapel

The church's dazzling highlight is the Cappella Cerasi with its two works by Caravaggio: the *Conversion of Saul* and the *Crucifixion of St Peter,* dramatically spotlit via the artist's use of light and shade. The former is the second version, as the first was rejected by the patron.

The central altarpiece painting is the *Assumption* by Annibale Carracci.

Interior of Chiesa di Santa Maria del Popolo

Chigi Chapel

Raphael designed the Cappella Chigi, dedicated to his patron Agostino Chigi, but never lived to see it completed. Bernini finished the job more than 100 years later, contributing statues of Daniel and Habakkuk to the altarpiece. Only the floor mosaics were retained from Raphael's original design, including that of a kneeling skeleton, placed there to remind the living of the inevitable.

Delle Rovere Chapel

The chapel, built in the late 15th century, features works by Pinturicchio and his school. Frescoes in the lunettes depict episodes from the life of St Jerome, while the main altarpiece shows the Nativity with St Jerome.

❶ Need to Know

Map p256; Piazza del Popolo; ⊙7am-noon & 4-7pm Mon-Sat, 7.30am-1.30pm & 4.30-7.30pm Sun; Ⓜ Flaminio

✕ Take a Break

Treat yourself to a sublime ice cream from the magnificent Fatamorgana (p129).

★ Top Tip

Look out for the oldest stained-glass windows in Rome.

What's Nearby?

Piazza del Popolo   Piazza

(Map p256; ⓂFlaminio) This dazzling piazza was laid out in 1538 to provide a grandiose entrance to what was then Rome's main northern gateway. It has since been remodelled several times, most recently by Giuseppe Valadier in 1823.

Guarding its southern approach are Carlo Rainaldi's twin 17th-century churches, **Chiesa di Santa Maria dei Miracoli** (Map p256) and **Chiesa di Santa Maria in Montesanto** (Map p256). In the centre, the 36m-high **obelisk** (Map p256) was brought by Augustus from ancient Egypt and originally stood in Circo Massimo.

Porta del Popolo   Landmark

(Map p256; ⓂFlaminio) On the northern flank of Piazza del Popolo, the Porta del Popolo was created by Bernini in 1655 to celebrate Queen Christina of Sweden's defection to Catholicism,

Interior of Basilica di San Giovanni in Laterano

Basilica di San Giovanni in Laterano

For a thousand years this landmark cathedral was the most important church in Christendom. It was the first Christian basilica built in the city, and until the early 14th century, was the pope's main place of worship. It's still Rome's official cathedral and the pope's seat as the bishop of Rome.

Great For...

ℹ️ Need to Know

Piazza di San Giovanni in Laterano 4; basilica/cloister free/€5; ⊘7am-6.30pm, cloister 9am-6pm; MSan Giovanni

★ **Top Tip**
Look down as well as up – the basilica has a beautiful inlaid marble floor.

The oldest of Rome's four papal basilicas, it was commissioned by the Emperor Constantine and consecrated by Pope Sylvester I in 324. From then until 1309, when the papacy moved to Avignon, it was the principal pontifical church, and the adjacent Palazzo Laterano was the pope's official residence. Both buildings fell into disrepair during the papacy's French interlude, and when Pope Gregory XI returned to Rome in 1377 he preferred to decamp to the fortified Vatican rather than stay in the official papal digs.

Over the centuries the basilica has been revamped several times, most notably by Borromini in the 17th century, and by Alessandro Galilei, who added the immense white facade in 1735.

The Facade

Surmounted by 15 7m-high statues – Christ with St John the Baptist, John the Evangelist and the 12 Apostles – Galilei's huge facade is an imposing work of late-baroque classicism. Behind the colossal columns there are five sets of doors in the portico. The **central bronze doors** were moved here from the Curia in the Roman Forum, while, on the far right, the **Holy Door** is only opened in Jubilee years.

The Interior

The enormous marble-clad interior owes much of its present look to Francesco Borromini, who was called in by Pope Innocent X to decorate it for the 1650 Jubilee. Divided into a central nave and four minor aisles, it's a breathtaking sight, measuring 130m

Portico in Basilica di San Giovanni in Laterano

(length) by 55.6m (width) by 30m (height). Up above, the spectacular **gilt ceiling** was created at different times, but the central section, which is set around Pope Pius IV's carved coat of arms, dates to the 1560s. Beneath your feet, the beautiful inlaid **mosaic floor** was laid down by Pope Martin V in 1425.

The **central nave** is lined with 18th-century sculptures of the apostles, each 4.6m high and each set in a heroic pose in its own dramatic niche. At the head of the nave, an elaborate Gothic **baldachin** stands over the papal altar. Dating to the 14th century, this towering ensemble is said to contain the relics of the heads of Saints Peter and Paul. In front, a double staircase leads down to the **confessio** and the Renaissance tomb of Pope Martin V.

Behind the altar, the massive **apse** is decorated with sparkling mosaics. Parts of these date to the 4th century, but most were added in the 1800s.

At the other end of the basilica, on the first pillar in the right-hand nave, is an incomplete Giotto fresco. While admiring this, cock your ear towards the next column, where a monument to Pope Sylvester II is said to creak when the death of a pope is imminent.

The Cloister

To the left of the altar, the basilica's 13th-century cloister is a lovely, peaceful place with graceful twisted columns set around a central garden. Lining the ambulatories are marble fragments from the original church, including the remains of a 5th-century papal throne and inscriptions of two papal bulls.

On the cloister's western side, four columns support a slab of marble that medieval Christians believed represented the height of Jesus.

> ☑ **Don't Miss**
>
> The serene cloister; well worth the small entrance fee as it's a lovely spot to collect your thoughts.

LONELY PLANET/GETTY IMAGES ©

> ✕ **Take a Break**
>
> There are few good eateries right by the basilica, so head towards the Colosseum for some tasty cafe fare at Cafè Cafè (p139).

Teatro, Ostia Antica

DAVID SOANES PHOTOGRAPHY/GETTY IMAGES ©

Day Trip: Ostia Antica

Rome's answer to Pompeii, the Scavi Archeologici di Ostia Antica is one of Italy's most underappreciated archaeological sites. The amazingly preserved ruins of Rome's main seaport provide a thrilling glimpse into the workings of an ancient town.

Great For...

☑ Don't Miss

The views over the site from atop the Terme di Nettuno.

Founded in the 4th century BC, Ostia (the name means the mouth, or *ostium,* of the Tiber) grew to become a great port and commercial centre with a population of around 50,000.

Decline set in after the fall of the Roman Empire, and by the 9th century the city had largely been abandoned, its citizens driven off by barbarian raids and outbreaks of malaria. Over subsequent centuries, it was plundered of marble and building materials, and its ruins were gradually buried in river silt, hence their survival.

To get to the site from Rome, take the Ostia Lido train from Stazione Porta San Paolo (next to Piramide metro station) and get off at Ostia Antica.

Roman column, Ostia Antica

❶ Need to Know

06 5635 0215; www.ostiaantica.benicultu
rali.it; Viale dei Romagnoli 717; adult/reduced
€8/4, plus possible exhibition supplement €3;
8.30am-6.15pm Tue-Sun summer, earlier
closing winter

✕ Take a Break

Try the **Ristorante Monumento** (06
565 00 21; www.ristorantemonumento.it; Piazza Umberto I 8; fixed-price lunch menu €14,
meals €25-30; 12.30-3.30pm & 8-11pm
Tue-Sun) in the picturesque borgo near
the entrance to the Scavi.

★ Top Tip

Come on a weekday when the site is
much quieter.

The Ruins

Near the entrance, **Porta Romana** gives
onto the **Decumanus Maximus**, the site's
central strip, which runs over 1km to Porta
Marina, the city's original sea-facing gate.

On the Decumanus, the **Terme di Nettuno** is a must-see. This baths complex, one
of 20 that originally stood in town, dates to
the 2nd century and boasts some superb
mosaics, including one of Neptune driving
his sea-horse chariot. In the centre of the
complex are the remains of an arcaded
palestra (gym).

Next to the Terme is the **Teatro**, an
amphitheatre built by Agrippa and later
enlarged to hold 4000 people.

The grassy area behind the amphitheatre
is the **Piazzale delle Corporazioni** (Forum

of the Corporations), home to the offices
of Ostia's merchant guilds. The mosaics
that line the perimeter – ships, dolphins,
a lighthouse, an elephant – are thought to
represent the businesses housed on the
square: ships and dolphins indicated ship-
ping agencies, while the elephant probably
referred to a business involved in the ivory
trade.

The Forum, Ostia's main square, is overlooked by what remains of the **Capitolium**,
a temple built by Hadrian and dedicated to
Jupiter, Juno and Minerva.

Nearby is another highlight: the **Ther-
mopolium**, an ancient cafe. Check out
the bar, frescoed menu, kitchen and small
courtyard where customers would have
relaxed next to a fountain.

Across the road are the remains of the
2nd-century-AD **Terme del Foro**, originally
the city's largest baths complex. Here, in
the *forica* (public toilet), you can see 20
well-preserved latrines set sociably in a
long stone bench.

Basilica superiore, Basilica di San Clemente

Basilica di San Clemente

Nowhere better illustrates the various stages of Rome's turbulent past than this fascinating, multi-layered church in the shadow of the Colosseum.

Great For...

☑ Don't Miss

The temple to Mithras, deep in the bowels of the basilica.

Basilica Superiore

The ground-floor basilica superiore contains some glorious works of medieval art. These include a golden 12th-century apse mosaic, the *Trionfo della Croce* (Triumph of the Cross), showing the Madonna and St John the Baptist standing by a cross on which Christ is represented by 12 white doves. Also impressive are Masolino's 15th-century frescoes in the **Cappella di Santa Caterina**, depicting a crucifixion scene and episodes from the life of St Catherine.

Basilica Inferiore

Steps lead down to the 4th-century basilica inferiore, mostly destroyed by Norman invaders in 1084, but with some faded 11th-century frescoes illustrating the life of San Clemente.

Basilica di San Clemente

EURASIA/ROBERTHARDING/GETTY IMAGES ©

ⓘ Need to Know

www.basilicasanclemente.com; Via di San Giovanni in Laterano; excavations adult/reduced €10/5; ⊘9am-12.30pm & 3-6pm Mon-Sat, 12.15-6pm Sun; 🚊Via Labicana

✕ Take a Break

Treat yourself to a slap-up trattoria meal at Il Bocconcino (p141).

★ Top Tip

Bring a sweater – the temperatures drops as you descend underground.

Follow down another level and you'll find yourself walking an ancient lane leading to a 1st-century Roman house and a dark, 2nd-century **temple to Mithras**, with an altar showing the god slaying a bull. Beneath it all, you can hear the eerie sound of a subterranean river flowing through a Republic-era drain.

What's Nearby?
Basilica di SS Quattro Coronati
Basilica

(Via dei Santissimi Quattro Coronati 20; ⊘10-11.45am & 4-5.45pm Mon-Sat, 4-5.45pm Sun; 🚊Via di San Giovanni in Laterano) This brooding fortified church harbours some lovely 13th-century frescoes and a delightful hidden cloister. The frescoes, in the **Oratorio di San Silvestro**, depict the story of the Donation of Constantine, a notorious

forged document with which the emperor Constantine ceded control of Rome and the Western Roman Empire to the papacy.

To access the Oratorio, ring the bell in the entrance courtyard. You might also have to ring for the cloister, which is situated off the northern aisle.

Chiesa di Santo Stefano Rotondo
Church

(www.santo-stefano-rotondo.it; Via di Santo Stefano Rotondo 7; ⊘10am-1pm & 2-5pm winter, 10am-1pm & 3-6pm summer; 🚊Via della Navicella) Set in its own secluded grounds, this haunting church boasts a porticoed facade and a round, columned interior. But what really gets the heart racing is the graphic wall decor – a cycle of 16th-century frescoes depicting the tortures suffered by many early Christian martyrs.

Describing them in 1846, Charles Dickens wrote: 'Such a panorama of horror and butchery no man could imagine in his sleep, though he were to eat a whole pig, raw, for supper.'

Terme di Caracalla

ALESSANDROCALZOLARO/GETTY IMAGES ©

Terme di Caracalla

The remains of the Terme di Caracalla, the emperor Caracalla's vast baths complex, are among Rome's most awe-inspiring ruins. The original 10-hectare complex comprised baths, gyms, libraries, shops and gardens.

Great For...

☑ **Don't Miss**

A white marble slab used in an ancient board game.

Inaugurated in AD 216, the baths remained in continuous use until 537, when the invading Visigoths cut off Rome's water supply. Excavations in the 16th and 17th centuries unearthed a number of important sculptures on the site, many of which found their way into the Farnese family's art collection.

In its heyday, the complex attracted between 6000 and 8000 people every day, while, underground, hundreds of slaves sweated in 9.5km of tunnels, tending to the intricate plumbing systems.

The Ruins

Most of the ruins are what's left of the central bathhouse. This was a huge rectangular edifice bookended by two *palestre* (gyms) and centred on a *frigidarium* (cold room), where bathers would stop after spells in the warmer *tepidarium* and dome-capped *caldaria* (hot room).

Inside the baths complex

MAC99/GETTY IMAGES ©

ℹ Need to Know

☑06 3996 7700; www.coopculture.it; Viale delle Terme di Caracalla 52; adult/reduced €6/3; ⊘9am-1hr before sunset Tue-Sun, 9am-2pm Mon; 🚊Viale delle Terme di Caracalla

✕ Take a Break

Head over to the Colosseum area for a light meal at Cafè Cafè (p139).

★ Top Tip

Opera fans should check for summer performances at the Terme.

As you traverse the ruins towards the *palestra orientale,* look out for a slab of white, pockmarked marble on your right. This is a board from an ancient game called 'tropa' (the hole game).

Underground, archaeologists have discovered a temple dedicated to the Persian god Mithras.

In summer the ruins are used to stage opera and ballet performances.

What's Nearby?

Villa Celimontana   Park

(⊘7am-sunset; 🚊Via della Navicella) With its grassy banks and colourful flower beds, this leafy park is a wonderful place to escape the crowds and enjoy a summer picnic. At its centre is a 16th-century villa housing the Italian Geographical Society.

Basilica di Santa Sabina   Basilica

(☑06 5 79 41; Piazza Pietro d'Illiria 1; ⊘6.30am-12.45pm & 3-8pm; 🚊Lungotevere Aventino) This solemn basilica, one of Rome's most beautiful medieval churches, was founded by Peter of Illyria in around AD 422. It was enlarged in the 9th century and again in 1216, just before it was given to the newly founded Dominican order – note the tombstone of Muñoz de Zamora, one of the order's founding fathers, in the nave floor. A 20th-century restoration returned it to its original look.

Priorato dei Cavalieri di Malta   Historic Building

(Piazza dei Cavalieri di Malta; ⊘closed to the public; 🚊Lungotevere Aventino) Fronting an ornate cypress-shaded piazza, the Roman headquarters of the Cavalieri di Malta (Knights of Malta) boast one of Rome's most celebrated views. It's not immediately apparent, but look through the keyhole in the Priorato's green door and you'll see the dome of St Peter's Basilica perfectly aligned at the end of a hedge-lined avenue.

SLOW IMAGES/GETTY IMAGES ©

Spanish Steps

Rising above Piazza di Spagna, the Spanish Steps provide a perfect people-watching perch and you'll almost certainly find yourself taking stock here at some point.

The Spanish Steps area has long been a magnet for foreigners. In the late 1700s it was much loved by English travellers on the Grand Tour, and was known locally as *'er ghetto de l'inglesi'* (the English ghetto). Keats lived for a short time in some rooms overlooking the Spanish Steps, and died here of tuberculosis at the age of 25. Later, in the 19th century, Charles Dickens visited, noting how artists' models would hang around in the hope of being hired to sit for a painting.

The Steps

Although Piazza di Spagna was named after the nearby Spanish embassy to the Holy See, the monumental 135-step staircase (known in Italian as the Scalinata della Trinità dei Monti) was designed by an Italian,

Great For...

☑ **Don't Miss**

The sweeping rooftop views from the top of the Steps.

Barcaccia and the Spanish Steps

Francesco de Sanctis, and built in 1725 with money bequeathed by a French diplomat.

Chiesa della Trinità dei Monti

The landmark **Chiesa della Trinità dei Monti** (Map p255; Piazza Trinità dei Monti; ☺6.30am-8pm Tue-Sun; MSpagna) was commissioned by King Louis XII of France and consecrated in 1585. Apart from the great rooftop views from outside, it boasts some wonderful frescoes by Daniele da Volterra. His *Deposizione* (Deposition), in the second chapel on the left, is regarded as a masterpiece of mannerist painting.

Piazza di Spagna

At the foot of the steps, the fountain of a sinking boat, the **Barcaccia** (1627), is believed to be by Pietro Bernini, father of the more famous Giani Lorenzo. The bees and

suns that decorate the structure, which was sunken to compensate for the low pressure of the feeder aqueduct, represent the Barbarini family who commissioned the fountain.

Opposite, **Via dei Condotti** is Rome's most exclusive shopping strip, while to the southeast, **Piazza Mignanelli** is dominated by the Colonna dell'Immacolata, built in 1857 to celebrate Pope Pius IX's declaration of the Immaculate Conception.

What's Nearby?

Keats–Shelley House   Museum
(Map p255; ☎06 678 42 35; www.keats-shelley-house.org; Piazza di Spagna 26; adult/reduced €5/4, ticket gives discount for Casa di Goethe; ☺10am-1pm & 2-6pm Mon-Fri, 11am-2pm & 3-6pm Sat; MSpagna) The Keats-Shelley House is where Romantic poet John Keats died of TB at the age of 25, in February 1821. A year later, fellow poet Percy Bysshe Shelley drowned off the coast of Tuscany. The small apartment evokes the impoverished lives of the poets, and is now a small museum crammed with memorabilia, from faded letters to death masks.

Auditorium Parco della Musica

ALEXANDRE ZVEIGER/SHUTTERSTOCK ©

Modern Architecture

Rome is best known for its classical architecture, but the city also boasts a string of striking modern buildings, many created and designed by the 21st century's top starchitects.

Great For...

☑ Don't Miss

The outlying EUR district is home to some impressive rationalist architecture.

Auditorium Parco della Musica
Cultural Centre

(☎06 8024 1281; www.auditorium.com; Viale Pietro de Coubertin 10; guided tours adult/reduced €9/7; ⊙11am-8pm Mon-Sat, 10am-6pm Sun; 🚊Viale Tiziano) Designed by archistar Renzo Piano and inaugurated in 2002, Rome's flagship cultural centre is an audacious work of architecture consisting of three grey pod-like concert halls set round a 3000-seat amphitheatre.

Excavations during its construction revealed remains of an ancient Roman villa, which are now on show in the Auditorium's small **Museo Archeologico** (⊙10am-8pm Mon-Sat summer, 11am-6pm Mon-Sat winter, 10am-6pm Sun year-round) **FREE**.

Guided tours (for a minimum of 10 people) depart hourly between 11.30am and 4.30pm Saturday and Sunday, and by arrangement from Monday to Friday.

Palazzo della Civiltà del Lavoro

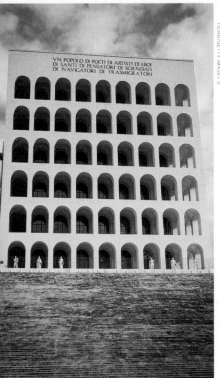

VN POPOLO DI POETI DI ARTISTI DI EROI
DI SANTI DI PENSATORI DI SCIENZIATI
DI NAVIGATORI DI TRASMIGRATORI

Museo Nazionale delle Arti del XXI Secolo (MAXXI)   Gallery

(☏06 320 19 54; www.fondazionemaxxi.it; Via Guido Reni 4a; adult/reduced €11/8; ⊙11am-7pm Tue-Sun, to 10pm Sat; ☒Viale Tiziano) As much as the exhibitions, the highlight of Rome's leading contemporary-art gallery is the Zaha Hadid–designed building it occupies. Formerly a barracks, the curved concrete structure is striking inside and out, with a multilayered geometric facade and a cavernous light-filled interior full of snaking walkways and suspended staircases.

The gallery has a small permanent collection but more interesting are the temporary exhibitions.

Museo d'Arte Contemporanea di Roma (MACRO)   Gallery

(☏06 06 08; www.museomacro.org; Via Nizza 138, cnr Via Cagliari; adult/reduced €9.50/7.50;

❶ Need to Know

The Auditorium and MAXXI can be accessed by tram 2 from Piazzale Flaminio.

✕ Take a Break

Enjoy splendid trattoria fare at Al Gran Sasso (p130) near the Museo dell'Ara Pacis.

★ Top Tip

Take in a gig at the Auditorium to experience its perfect acoustics.

⊙10.30am-7.30pm Tue-Sun; ☒Via Nizza) Along with MAXXI, this is Rome's most important contemporary-art gallery. Occupying a converted Peroni brewery, it hosts temporary exhibitions and displays works from its permanent collection of post-1960s Italian art.

Vying with the exhibits for your attention is the museum's sleek black-and-red interior design. The work of French architect Odile Decq, it retains much of the building's original structure while also incorporating a sophisticated steel-and-glass finish.

Museo dell'Ara Pacis   Museum

(☏06 06 08; www.arapacis.it; Lungotevere in Auga; adult/reduced €10.50/8.50, audioguide €4; ⊙9am-7pm, last admission 6pm; Ⓜ Flaminio) The first modern construction in Rome's historic centre since WWII, Richard Meier's controversial and widely detested glass-and-marble pavilion houses the *Ara Pacis Augustae* (Altar of Peace), Augustus' great monument to peace. One of the most important works of ancient Roman sculpture, the vast marble altar – measuring 11.6m by 10.6m by 3.6m – was completed in 13 BC.

Palazzo della Civiltà del Lavoro   Historic Building

(Palace of the Workers; Quadrato della Concordia; Ⓜ EUR Magliana) Dubbed the Square Colosseum, the Palace of the Workers is EUR's architectural icon, a rationalist masterpiece clad in gleaming white travertine.

IZZET KERIBAR/GETTY IMAGES ©

Basilica di Santa Maria Maggiore

One of Rome's four patriarchal basilicas, this monumental church stands on the summit of the Esquiline Hill, on the site of a miraculous snowfall in the summer of AD 358.

Great For...

☑ **Don't Miss**

The luminous 13th-century apse mosaics by Jacopo Torriti.

The basilica, much altered over the centuries, is something of an architectural hybrid, with a 14th-century Romanesque belfry, an 18th-century baroque facade, a largely baroque interior and a series of glorious 5th-century mosaics.

Exterior

Outside, the exterior is decorated with glimmering 13th-century mosaics, protected by Ferdinand Fuga's 1741 baroque loggia. Rising behind, the belfry, Rome's tallest, tops out at 75m.

On the piazza in front of the church, the 18.78m-high column originally stood in the Basilica of Massenzio in the Roman Forum.

Interior

The vast interior retains its original structure, despite the basilica's many overhauls.

Interior of Basilica di Santa Maria Maggiore

ℹ️ Need to Know

Map p255; Piazza Santa Maria Maggiore; basilica/museum/loggia/archaeological site free/€3/5/5; ⏱7am-7pm, museum & loggia 9am-5.30pm; 🚌Piazza Santa Maria Maggiore

✕ Take a Break

Relax over a filling meal at the highly rated Trattoria Monti (p135).

★ Top Tip

Come on 5 August to see the historic snowfall re-created with thousands of white petals.

Particularly spectacular are the **5th-century mosaics** in the **triumphal arch** and **nave**, depicting Old Testament scenes. The central image in the **apse**, signed by Jacopo Torriti, dates from the 13th century and represents the coronation of the Virgin Mary. Beneath your feet, the nave floor is a fine example of 12th-century Cosmati paving.

The **baldachin** over the high altar is heavy with gilt cherubs; the altar itself is a porphyry sarcophagus, which is said to contain the relics of St Matthew and other martyrs. The *Madonna col Bambino* (Madonna and Child) panel above the altar is believed to date from the 12th to 13th centuries.

A simple stone plaque embedded in the floor to the right of the altar marks the spot where Gian Lorenzo Bernini and his father Pietro are buried. Steps lead down to the **confessio** where a statue of Pope Pius IX

kneels before a reliquary containing a fragment of Jesus' manger.

Through the souvenir shop on the right-hand side of the church is a **museum** with a glittering collection of religious artefacts. Most interesting, however, is the upper loggia, where you'll get a close look at the facade's iridescent 13th-century mosaics, created by Filippo Rusuti. You'll also see Bernini's helical staircase.

What's Nearby?

Basilica di San Pietro in Vincoli   Basilica

(Map p252; Piazza di San Pietro in Vincoli 4a; ⏱8am-12.20pm & 3-7pm summer, to 6pm winter; Ⓜ Cavour) Pilgrims and art lovers flock to this 5th-century basilica for two reasons: to marvel at Michelangelo's colossal *Moses* (1505) sculpture and to see the chains that supposedly bound St Peter when he was imprisoned in the Carcere Mamertino (near the Roman Forum).

Access to the church is via a flight of steps through a low arch that leads up from Via Cavour.

Interior of Basilica di Santa Maria in Trastevere

Basilica di Santa Maria in Trastevere

The glittering Basilica di Santa Maria in Trastevere is said to be the oldest church dedicated to the Virgin Mary in Rome. Inside, its golden mosaics are a spectacle to behold.

Great For...

☑ **Don't Miss**

The Cappella Avila and its cleverly constructed 17th-century dome.

Dating to the early 3rd century, the basilica was commissioned by Pope Callixtus III on the site where, according to legend, a fountain of oil had miraculously sprung from the ground. The basilica has been much altered over the centuries and its current Romanesque form is the result of a 12th-century revamp. The portico came later, added by Carlo Fontana in 1702.

The Exterior

Rising above the four papal statues on Domenico Fontana's 18th-century **porch**, the basilica's restrained 12th-century **facade** is most notable for its beautiful medieval mosaic. This glittering gold banner depicts Mary feeding Jesus surrounded by 10 women bearing lamps.

Towering above the church is a 12th-century Romanesque **bell tower**, complete

Golden ceiling

JULIAN ELLIOTT PHOTOGRAPHY/GETTY IMAGES ©

❶ Need to Know

Piazza Santa Maria in Trastevere; ⏰7.30am-9pm; 🚃Viale di Trastevere, 🚋Viale di Trastevere

✕ Take a Break

Enjoy a tasty meal at the hit foodie hotspot Pianostrada Laboratorio di Cucina (p138).

★ Top Tip

Take some coins to drop in the light box and illuminate the mosaics.

with its very own mosaic – look in the small niche near the top.

Mosaics & Interior Design

The basilica's main drawcard is its golden 12th-century mosaics. In the **apse**, look out for the dazzling depiction of Christ and his mother flanked by various saints, and, on the far left, Pope Innocent II holding a model of the church. Beneath this is a series of six mosaics by Pietro Cavallini (c 1291) illustrating the life of the Virgin.

The interior boasts a typical 12th-century design with three naves divided by 21 **Roman columns**, some plundered from the Terme di Caracalla. On the right of the altar, near a spiralling Paschal candlestick, is an inscription, *Fons Olei,* which marks the spot where the miraculous oil fountain supposedly sprung. The spiralling **Cosmatesque**

floor was relaid in the 1870s, a re-creation of the 13th-century original. Up above, the coffered **golden ceiling** was designed by Domenichino in 1617.

Also worth a look is the **Cappella Avila**, the last chapel on the left, with its stunning 17th-century dome. Antonio Gherardi's clever design depicts four angels holding the circular base of a large lantern whose columns rise to give the effect of a second cupola within a larger outer dome.

Piazza Santa Maria in Trastevere

Outside the basilica, Piazza Santa Maria in Trastevere is the neighbourhood's focal square. By day it's full of mums with strollers, chatting locals and guidebook-toting tourists; by night it's the domain of foreign students, young Romans and out-of-towners, all out for a good time. The fountain in the centre of the square is of Roman origin and was restored by Carlo Fontana in 1692.

Ceiling fresco, Chiesa del Gesù

JSSIII/GETTY IMAGES ©

Chiesa del Gesù

An imposing example of Counter-Reformation architecture, Rome's most important Jesuit church is a treasure trove of glorious baroque art.

The church, which was consecrated in 1584, is fronted by an impressive and much-copied facade by Giacomo della Porta. But more than the masonry, the star turn here is the lavish marble-clad interior. Of the art on display, the most astounding work is the hypnotic *Trionfo del Nome di Gesù* (Triumph of the Name of Jesus; 1679), the swirling ceiling fresco by Giovanni Battista Gaulli. The artist, better known as Il Baciccia, also created much of the stucco decoration and the cupola frescoes.

In the northern transept, the **Cappella di Sant'Ignazio** houses the tomb of Ignatius Loyola, the Spanish soldier who founded the Jesuits in 1540. Designed by baroque maestro Andrea Pozzo, the altar-tomb is an opulent marble-and-bronze affair with lapis lazuli–encrusted columns, and, on top, a lapis lazuli globe representing the Trinity.

Great For...

☑ **Don't Miss**

Andrea Pozzo's lavish tomb of Jesuit founder St Ignatius Loyola.

Chiesa del Gesù facade

Corso Vittorio Emanuele II; Via del Plebiscito; Piazza Venezia; Piazza del Gesù; **Chiesa del Gesù**; Via d'Aracoeli

❶ Need to Know

Map p250; www.chiesadelgesu.org; Piazza del Gesù; ⊙7am-12.30pm & 4-7.45pm, St Ignatius rooms 4-6pm Mon-Sat, 10am-noon Sun; ⊡Largo di Torre Argentina

✕ Take a Break

Towards the Pantheon, La Ciambella (p126) is a great spot for a pasta lunch.

★ Top Tip

Have some coins to hand for the light machines in the dark interior.

On either side are sculptures whose titles neatly encapsulate the Jesuit ethos: to the left, *Fede che vince l'Idolatria* (Faith Defeats Idolatry); to the right, *Religione che flagella l'Eresia* (Religion Lashing Heresy).

The Spanish saint lived in the church from 1544 until his death in 1556. You can visit his **private rooms**, together with a corridor adorned with Andrea Pozzo frescoes, to the right of the main church.

What's Nearby?

Museo Nazionale
Romano: Crypta Balbi   Museum

(Map p250; ☑06 3996 7700; www.coopculture. it; Via delle Botteghe Oscure 31; adult/reduced €7/3.50; ⊙9am-7.45pm Tue-Sun; ⊡Via delle Botteghe Oscure) The least known of the Museo Nazionale Romano's four museums, the Crypta Balbi sits over the ruins of several medieval buildings, themselves set atop the Teatro di Balbo (13 BC). Archaeological finds illustrate the urban development of the surrounding area, while the museum's underground excavations, visitable by guided tour, provide an interesting insight into Rome's multilayered past.

Palazzo Venezia   Palace

(Map p250; Piazza Venezia; ⊡Piazza Venezia) Built between 1455 and 1464, this was the first of Rome's great Renaissance palaces. For centuries it served as the embassy of the Venetian Republic, but it's most readily associated with Mussolini, who installed his office here in 1929, and famously made speeches from the balcony. Nowadays, it's home to the tranquil **Museo Nazionale del Palazzo Venezia** (Map p250; ☑06 678 01 31; http://museopalazzovenezia.beniculturali. it; Via del Plebiscito 118; adult/reduced €5/2.50; ⊙8.30am-7.30pm Tue-Sun; ⊡Piazza Venezia) and its eclectic collection of Byzantine and early Renaissance paintings, furniture, ceramics, bronze figures, weaponry and armour.

DALLAS STRIBLEY/GETTY IMAGES ©

PHOTOGOLFER/SHUTTERSTOCK ©

Galleria Doria Pamphilj

Hidden behind the grimy grey exterior of Palazzo Doria Pamphilj, this wonderful gallery boasts one of Rome's richest private art collections, with works by Raphael, Tintoretto, Brueghel, Titian, Caravaggio, Bernini and Velázquez.

Great For...

☑ Don't Miss

The *Ritratto di papa Innocenzo X*, generally considered the gallery's greatest masterpiece.

Palazzo Doria Pamphilj dates to the mid-15th century, but its current look was largely the work of the current owners, the Doria Pamphilj family, who acquired it in the 18th century. The Pamphilj's golden age, during which the family collection was started, came during the papacy of one of their own, Innocent X (r 1644–55).

The opulent picture galleries, decorated with frescoed ceilings and gilded mirrors, are hung with floor-to-ceiling paintings. Masterpieces abound, but look out for Titian's *Salomè con la testa del Battista* (Salome with the Head of John the Baptist) and two early Caravaggios: *Riposo durante la fuga in Egitto* (Rest During the Flight into Egypt) and *Maddalene Penitente* (Penitent Magdalen). The undisputed star, though, is Velázquez' **Ritratto di papa Innocenzo X**, his portrait of an implacable Pope Innocent X, who grumbled that the depiction was

Interior, Galleria Doria Pamphilj

❶ Need to Know

Map p250; ☎06 679 73 23; www.dopart.it; Via del Corso 305; adult/reduced €11/7.50; ⊗9am-7pm, last admission 6pm; 🚇Via del Corso

✖ Take a Break

A short walk north, Osteria dell'Ingegno (p128) offers seasonal pastas and a piazza-side setting.

★ Top Tip

Make sure to pick up the free audioguide.

'too real'. For a comparison, check out Gian Lorenzo Bernini's sculptural interpretation of the same subject.

The excellent free audioguide, narrated by Jonathan Pamphilj, brings the place alive with family anecdotes and background information.

What's Nearby?

Chiesa di Sant'Ignazio di Loyola   Church

(Map p250; Piazza di Sant'Ignazio; ⊗7.30am-7pm Mon-Sat, 9am-7pm Sun; 🚇Via del Corso) Flanking a delightful rococo piazza, this important Jesuit church boasts a Carlo Maderno facade and two celebrated *trompe l'œil* frescoes by Andrea Pozzo (1642–1709). One cleverly depicts a fake dome, whilst the other, on the nave ceiling, shows St Ignatius Loyola being welcomed into paradise by Christ and the Madonna.

Piazza Colonna   Piazza

(Map p250; 🚇Via del Corso) Together with the adjacent Piazza di Montecitorio, this stylish piazza is Rome's political nerve centre. On its northern flank, the 16th-century **Palazzo Chigi** (Map p250; www.governo.it; ⊗guided visits 9am-1pm Sat Oct-May, bookings required) **FREE** has been the official residence of Italy's prime minister since 1961. In the centre, the 30m-high **Colonna di Marco Aurelio** (Map p250) was completed in AD 193 to honour Marcus Aurelius' military victories.

Palazzo di Montecitorio   Historic Building

(Map p250; ☎800 012955; www.camera.it; Piazza di Montecitorio; ⊗guided visits noon-2.30pm 1st Sun of month; 🚇Via del Corso) **FREE** Home to Italy's Chamber of Deputies, this baroque *palazzo* was built by Bernini in 1653, expanded by Carlo Fontana in the late 17th century, and given an art nouveau facelift in 1918. Visits take in the mansion's lavish reception rooms and the main chamber where the 630 deputies debate beneath a beautiful Liberty-style skyline.

Sunset over the Teatro di Marcello

Life in the Ghetto

The Jewish Ghetto, centred on lively Via Portico d'Ottavia, is an atmospheric area studded with artisans' studios, vintage clothes shops, kosher bakeries and popular trattorias.

Great For...

☑ Don't Miss

Poking around the ruins beneath the landmark Teatro di Marcello.

Rome's Jewish community harks back to the 2nd century BC, making it one of the oldest in Europe. Confinement in the Ghetto was first enforced in 1555 when Pope Paul IV ushered in a period of official intolerance that lasted, on and off, until the 20th century.

Museo Ebraico di Roma
Synagogue, Museum

(Jewish Museum of Rome; Map p250; ☎06 6840 0661; www.museoebraico.roma.it; Via Catalana; adult/reduced €11/8; ☉10am-6.15pm Sun-Thu, 9am-3.15pm Fri summer, 10am-4.15pm Sun-Thu, 9am-1.15pm Fri winter; ☐Lungotevere de' Cenci) The historical, cultural and artistic heritage of Rome's Jewish community is chronicled in this small but engrossing museum. Housed in the city's early 20th-century synagogue, Europe's second largest, it displays parchments, precious fabrics,

Fontana della Tartarughe

GORAN BOGICEVIC/SHUTTERSTOCK ©

marble carvings, and a collection of 17th- and 18th-century silverware. Documents and photos attest to life in the Ghetto and the hardships suffered by the city's Jewry during WWII.

Fontana delle Tartarughe Fountain (Map p250; Piazza Mattei; 🚌Via Arenula) This playful, much-loved fountain features four boys gently hoisting tortoises up into a bowl of water. Created by Giacomo della Porta and Taddeo Landini in the late 16th century, it's the subject of a popular local legend, according to which it was created in a single night.

The story goes that the Duke of Mattei had it built to save his engagement and prove to his prospective father-in-law that despite gambling his fortune away he was still a good catch. And amazingly, it worked.

The father was impressed and allowed Mattei to marry his daughter.

In reality, the fountain was no overnight sensation and took three years to craft (1581–1584). The tortoises, after whom it's named, were added by Bernini during a restoration in 1658.

Area Archeologica del Teatro di Marcello e del Portico d'Ottavia

Archaeological Site (Map p250; entrances Via del Teatro di Marcello 44 & Via Portico d'Ottavia 29; ⏰9am-7pm summer, 9am-6pm winter; 🚌Via del Teatro di Marcello) **FREE** To the east of the Jewish Ghetto, the **Teatro di Marcello** (Theatre of Marcellus; Map p250; Via del Teatro di Marcello) is the star turn of this dusty archaeological area. This 20,000-seat mini-Colosseum was planned by Julius Caesar and completed in 11 BC by Augustus, who named it after a favourite nephew, Marcellus. In the 16th century a *palazzo,* which now contains several exclusive apartments, was built on top of the original structure.

Iconic Treasures & Ruins

Follow in the footsteps of an ancient Roman on this whistle-stop tour of the city's iconic treasures. The route transports you back to Rome's glorious golden age.

Start: M Colosseo
Distance: 1.5km
Duration: 3 hours plus

6 It's worth stopping off at **Il Vittoriano** (p75), the massive mountain of white marble, for its unforgettable 360-degree views over the city.

RICHARD I'ANSON/SHUTTERSTOCK ©

4 The Michelangelo-designed **Piazza del Campidoglio** (p74) sits atop the Capitoline hill, one of the seven hills on which Rome was founded.

ANSHAR/SHUTTERSTOCK ©

5 One of Rome's top museum complexes, the **Capitoline Museums** (p72) are home to the city's finest ancient sculpture.

✕ Take a Break

The Caffè Capitolino (p124) is a refined spot for an uplifting coffee.

2 The **Palatino** (p60) was the site of the emperor's palace and home to the cream of imperial society.

Piazza Venezia
Piazza di San Marco
Piazza
Piazza d'Ara Coeli
6
FINISH
Via di San Pietro in Carcere
Aracoeli stairs
Via d'Aracoeli
Via del Teatro di Marcello
4
5
Palazzo Senatorio
Campidoglio (Capitoline Hill)
Via del Foro Romano
Via di San Teodoro

3 The **Roman Forum** (p80) was the empire's nerve centre, a hive of law courts, temples, piazzas and shops.
FRANCESCO IACOBELLI/GETTY IMAGES ©

Classic Photo of the Colosseum – great from any angle

1 More than any other monument, it's the **Colosseum** (p36) that symbolises the power and glory of ancient Rome.
JAMES EMMERSON/ROBERTHARDING/GETTY IMAGES ©

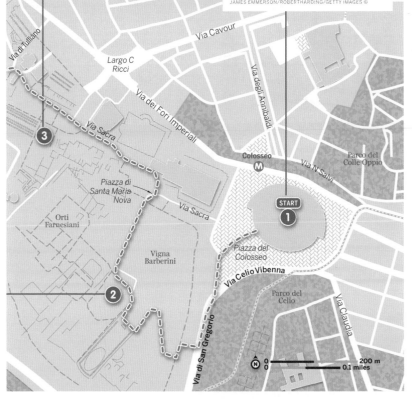

Centro Storico Piazzas

Rome's historic centre boasts some of the city's most celebrated piazzas and beautiful but lesser known squares. Together they encapsulate much of the city's beauty, history and drama.

Start: 🚊 Via del Corso
Distance: 1.5km
Duration: 3.5 hours

Classic Photo of Piazza della Rotonda with the Pantheon in the background

4 It's a short walk along Via del Seminario to Piazza della Rotonda, where the **Pantheon** (p50) needs no introduction.

DAVID SOANES PHOTOGRAPHY/GETTY IMAGES ©

5 Piazza Navona (p64) is Rome's great showpiece square where you can compare the two giants of Roman baroque: Gian Lorenzo Bernini and Francesco Borromini.

BASIC ELEMENTS PHOTOGRAPHY/GETTY IMAGES ©

7 Just beyond the Campo, the more sober Piazza Farnese is overshadowed by the austere facade of the Renaissance **Palazzo Farnese** (p116).

1 Piazza Colonna (p111) is dominated by the 30m-high Colonna di Marco Aurelio and flanked by Palazzo Chigi, the official residence of the Italian PM.
FRED MATOS/GETTY IMAGES ©

2 Follow Via dei Bergamaschi to **Piazza di Pietra**, a refined space overlooked by the 2nd-century Tempio di Adriano.

3 Continue down Via de' Burro to Piazza di Sant'Ignazio, location of the **Chiesa di Sant'Ignazio di Loyola** (p111), with its celebrated *trompe l'œil* frescoes.

✗ **Take a Break**
Caffè Sant'Eustachio (p170) is reckoned by many to serve the city's best coffee.

6 Over on the other side of Corso Vittorio Emanuele II, **Campo de' Fiori** (p67) hosts a noisy market and boisterous drinking scene.
CHRISTIAN MUELLER/SHUTTERSTOCK ©

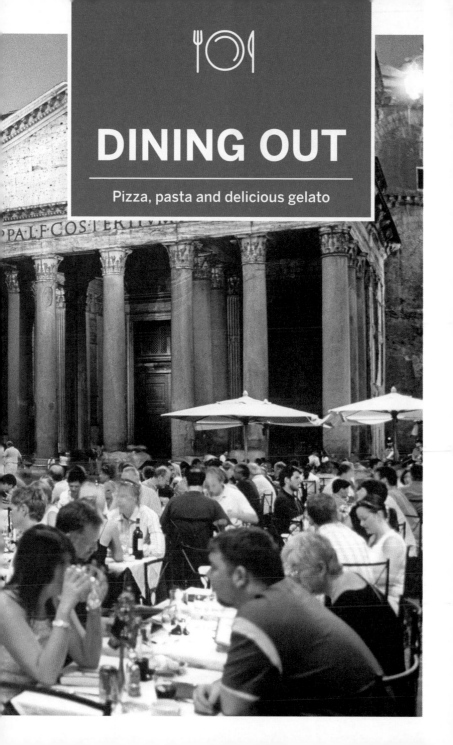

DINING OUT

Pizza, pasta and delicious gelato

Dining Out

Food is central to the Roman passion for life. Everyone has an opinion on it and the city teems with trattorias, pizzerias, fine-dining restaurants and gourmet gelaterie.

Over recent decades, Rome's dining scene has become increasingly sophisticated as cucina creativa *(creative cooking) has taken off and the city's gourmet restaurants have upped their game. But the bedrock of the Roman foodscape has always been, and still remains, the family-run trattorias that pepper the city's streets and piazzas. These simple eateries, often with rickety wooden tables and* nonna *(grandma) at the stove, have been feeding visitors for centuries and are still the best bet for classic, seasonal Roman fare.*

In This Section

Price Ranges

The following prices refer to a meal consisting of a *primo* (first course), *secondo* (second course) and *dolce* (dessert), plus a glass of wine.

€	less than €25
€€	€25–45
€€€	more than €45

Tipping

Although service is included, leave a tip: from 5% in a pizzeria to 10% in a restaurant.

Vatican City, Borgo & Prati
Sophisticated restaurants,
delicious takeaways,
heavenly gelaterie (p132)

Villa Borghese & Northern Rome
Park cafes and smart, fashionable
restaurants (p141)

Tridente, Trevi & the Quirinale
Classy neighbourhood
eateries, great gelaterie
and upmarket cafes (p129)

Centro Storico
Romantic hideaways,
old-school trattorias,
top pizzerias (p124)

Monti, Esquilino & San Lorenzo
Ethnic eats, cool bars,
boho restaurants (p135)

Ancient Rome
Hidden gems among
the tourist traps (p124)

Trastevere & Gianicolo
Touristy but terrific
trattorias, gelaterie, bars
and pizzerias (p138)

San Giovanni & Testaccio
Traditional Roman cuisine,
good cheap eats (p139)

Southern Rome
Trend-setting foodie venues in ex-
industrial Ostiense district (p143)

Useful Phrases

I'd like... vorrei (vo.*ray*...)

a table un tavolo (oon *ta*.vo.lo)

the menu il menù (eel me.*noo*)

two beers due birre (doo.e *bee*.re)

What would you recommend? Cosa
mi consiglia? (*ko*.za mee kon.*see*.lya)

Can you bring me the bill, please? Mi
porta il conto, per favore? (mee *por*.ta
eel *kon*.to per fa.vo.re)

Classic Dishes

Bucatini all'amatriciana Thick
spaghetti with tomato sauce, onions,
pancetta, cheese and chilli.

Cacio e pepe Pasta mixed with pecorino romano cheese, black pepper and
olive oil.

Carciofi alla giudia Deep-fried 'Jewish-
style' artichokes.

Saltimbocca alla romana Veal cutlet
with prosciutto (ham) and sage.

The Best...

Experience Rome's top restaurants and cafes

Roman

Flavio al Velavevodetto (p140) Classic *cucina romana*, served in huge portions.

Da Felice (p140) In the heartland of Roman cuisine, and sticking to a traditional weekly timetable.

Armando al Pantheon (p127) Family-run trattoria offering hearty Roman cuisine in the shadow of the Pantheon.

Ristorante L'Arcangelo (p133) A creative, contemporary take on Roman dishes.

Creative Cuisine

Metamorfosi (p142) Michelin-starred cuisine by wonder-chef Roy Carceres.

All'Oro (p132) Food as art at chef Riccardo Di Giacinto's glamorous Michelin-starred eatery.

Glass Hostaria (p139) Wonderful, innovative food in a contemporary setting in Trastevere.

Open Colonna (p137) Antonello Colonna's glass-roofed restaurant offers creative takes on Roman classics.

Pizzerias

Pizzeria Da Remo (p140) Spartan but stunning, the frenetic Roman pizzeria experience in Testaccio.

Pizza Ostiense (p143) New on the scene, but offering classic Roman neighbourhood pizza.

Pizzeria Ivo (p138) Always busy, fiercely traditional, loud-and-gruff Trastevere pizzeria.

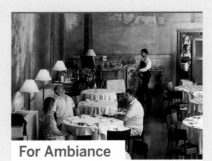

For Ambiance

Aroma (p141) The Michelin-starred rooftop restaurant of the Palazzo Manfredi hotel has 'marry me' views over the Colosseum.

La Veranda (pictured above; p135) A location in Paolo Sorrentino's *The Great Beauty*; dine beneath 15th-century Pinturicchio frescoes.

Open Colonna (p137) Restaurant on a mezzanine under a soaring glass ceiling in the Palazzo degli Esposizioni.

Regional

Enoteca Regionale Palatium (p130) Wine bar showcasing the best of Lazio food and drink.

Colline Emiliane (p130) Fantastic roasted meats and hearty pastas.

Trattoria Monti (p135) Top-notch traditional cooking from the Marches, including heavenly fried things.

Terre e Domus (p124) All ingredients are sourced from the surrounding Lazio region.

Eating with Locals

Pizzeria Da Remo (p140) The full neighbourhood Roman pizza experience, with lightning-fast waiters serving paper-thin pizzas.

Da Felice (p140) Traditional local cooking in Testaccio, the heartland of Roman cuisine.

Antico Forno Urbani (p126) Queue up with the locals for *pizza al taglio* (by the slice) in the Ghetto.

Pizza Ostiense (p143) Fabulous thin-crust pizza in Rome's ex-industrial, hip neighbourhood of Ostiense.

Pastries

Pasticceria De Bellis (p125) Work-of-art cakes, pastries and *dolci* (sweets) at this chic *pasticceria* (pastry shop).

Andreotti (p143) Poem-worthy treats from buttery *crostate* (tarts) to the piles of golden *sfogliatelle romane* (ricotta-filled pastries).

Innocenti (p138) Classic old-school Trastevere bakery, with piled-high biscuits such as *brutti ma buoni* (ugly but good).

★ Lonely Planet's Top Choices

Metamorfosi (p142) Michelin-starred, chic yet informal.

Glass Hostaria (p139) Italian cuisine as a creative art in Trastevere.

Casa Coppelle (p126) Creative Italian- and French-inspired food in romantic surroundings.

Flavio al Velavevodetto (p140) For the real *cucina romana* (Roman kitchen).

L'Asino d'Oro (p135) Fantastic food, stunning value and Umbrian flavours.

Fatamorgana (p129) Incredible artisanal gelato, in Tridente, Vatican, Monti and Trastevere.

✕ Ancient Rome

Caffè Capitolino — Cafe €

(Map p252; Piazzale Caffarelli 4; ⊙9am-7.30pm Tue-Sun; ⊟Piazza Venezia) The Capitoline Museums' charming terrace cafe is a good place to relax over a drink or light snack (*panini,* salads and pizza) and enjoy wonderful views across the city's rooftops. Although part of the museum complex, you don't need a ticket to come here as it's accessible via an independent entrance on Piazzale Caffarelli.

Terre e Domus — Lazio Cuisine €€

(Map p252; ☑06 6994 0273; Via Foro Traiano 82-4; meals €30; ⊙7.30am-12.30am Mon-Sat; ⊟Via dei Fori Imperiali) This modern white-and-glass restaurant is the best option in the touristy Forum area. Overlooking the Colonna di Traiano, it serves a menu of traditional staples, all made with ingredients sourced from the surrounding Lazio region, and a thoughtful selection of regional wines. Lunchtime can be busy but it quietens down in the evening.

Ristorante Roof Garden Circus — Ristorante €€€

(☑06 678 78 16; www.fortysevenhotel.com; Hotel Forty Seven, Via Petroselli 47; meals €50; ⊙12.30-3pm & 7.30-11.30pm; ⊟Via Petroselli) The rooftop of the Forty Seven hotel sets the romantic stage for chef Vito Grippa's menu of classic Roman dishes and contemporary Italian cuisine. With the Aventino hill rising in the background, you can tuck into stalwarts such as spaghetti *aglio e olio* (with garlic and olive oil) or push the boat out and opt for something richer like roast guinea fowl with black truffles.

✕ Centro Storico

Forno Roscioli — Pizza, Bakery €

(Map p250; Via dei Chiavari 34; pizza slices from €2, snacks from €1.50; ⊙7am-7.30pm Mon-Sat; ⊟Via Arenula) This is one of Rome's top bakeries, much loved by lunching locals who crowd here for luscious sliced pizza, prize pastries and hunger-sating *supplì*. There's also a counter serving hot pastas and vegetable side dishes.

Spaghetti *aglio e olio*

Forno di Campo de' Fiori
Pizza, Bakery €

(Map p250; Campo de' Fiori 22; pizza slices about €3; ⏰7.30am-2.30pm & 4.45-8pm Mon-Sat; 🚇Corso Vittorio Emanuele II) This buzzing bakery on Campo de' Fiori does a roaring trade in *panini* and delicious fresh-from-the-oven *pizza al taglio* (by the slice). Aficionados swear by the *pizza bianca* ('white' pizza with olive oil, rosemary and salt), but the *panini* and *pizza rossa* ('red' pizza, with olive oil, tomato and oregano) taste plenty good, too.

Supplizio
Fast Food €

(Via dei Banchi Vecchi 143; supplì €3-5; ⏰noon-4pm Mon-Sat plus 5.30-10pm Mon-Thu, to 11pm Fri & Sat; 🚇Corso Vittorio Emanuele II) Rome's favourite snack, the *supplì* (a fried croquette filled with rice, tomato sauce and mozzarella), gets a gourmet makeover at this elegant new street-food joint. Sit back on the vintage leather sofa and dig into the classic article or throw the boat out and try something different, maybe a mildly spicy fish *supplì* stuffed with anchovies, tuna, parsley, and just a hint of orange.

Chiostro del Bramante Caffè
Cafe €

(Map p250; www.chiostrodelbramante.it; Via Arco della Pace 5; meals €15-20; ⏰10am-8pm Mon-Fri, to 9pm Sat & Sun; 🛜; 🚇Corso del Rinascimento) Many of Rome's galleries and museums have in-house cafes but few are as beautifully located as the Chiostro del Bramante Caffè on the 1st floor of Bramante's elegant Renaissance cloister. With outdoor tables overlooking the central courtyard and an all-day menu offering everything from cakes and coffee to baguettes, light lunches and aperitifs, it's a great spot for a break.

Gelateria del Teatro
Gelateria €

(Map p250; Via dei Coronari 65; gelato from €2.50; ⏰11.30am-midnight; 🚇Corso del Rinascimento) All the ice cream served at this excellent gelateria is prepared on-site – look through the window and you'll see how. There are about 40 flavours to choose from, all made from thoughtfully sourced

🍴 Where to Eat

Take your pick according to your mood and your pocket, from the frenetic energy of a Roman pizzeria to the warm familiarity of a local trattoria, run for generations by the same family, or from a bar laden with sumptuous *aperitivi* to a restaurant where both presentation and the flavours are a work of art.

Romans rarely drink without eating, and you can eat well at many *enoteche*, wine bars that usually serve snacks (such as cheeses or cold meats, bruschette and crostini) and hot dishes. Some, such as Enoteca Regionale Palatium (p130) or Casa Bleve (p129), offer full-scale dining.

Traditionally, trattorias were family-run places that offered a basic, affordable local menu, while *osterie* usually specialised in one dish and *vino della casa* (house wine). There are still lots of these around. *Ristoranti* offer more choices and smarter service, and are more expensive.

ingredients, including some excellent fruit combos and spicy chocolate.

Baguetteria del Fico
Sandwiches €

(Map p250; Via della Fossa 12; panini €5-7; ⏰11am-2am; 🚇Corso del Risorgimento) A designer baguette bar ideal for a midday bite or late snack. Choose your bread, then select from the rich array of fillers – cured meats, cheeses, marinated vegetables, salads, homemade sauces. For liquid sustenance, there's a choice of bottled craft beers.

Pasticceria De Bellis
Pasticceria €

(Map p250; Piazza del Paradiso 56-57; pastries €4; ⏰9am-8pm Tue-Sun; 🚇Corso Vittorio Emanuele II) The beautifully crafted cakes, pastries and *dolci* made at this chic pasticceria are miniature works of art. Curated in every detail, they look superb and taste magnificent. You'll find traditional offerings

🍽 Roman Cuisine

Like most Italian cuisines, Roman cooking was born of careful use of local ingredients – making use of the cheaper cuts of meat, like *guanciale* (pig's cheek), and greens that could be gathered wild from the fields.

There are a few classic dishes that are served by almost every trattoria and restaurant in Rome. These carb-laden comfort foods are seemingly simple, yet notoriously difficult to prepare well. Iconic Roman dishes include carbonara (pasta with lardons, egg and Parmesan), *alla gricia* (with pig's cheek and onions), *amatriciana* (invented when an enterprising chef from Amatrice added tomatoes to *alla gricia*) and *cacio e pepe* (with cheese and pepper).

The number of special-occasion, creative restaurants is ever rising in Rome, with a buzz around openings such as chef Riccardo Di Giacinto's All'Oro (p132). Roy Carceres continues to wow at Metamorfosi (p142), and Cristina Bowerman, director of Trastevere's Glass Hostaria (p139), is one of the few Italian female chefs to have received a Michelin star.

Another relatively new concept in Rome is all-day dining, with a few notable all-things-to-all-people restaurants including Porto Fluviale (p143) and the multistorey mall Eataly (p143), which has restaurants to suit almost every mood, from a hankering for *fritti* (fried things) to fine dining.

Guanciale
CLAUDIO RAMPININI/GETTY IMAGES ©

alongside unique creations such as the Assoluta, a decadent concoction combining several chocolate mousses.

Alfredo e Ada   Trattoria €
(☎06 687 88 42; Via dei Banchi Nuovi 14; meals €25; ◷noon-3pm & 7-10pm Tue-Sat; ☐Corso Vittorio Emanuele II) For an authentic trattoria meal, search out this much-loved local eatery. It's distinctly no-frills with spindly, marble-topped tables and homey clutter, but there's a warm, friendly atmosphere and the traditional Roman food is filling and flavoursome.

Antico Forno Urbani   Pizza, Bakery €
(Map p250; Piazza Costaguti 31; pizza slices from €1.50; ◷7.40am-2.30pm & 5-8.45pm Mon-Fri, 9am-1.30pm Sat & Sun; ☐Via Arenula) A popular kosher bakery, this Ghetto institution makes some of the best *pizza bianca* in town, as well as freshly baked bread, biscuits and focaccias. It gets very busy but once you catch a whiff of the yeasty odours wafting off the counter, there's nothing for it but to grab a ticket and wait your turn.

Casa Coppelle   Ristorante €€
(Map p250; ☎06 6889 1707; www.casacoppelle. it; Piazza delle Coppelle 49; meals €45; ◷12-3.30pm & 6.30-11.30pm; ☐Corso del Rinascimento) Exposed brick walls, flowers and subdued lighting set the stage for creative Italian- and French-inspired food at this intimate, romantic restaurant. There's a full range of starters and pastas, but the real tour de force are the deliciously tender steaks and rich meat dishes. Service is attentive and the setting, on a small piazza near the Pantheon, memorable. Book ahead.

La Ciambella   Italian €€
(Map p250; www.laciambellaroma.com; Via dell'Arco della Ciambella 20; fixed-price lunch menus €10-25, meals €30; ◷7.30am-midnight; ☐Largo di Torre Argentina) From breakfast pastries and lunchtime pastas to afternoon tea, Neapolitan pizzas and aperitif cocktails, this all-day eatery is a top find. Central but as yet undiscovered by the tourist

Pastries in Centro Storico (p124)

hordes, it's a spacious, light-filled spot set over the ruins of the Terme di Agrippa, visible through transparent floor panels. The mostly traditional food is spot on, and the atmosphere laid-back and friendly.

Armando al Pantheon   Trattoria €€

(Map p250; ☑06 6880 3034; www.armandoal pantheon.it; Salita dei Crescenzi 31; meals €40; ☺12.30-3pm & 7-11pm Mon-Fri, 12.30-3pm Sat; ☒Largo di Torre Argentina) An institution in these parts, Armando al Pantheon is a rare find – a genuine family-run trattoria in the touristy Pantheon area. It's been on the go for more than 50 years and has served its fair share of celebs, but it hasn't let fame go to its head and it remains one of the best bets for earthy Roman cuisine. Reservations essential.

Renato e Luisa   Trattoria €€

(Map p250; ☑06 686 96 60; www.renatoeluisa. it; Via dei Barbieri 25; meals €45; ☺8pm-midnight Tue-Sun; ☒Largo di Torre Argentina) Highly rated locally, this small backstreet trattoria is always packed. Chef Renato takes a creative approach to classic Roman cooking, result-

ing in dishes that are modern and seasonal yet undeniably local, such as his signature *cacio e pepe e fiori di zucca* (pasta with pecorino cheese, black pepper and courgette flowers). Bookings recommended.

Ditirambo   Italian €€

(Map p250; ☑06 687 16 26; www.ristorante ditirambo.it; Piazza della Cancelleria 72; meals €40; ☺1-3pm & 7.20-10.30pm, closed Mon lunch; ☒Corso Vittorio Emanuele II) Since opening in 1996, Ditirambo has won an army of fans with its informal trattoria vibe and seasonal, organic cuisine. Dishes cover many bases, ranging from old-school favourites to thoughtful vegetarian offerings and more exotic fare such as pasta with Sicilian prawns, basil and lime. Book ahead.

Grappolo D'Oro   Italian €€

(Map p250; ☑06 689 70 80; www.hosteria grappolodoro.it; Piazza della Cancelleria 80; tasting menu €28, meals €35-40; ☺12.45-3pm & 7-11.30pm, closed Wed lunch; ☒Corso Vittorio Emanuele II) This informal eatery stands out among the many lacklustre options around Campo de' Fiori. The emphasis is on

MONCHERIE GETTY IMAGES ©

> *toppings loaded atop thin, crispy, light-as-air, slow-risen bread that verge on the divine*

traditional Roman cuisine, albeit with the occasional twist, so look out for artichoke starters, pastas littered with pecorino, pancetta and black pepper, and mains of no-nonsense braised and grilled meats.

Matricianella   Trattoria €€
(☎06 683 21 00; www.matricianella.it; Via del Leone 2/4; meals €40; ⏱12.30-3pm & 7.30-11pm Mon-Sat; 🚇Via del Corso) With its gingham tablecloths, chintzy murals and fading prints, Matricianella is an archetypal trattoria, much loved for its traditional Roman cuisine. Its loyal clientele go crazy for ever-green crowd-pleasers like battered vegetables, artichoke *alla giudia* (fried, Jewish style), and *saltimbocca* (veal cutlet with ham and sage). Booking is essential.

Osteria dell'Ingegno   Italian €€
(Map p250; ☎06 678 06 62; www.osteriaingegno.it; Piazza di Pietra 45; meals €40; ⏱noon-

midnight; 🚇Via del Corso) A boho-chic restaurant–wine bar with a colourful art-filled interior and a prime location on a charming central piazza. The menu hits all the right notes with a selection of seasonal pastas, creative mains, salads and home-made desserts, while the 300-strong wine list boasts some interesting Italian labels. *Aperitivo* is served daily from 5pm to 8pm.

Salumeria Roscioli   Italian €€€
(Map p250; ☎06 687 52 87; Via dei Giubbonari 21; meals €55; ⏱12.30-4pm & 7pm-midnight Mon-Sat; 🚇Via Arenula) The name Roscioli has long been a byword for foodie excellence, and this luxurious deli-restaurant is the place to experience it. Under a coffered ceiling, you'll find a display of mouth-watering Italian and foreign delicacies, while behind, in the small restaurant, diners sit down to sophisticated Italian food and some truly outstanding wines.

La Rosetta   Seafood €€€
(Map p250; ☎06 686 10 02; www.larosetta.com; Via della Rosetta 8; lunch menu €65, meals €90-120; ⏱12.15-2.45pm & 7-10.45pm, closed 3 weeks

Aug; 🚇Corso del Rinascimento) Food fads might come and go but La Rosetta remains what it has long been, one of Rome's top fish restaurants. Hidden down a sidestreet near the Pantheon, it offers classic seafood dishes and a choice of raw delicacies alongside more elaborate modern creations. Bookings essential.

Casa Bleve Ristorante, Wine Bar €€€
(Map p250; 📞06 686 59 70; www.casableve. it; Via del Teatro Valle 48-49; meals €50-65; 🕒12.30-3pm & 7.30-10.30pm Mon-Sat; 🚇Largo di Torre Argentina) Ideal for a special-occasion dinner, this palatial restaurant–wine bar dazzles with its column-lined dining hall and stained-glass roof. Its wine list, one of the best in town, accompanies a small but considered menu of hard-to-find cheeses, cold cuts, seasonal pastas and refined main courses.

Piperno Ristorante €€€
(Map p250; 📞06 6880 6629; www.ristorante piperno.it; Via Monte de' Cenci 9; meals €50-55; 🕒12.45-2.20pm & 7.45-10.20pm, closed Mon & Sun dinner; 🚌Via Arenula) This historic Ghetto restaurant, complete with its smart old-school look, is a top spot to get to grips with traditional Jewish-Roman cooking. Signature dishes include wonderful deep-fried *filetti di baccalà* (cod fillets) and *animelle di agnello con carciofi* (lamb sweetbreads with artichokes). To finish off, try the *tortino al cioccolato* (chocolate cake). Booking recommended.

✕ Tridente, Trevi & the Quirinale

Fatamorgana Gelateria €
(Map p256; Via Laurina 10; 🕒noon-11pm; 🚇Flaminio) The wonderful all-natural Fatamorgana, purveyors of arguably Rome's best artisanal ice cream, now has this handy central branch. Innovative and classic tastes of heaven abound, including flavours such as pear and caramel, all made from the finest seasonal ingredients.

Il Caruso Gelateria €
(Via Collina 15; 🕒noon-9pm; 🚇Repubblica) Spot Il Caruso by the gelato-licking hordes outside. This best-kept-secret artisanal gelateria only does a few strictly seasonal flavours, but they're created to perfection. Try the incredibly creamy pistachio. It also offers two types of *panna:* the usual whipped cream or the verging-on-sublime *zabaglione* (egg and marsala custard) combined with whipped cream.

Dei Gracchi Gelateria €
(Map p256; Via di Ripetta 261; ice cream from €2; 🕒11.30am-10pm, to midnight Jun-Sep; 🚇Flaminio) A new outpost of the venerable Gelataria dei Gracchi, close to the Vatican, this serves up superb ice cream made from the best ingredients, with an excellent array of classic flavours. It's handily located just off Piazza del Popolo, so you can take your pick and then wander around the square as you revel in your excellent selection.

Gina Cafe €
(Map p255; 📞06 678 02 51; Via San Sebastian-ello 7a; snacks €8-16; 🕒11am-8pm; 🚇Spagna) Around the corner from the Spanish Steps, this is an ideal place to drop once you've shopped. Comfy white seats are strewn with powder-blue cushions, and it gets packed by a Prada-clad crowd, gossiping and flirting over sophisticated salads and perfect *panini*. You can also order a €40/60 regular/deluxe picnic-for-two to take up to Villa Borghese.

Canova Tadolini Cafe €
(Map p256; 📞06 3211 0702; Via del Babuino 150a/b; 🕒9am-10.30pm Mon-Sat; 🚇Spagna) In 1818 sculptor Canova signed a contract for this studio that agreed it would be forever preserved for sculpture. The place is still stuffed with statues and it's a unique experience to sit among the great maquettes and sup an upmarket tea or knock back some wine and snacks.

Caffè Greco Cafe €
(📞06 679 17 00; Via dei Condotti 86; 🕒9am-9pm; 🚇Spagna) Caffè Greco opened in 1760 and is still working the look: penguin

🍽 Pizza

Remarkably, pizza was only introduced to Rome post-WWII, by southern immigrants. It caught on. Every Roman's favourite casual (and cheap) meal is the gloriously simple pizza, with Rome's signature wafer-thin bases, covered in fresh, bubbling toppings, slapped down on tables by waiters on a mission. Pizzerias often only open in the evening, as their wood-fired ovens take a while to get going. Most Romans will precede their pizza with a starter of bruschetta or *fritti* (mixed fried foods, such as zucchini flowers, potato, olives etc) and wash it all down with beer. Some places in Rome serve pizza with a thicker, fluffier base, which is the Neapolitan style.

For a snack on the run, Rome's *pizza al taglio* (by the slice) places are hard to beat, with toppings loaded atop thin, crispy, light-as-air, slow-risen bread that verge on the divine. There's been an outbreak of gourmet pizza places in the last decade, with Gabriele Bonci's Pizzarium (p132) leading the way near the Vatican.

STUART MCCALL/GETTY IMAGES ©

waiters, red flock and age-spotted gilt mirrors. Casanova, Goethe, Wagner, Keats, Byron, Shelley and Baudelaire were all once regulars. Now there are fewer artists and lovers and more shoppers and tourists. Prices reflect this, unless you do as the locals do and have a drink at the bar (*caffè* bar/seated €1.50/6).

Colline Emiliane   Italian €€

(Map p255; ☑06 481 75 38; Via degli Avignonesi 22; meals €50; ⊗12.45-2.45pm Tue-Sun & 7.30-10.45pm Tue-Sat, closed Aug; ⓂBarberini) This welcoming, tucked-away restaurant just off Piazza Barberini flies the flag for Emilia-Romagna, the well-fed Italian province that has blessed the world with Parmesan, balsamic vinegar, bolognese sauce and Parma ham. This is a consistently excellent place to eat; there are delicious meats, homemade pasta and rich *ragù*. Try to save room for dessert too.

Al Gran Sasso   Trattoria €€

(Map p256; ☑06 321 48 83; www.algransasso.com; Via di Ripetta 32; meals €35; ⊗12.30-2.30pm & 7.30-11.30pm Sun-Fri; ⓂFlaminio) A top lunchtime spot, this is a classic, dyed-in-the-wool trattoria specialising in old-school country cooking. It's a relaxed place with a welcoming vibe, garish murals on the walls (strangely often a good sign) and tasty, value-for-money food. The fried dishes are excellent, or try one of the daily specials, chalked up on the board outside.

Il Margutta RistorArte   Vegetarian €€

(Map p256; ☑06 678 60 33; www.ilmargutta.it; Via Margutta 118; meals €40; ⊗12.30-3pm & 7-11.30pm; ☑; ⓂSpagna, Flaminio) Vegetarian restaurants in Rome are rarer than parking spaces, and this airy art gallery–restaurant is an unusually chic way to eat your greens. Dishes are excellent and most produce is organic, with offerings such as artichoke hearts with potato cubes and smoked provolone cheese. Best value is the weekday (€15 to €18) and weekend (€25) buffet brunch. There's a vegan menu, and live music, on weekends.

Enoteca Regionale Palatium   Ristorante, Wine Bar €€€

(☑06 692 02 132; Via Frattina 94; meals €55; ⊗11am-11pm Mon-Sat, closed Aug; ⓠVia del Corso) A rich showcase of regional bounty, run by the Lazio Regional Food Authority, this sleek wine bar serves excellent local specialities, such as *porchetta* (pork

★ **The Culinary Calendar**

According to the culinary calendar (initiated by the Catholic Church), fish is eaten on Friday and *baccalà* (salted cod) is often eaten with *ceci* (chickpeas), usually on Wednesday. Thursday is gnocchi day.

Clockwise from top: Roman restaurant;
Making pasta; Salami varieties

roasted with herbs) or *gnocchi alla Romana con crema da zucca* (potato dumplings Roman-style with cream of pumpkin), as well as an impressive array of Lazio wines (try lesser-known drops such as Aleatico). *Aperitivo* is a good bet, too.

There's also a tantalising array of artisanal cheese and delicious salami and cold cuts.

Imàgo
Italian €€€

(Map p255; ☑06 6993 4726; www.imagorestau rant.com; Piazza della Trinità dei Monti 6; tasting menus €120-140; ⊗7-10.30pm; Ⓜ Spagna; 🗷) Even in a city of great views, the panoramas from the Hassler Hotel's Michelin-starred romantic rooftop restaurant are special (request the corner table), extending over a sea of roofs to the great dome of St Peter's Basilica. Complementing the views are the bold, mod-Italian creations of culinary whizz, chef Francesco Apreda. Book ahead.

Babette
Italian €€€

(Map p256; ☑06 321 15 59; Via Margutta 1; meals €45-55; ⊗1-3pm Tue-Sun, 7-10.45pm daily, closed Jan & Aug; 🗷; Ⓜ Spagna, Flaminio) Babette is run by two sisters who used to produce a fashion magazine, which accounts for its effortlessly chic interior of exposed brick walls and vintage painted signs. You're in for a feast too, as the cooking is delicious, with a sophisticated, creative French twist (think *tortiglioni* with courgette and pistachio pesto). The *torta Babette* is the food of the gods, a light-as-air lemon cheesecake.

The weekend lunch buffet (adult/child €28/18) is a good deal, including water, bread, dessert and coffee.

All'Oro
Italian €€€

(Map p256; Via del Vantaggio 14; tasting menu €98, meals €90; Ⓜ Flaminio) A Michelin-starred fine-dining restaurant, All'Oro established itself under chef Riccardo Di Giacinto in the upmarket suburb of Parioli. It's now transferred to the contemporary art-styled First Luxury Art Hotel, with white surroundings and sophisticated dishes such as ravioli

filled with mascarpone, duck ragout and red wine reduction and roasted suckling pig with potatoes and black truffle souce.

✖ Vatican City, Borgo & Prati

Pizzarium
Pizza €

(Via della Meloria 43; pizza slices from €3; ⊗11am-10pm; Ⓜ Cipro–Musei Vaticani) Pizzarium, or 'Bonci pizza rustica #pizzarium', as it has recently rebranded itself, serves some of Rome's best sliced pizza. Scissor-cut squares of meticulously crafted dough are topped with original combinations of seasonal ingredients and served on paper trays for immediate consumption. There's also a daily selection of freshly fried *supplì* (crunchy rice croquettes).

Gelarmony
Gelateria €

(Via Marcantonio Colonna 34; gelato €1.50-3; ⊗10am-late; Ⓜ Lepanto) Sweet-tooths are spoiled for choice at this popular Sicilian gelateria. There's an ample selection of fruit and cream gelati but for a typically Sicilian flavour go for pistachio or cassata.

Fa-Bìo
Sandwiches €

(☑06 6452 5810; www.fa-bio.com; Via Germanico 43; sandwiches €5; ⊗10am-5.30pm Mon-Fri, to 4pm Sat) 🖝 Sandwiches, salads and smoothies are all prepared with speed, skill and fresh organic ingredients at this tiny takeaway. Locals and in-the-know visitors come to grab a quick lunchtime bite, and if you can squeeze in the door you'd do well to follow suit.

Old Bridge
Gelateria €

(www.gelateriaoldbridge.com; Viale dei Bastioni di Michelangelo 5; gelato €2-5; ⊗9am-2am Mon-Sat, 2.30pm-2am Sun; 🚇 Piazza del Risorgimento, 🚇 Piazza del Risorgimento) Ideal for a pre- or post-Vatican pick-me-up, this tiny gelateria has been cheerfully dishing up huge portions of delicious gelato for over 20 years. Alongside all the traditional flavours, there are also yoghurts and refreshing sorbets.

Romeo
Pizza, Ristorante €€

(☑06 3211 0120; www.romeo.roma.it; Via Silla 26a; pizza slices €2.50, meals €45; ☺9am-midnight; ⓂOttaviano–San Pietro) This chic, contemporary outfit is part bakery, part deli, part takeaway and part restaurant. For a quick bite, there's delicious sliced pizza or you can have a *panino* made up at the deli counter; for a full restaurant meal, the à la carte menu offers a mix of traditional Italian dishes and forward-looking international creations.

Il Sorpasso
Italian €€

(www.sorpasso.info; Via Properzio 31-33; meals €20-35; ☺7am-1am Mon-Fri, 9am-1am Sat; ☐Piazza del Risorgimento) A bar-restaurant hybrid sporting a vintage cool look – vaulted stone ceilings, hanging hams, white bare-brick walls – Il Sorpasso is a hot ticket right now. Open throughout the day, it caters to a fashionable neighbourhood crowd, serving everything from pasta specials to aperitifs, *trappizini* (pyramids of stuffed pizza), and a full dinner menu.

Velavevodetto Ai Quiriti
Lazio Cuisine €€

(☑06 3600 0009; www.ristorantevelavevodetto.it; Piazza dei Quiriti 5; meals €35; ☺12.30-2.30pm & 7.30-11.30pm; ⓂLepanto) This welcoming restaurant continues to win diners over with its unpretentious, earthy food and honest prices. The menu reads like a directory of Roman staples, and while it's all pretty good, standout choices include *fettuccine con asparagi, guanciale e pecorino* (pasta ribbons with asparagus, guanciale and pecorino cheese) and *polpette di bollito* (fried meat balls).

Del Frate
Ristorante €€

(☑06 323 64 37; www.enotecadelfrate.it; Via degli Scipioni 122; meals €40; ☺noon-3pm & 6-11.45pm Mon-Sat; ⓂOttaviano–San Pietro) Locals love this upmarket wine bar with its simple wooden tables and high-ceilinged brick-arched rooms. There's a formidable wine and cheese list with everything from Sicilian ricotta to Piedmontese Gorgonzola,

🍽 Fast Food

Fast food is a long-standing Roman tradition, with plenty of street-food favourites.

A *tavola calda* (hot table) offers cheap, pre-prepared pasta, meat and vegetable dishes, while a *rosticceria* sells mainly cooked meats. Neither make for a romantic meal, but they're often very tasty.

Another favourite on the run are *arancini*, fried risotto balls that have fillings such as mozzarella and ham. These originate from Sicily, but are much loved in Rome too, where they're known as *supplì*.

Fast food is the latest Roman tradition to be reinvented, with a new-fangled offering of gourmet snacks that riff on family favourites. These days you'll find hip new places serving *supplì* or *fritti* (fried things) with a twist. And these are no victory of style over substance – the new guard takes their gastronomy just as seriously as the old.

Arancini

and a small but refined menu of tartars, salads, fresh pastas and main courses.

Ristorante L'Arcangelo
Ristorante €€€

(☑06 321 09 92; www.larcangelo.com; Via Belli 59-61; tasting menus lunch/dinner €25/55, meals €60; ☺12.30-2.30pm Mon-Fri, 8-11pm Mon-Sat; ☐Piazza Cavour) Styled as an informal bistro with wood-panelling, leather banquettes

Rome on a Plate

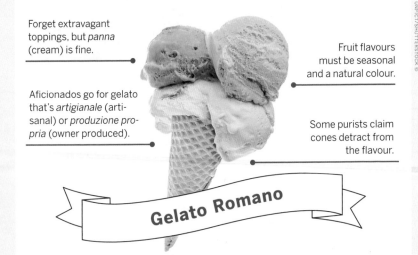

Forget extravagant toppings, but *panna* (cream) is fine.

Fruit flavours must be seasonal and a natural colour.

Aficionados go for gelato that's *artigianale* (artisanal) or *produzione propria* (owner produced).

Some purists claim cones detract from the flavour.

Gelato Romano

Get Your Ice Cream!

Gelato is one of Rome's great social unifiers. Everyone, from elegant matrons to politicians and toddlers, adores the stuff and the city's gelaterie cater to locals as much as tourists. The best are often small with a limited choice of freshly made seasonal flavours. Once you've got yours, hit the streets and stroll as you slurp, trying not to drip the ice cream all over yourself.

Gelato display
XUAN CHE/GETTY IMAGES ©

★ Top Five Gelaterie

Fatamorgana (p129) Rome's finest artisanal flavours, now in multiple central locations.

Gelateria del Teatro (p125) Around 40 choices of delicious ice cream, all made on-site.

Il Caruso (p129) A small but perfect selection of creamy flavours.

Gelarmony (p132) A Sicilian gelataria with many great tastes, including typically Sicilian pistachio or cassata.

Dei Gracchi (p129) A taste of heaven in several locations across Rome.

and casual table settings, L'Arcangelo enjoys a stellar local reputation. The highlight for many are the classic Roman staples such as carbonara and *amatriciana,* but there's also a limited selection of more innovative modern dishes. The wine list is a further plus, boasting some interesting Italian labels.

Enoteca La Torre   Ristorante €€€

(☎06 4566 8304; www.enotecalatorreroma. com; Villa Laetitia, Lungotevere delle Armi 22; fixed-price lunch menu €55, meals €110; ☺12.30-2.30pm Tue-Sat, 7.30-10pm Mon-Sat; ☐Lungotevere delle Armi) The art-nouveau Villa Laetitia provides the romantic setting for this refined Michelin-starred restaurant. A relative newcomer to the capital's fine-dining scene, chef Danilo Ciavattino has quickly established himself with his original culinary style and love of authentic country flavours.

Settembrini   Ristorante €€€

(☎06 323 26 17; www.viasettembrini.it; Via Settembrini 25; menus lunch €28-38, dinner €48-65; ☺12.30-3pm Mon-Fri, 8-11pm Mon-Sat; ☐Piazza Giuseppe Mazzini) All labels, suits and media gossip, this fashionable restaurant is part of the ever-growing Settembrini empire. Next door is a stylish all-day cafe, while over the way, Libri & Cucina is a laid-back bookshop eatery, and L'Officina an upscale food store. At the casually chic main restaurant expect contemporary Italian cuisine and quality wine to match.

La Veranda   Ristorante €€€

(☎06 687 29 73; www.laveranda.net; Borgo Santo Spirito 73; meals €60-70, brunch €18-27; ☺12.30-3pm & 7.30-11pm Tue-Sun; ☐Piazza Pia) A location in Paolo Sorrentino's Oscar-winning film *The Great Beauty,* this fine-dining restaurant sets a memorable stage for quality Italian cuisine. Inside, you can dine under 15th-century Pinturicchio frescoes, while in the warmer months, you can opt for a shady table in the garden. To enjoy the atmosphere for a snip of the regular price, stop by for Sunday brunch.

✖ Monti, Esquilino & San Lorenzo

Panella l'Arte del Pane   Bakery, Cafe €

(☎06 487 24 35; Via Merulana 54; snacks about €3.50; ☺8am-11pm Mon-Thu, to midnight Fri & Sat, 8.30am-4pm Sun; Ⓜ Vittorio Emanuele) With a magnificent array of *pizza al taglio, arancini,* focaccia, fried croquettes and pastries, this smart bakery-cum-cafe is good any time of the day. The outside tables are ideal for a leisurely breakfast or chilled evening drink, or you can perch on a high stool and lunch on something from the sumptuous counter display.

Roscioli   Pizza, Bakery €

(Via Buonarroti 48; pizza slices €3.50; ☺7am-8pm Mon-Sat; Ⓜ Vittorio Emanuele) Off-the-track branch of this splendid deli-bakery-pizzeria, with delish *pizza al taglio,* pasta dishes and other goodies that make it ideal for a swift lunch or picnic stock-up. It's on a road leading off Piazza Vittorio Emanuele II.

L'Asino d'Oro   Italian €€

(Map p255; ☎06 4891 3832; Via del Boschetto 73; meals €45; ☺12.30-2.30pm Sat, 7.30-11pm Tue-Sat; Ⓜ Cavour) This fabulous restaurant was transplanted from Orvieto and its Umbrian origins resonate in Lucio Sforza's delicious, exceptional cooking. It's unfussy yet innovative, with dishes featuring lots of flavourful contrasts, such as lamb meatballs with pear and blue cheese. Save room for the amazing desserts. For such excellent food, this intimate, informal yet classy place is one of Rome's best deals. Hours are changeable so call ahead.

Trattoria Monti   Ristorante €€

(☎06 446 65 73; Via di San Vito 13a; meals €40-45; ☺1-3pm Tue-Sun, 8-11pm Tue-Sat, closed Aug; Ⓜ Vittorio Emanuele) The Camerucci family runs this elegant brick-arched place, proffering top-notch traditional cooking from the Marches region. There are wonderful *fritti* (fried things), delicate pastas and ingredients such as *pecorino di fossa* (sheep's cheese aged in caves), goose, swordfish and truffles. Try the egg-yolk *tortelli* pasta. Desserts are delectable, including apple pie with *zabaglione*. Word has spread, so book ahead.

Temakinho
Sushi €€

(Map p252; www.temakinho.com; Via dei Serpenti 16; meals €40; ⊗12.30-3.30pm & 7pm-midnight; ⓂCavour) In a city where food is still mostly resolutely (though deliciously) Italian, this Brazilian-Japanese hybrid serves up sushi and ceviche, and makes for a refreshing, sensational change. As well as delicious, strong *caipirinhas*, which combine Brazilian *cachaça*, sugar, lime and fresh fruit, there are *'sakehinhas'* made with sake. It's very popular; book ahead.

Tram Tram
Osteria €€

(☑06 49 04 16; www.tramtram.it; Via dei Reti 44; meals around €45; ⊗12.30-3.30pm & 7.30-11.30pm Tue-Sun; ⓆVia Tiburtina) This trendy yet old-style lace-curtained trattoria takes its name from the trams that rattle past outside. It's a family-run concern whose menu is an unusual mix of Roman and Pugliese (southern Italian) dishes, featuring taste sensations such as *tiella riso, patata e cozze* (baked rice dish with rice, potatoes and mussels). Book ahead.

Da Valentino
Trattoria €€

(Map p255; ☑06 488 06 43; Via del Boschetto; meals €25-30; ⊗1-2.45pm & 7.30-11.30pm Mon-Sat; ⓂCavour) The vintage 1930s sign outside says 'Birra Peroni', and inside the lovely old-fashioned feel indicates that not much has changed here for years, with black-and-white photographs on the walls, white tablecloths and tiled floors. Come here when you're in the mood for grilled *scamorza* (a type of Italian cheese, similar to mozzarella), as this is the main focus of the menu, with myriad variations: served with tomato and rocket, tomato and Gorgonzola, cheese and artichokes, grilled meats, hamburgers and so on.

Primo
Italian €€

(☑06 701 38 27; www.primoalpigneto.it; Via del Pigneto 46; meals around €45; ⊗7.30pm-2am Tue-Sat, lunch Sun; 🛜; ⓆVia Prenestina) Flagship of the Pigneto scene, Primo is still buzzing after several years, with outdoor

ANGELO CAVALLI/ROBERTHARDING/GETTY IMAGES ©

tables and an industrial brasserie-style interior. Service is slow, though.

Doozo   Japanese €€
(Map p255; ☎06 481 56 55; Via Palermo 51; set lunch €16-26, set dinner €15-28; ☺12.30-3pm & 7.30-11pm Tue-Sat, 7.30-10.30pm Sun; ▣Via Nazionale) Doozo (meaning 'welcome') is a spacious, Zen restaurant-bookshop and gallery that offers tofu, sushi, *soba* (buckwheat noodle) soup and other Japanese delicacies, plus beer and green tea in wonderfully serene surroundings. It's a little oasis, particularly the shady courtyard garden.

Open Colonna   Italian €€€
(Map p255; ☎06 4782 2641; www.antonellocolonna.it; Via Milano 9a; meals €20-80; ☺12.30-3.30pm Tue-Sun, 8-11.30pm Tue-Sat; ❄; ▣Via Nazionale) Spectacularly set at the back of Palazzo delle Esposizioni, superchef Antonello Colonna's superb restaurant is tucked onto a mezzanine floor under an extraordinary glass roof. The cuisine is new Roman: innovative takes on traditional dishes, cooked with wit and flair. The best thing? There's a more basic but still

delectable fixed two-course lunch for €16, and Saturday and Sunday brunch is €30, served in the dramatic, glass-ceilinged hall, with a terrace for sunny days.

Agata e Romeo   Italian €€€
(☎06 446 61 15; Via Carlo Alberto 45; meals €120; ☺12.30-2.30pm & 7.30-11.30pm Mon-Fri; ⒨Vittorio Emanuele) This elegant, restrained place was one of Rome's gastronomic pioneers and still holds its own as one of the city's most gourmet takes on Roman cuisine. Chef Agata Parisella prepares the menus and runs the kitchen, offering creative uses of Roman traditions; husband Romeo curates the wine cellar; and daughter Maria Antonietta chooses the cheeses. Bookings essential.

Pastificio San Lorenzo Italian €€€
(☎06 9727 3519; Via Tiburtina 135; meals €50; ☺from 7pm; ▣Via Tiburtina, ▣Via dei Reti) The biggest buzz in San Lorenzo is to be found at this brasserie-style restaurant, housed in a corner of the former pasta factory that is now Rome's contemporary art hub as it's also home to a collective of artists' studios. The place is packed, the

★ Top Five for Street Food
Pizzarium (p132)

Supplizio (p125)

Forno Roscioli (p124)

Forno di Campo de' Fiori (p125)

Trapizzino (p140)

From left: Restaurants on Piazza della Rotonda; Al fresco dining in a Roman laneway; Food stall, Piazza di Spagna

GARY YEOWELL/GETTY IMAGES ©

RACHEL LEWIS/GETTY IMAGES ©

vibe is 'this is where it's at', and the food....is fine – nothing to shout about, but perfectly scrumptious old favourites with pappadelle and *ragù*, served up in a stylish fashion with equivalent prices.

✕ Trastevere & Gianicolo

Fatamorgana – Trastevere   Gelateria €
(Via Roma Libera 11, Piazza San Cosimato; cones/tubs from €2; ⊘noon-midnight summer, to 10.30pm winter; 🚊Viale di Trastevere, 🚊Viale di Trastevere) One of several Fatamorgana outlets across Rome, this is one of the finest among the city's gourmet gelatarie. Quality natural ingredients are used to produce creative flavour combos such as pineapple and ginger or pear and Gorgonzola. Gluten-free.

Innocenti   Bakery €
(☑06 580 39 26; Via delle Luce 21; ⊘8am-8pm Mon-Sat, 9.30am-2pm Sun; 🚊Viale di Trastevere, 🚊Viale di Trastevere) It's at reassuring spots like this that you can feel that the world never changes, in some corners at least. Here you can buy light-as-air *crostata*, and stock up on biscuits such as *brutti ma buoni* (ugly but good).

Panetteria Romana   Pizza €
(Via della Lungaretta 28-31; pizza slices from around €2.50; ⊘8am-3.30pm & 4.30-7.30pm Mon-Fri, 9am-3pm Sat) Run by the Conti family since the 19th century, this venerable bakery is a handy address for pizza by the slice, cakes and biscuits in Trastevere, especially as you can grab a quick lunch here, eating in at the high tables and stools.

Pianostrada Laboratorio di Cucina   Italian €
(Vicolo del Cedro; meals €25; ⊘1-4pm & 7.30-11.30pm Tue-Sun; 🚊Piazza Trilussa) A diminutive, tucked-away place, this all-female-run foodie stop has been attracting attention with its delicious meals such as parmigiana with aubergine and pumpkin, meatballs, burgers, pasta with swordfish

and wild fennel, and gourmet sandwiches. It's all exquisitely made and conceived, so squeeze in along the bar or take one of the tiny tables with barstools.

Da Corrado   Roman €
(Via della Pelliccia 39; meals €25; ⊘12.30-2.30pm & 7-11pm Mon-Sat; 🚊Viale di Trastevere, 🚊Viale di Trastevere) Don't expect refined service or a fancy interior. This is a proper Roman old-school trattoria, with no outdoor seating, but an unfussy, rough-and-ready atmosphere. It's packed with locals, feasting on hearty Roman soul food, such as *amatriciana*.

Pizzeria Ivo   Pizza €
(☑06 581 70 82; Via di San Francesco a Ripa 158; pizzas from €7; ⊘7pm-midnight Wed-Mon; 🚊Viale di Trastevere, 🚊Viale di Trastevere) One of Trastevere's most famous pizzerias, Ivo's has been slinging pizzas for some 40 years, and still the hungry come. With the TV on in the corner and the tables full (a few outside on the cobbled street), Ivo is a noisy and vibrant place, and the waiters fit the gruff-and-fast stereotype.

Da Olindo   Trattoria €
(☑06 581 88 35; Vicolo della Scala 8; meals €25; ⊘7.30-11pm Mon-Sat; 🚊Viale di Trastevere) This is your classic family affair; the menu is short, cuisine robust, portions huge, and the atmosphere lively. Expect *baccalà con patate* on Fridays and gnocchi on Thursdays, but other dishes – such as *coniglio all cacciatore* (rabbit, hunter-style) or *polpette al sugo* (meatballs in sauce) – whichever day you like.

La Gensola   Sicilian €€
(☑06 581 63 12; Piazza della Gensola 15; meals €45; ⊘12.30-3pm & 7.30-11.30pm, closed Sun mid-Jun–mid-Sep; 🚊Viale di Trastevere, 🚊Viale di Trastevere) This tranquil, classy yet unpretentious trattoria thrills foodies with delicious food that has a Sicilian slant and emphasis on seafood, including an excellent tuna tartare, linguine with fresh anchovies and divine *zuccherini* (tiny fish) with fresh mint.

Le Mani in Pasta   Ristorante €€

(📞06 581 60 17; Via dei Genovesi 37; meals €35; 🕐12.30-3pm & 7.30-11pm Tue-Sun; 🚌Viale di Trastevere, 🚃Viale di Trastevere) Popular and lively, this rustic, snug place has arched ceilings and an open kitchen that serves up delicious fresh pasta dishes such as *fettucine con ricotta e pancetta*. The grilled meats are great, too.

Glass Hostaria   Italian €€€

(📞06 5833 5903; Vicolo del Cinque 58; meals €90; 🕐7.30-11.30pm Tue-Sun; 🚌Piazza Trilussa) Trastevere's foremost foodie address, the Glass is a modernist-styled, sophisticated setting decorated in warm wood and contemporary gold, with fabulous cooking to match. Chef Cristina Bowerman creates inventive, delicate dishes that combine with fresh ingredients and traditional elements to delight and surprise the palate. There are tasting menus at €75, €80 and €100.

Paris   Ristorante €€€

(📞06 581 53 78; www.ristoranteparis.it; Piazza San Calisto 7a; meals €45-55; 🕐7.30-11pm Mon, 12.30-3pm & 7.30-11pm Tue-Sun; 🚌Viale di Trastevere, 🚃Viale di Trastevere) An old-school restaurant set in a 17th-century building with tables on a small piazza, Paris – named for its founder, not the French capital – is the best place outside the Ghetto to sample Roman-Jewish cuisine. Signature dishes include *gran fritto vegetale con baccalà* (deep-fried vegetables with salt cod) and *carciofi alla giudia* (fried artichoke).

✗ San Giovanni & Testaccio

Cafè Cafè   Bistro €

(📞06 700 87 43; www.cafecafebistrot.it; Via dei Santissimi Quattro Coronati 44; meals €15-20; 🕐9.30am-11pm; 🚌Via di San Giovanni in Laterano) Cosy, relaxed and welcoming, this cafe-bistro is a far cry from the usual impersonal eateries in the Colosseum area. With its rustic wooden tables, butternut walls and wine bottles, it's a charming spot to recharge your batteries over tea and

🍽 Roman-Jewish Cuisine

If you thought fried fish was exclusive to British takeaways, think again. Deep-frying is a staple of *cucina ebraico-romanesca* (Roman-Jewish cuisine), a form of cooking that developed between the 16th and 19th centuries when Rome's Jews were confined to the city's Ghetto. To add flavour to their limited ingredients they began to fry everything from mozzarella to *baccalà* (salted cod). To delicious effect. Particularly addictive are locally grown artichokes, which are flattened out to form a kind of flower shape and then deep-fried and salted.

For the best place to try these *carciofi alla guidia* (crisp fried artichokes) and other Roman-Jewish staples, head to Via del Portico d'Ottavia, the main strip through the Jewish Ghetto. Lined with trattorias and restaurants, it's a lively hangout, especially on hot summer nights when diners crowd the many sidewalk tables. For a taste of typical Ghetto cooking, try **Nonna Betta** (Map p250; 📞06 6880 6263; www.nonnabetta. it; Via del Portico d'Ottavia 16; meals €30-35; 🕐noon-4pm & 6-11pm, closed Fri dinner & Sat lunch; 🚌Via Arenula), a small tunnel of a trattoria serving traditional kosher food. Further down the road, the unmarked **Cremeria Romana** (Map p250; Via del Portico d'Ottavia 1b; gelato €2-5; 🕐8am-11pm Sun-Thu, to 4pm Fri, 6pm-midnight Sat; 🚌Via Arenula) has a small selection of tasty kosher gelato.

Carciofi alla guidia
MANAKIN/GETTY IMAGES ©

🍴 Offal Specialities

The hallmark of an authentic Roman menu is the presence of offal. The Roman love of nose-to-tail eating arose in Testaccio, a traditionally working-class district clustered around the city's former slaughterhouse. In the past, butchers who worked there would often be paid in cheap cuts of meat as well as money. As a result, local cooks came up with recipes to make the best possible use of these unfashionable scraps. The Roman staple *coda alla vaccinara*, which translates as 'oxtail cooked butcher's style', is cooked for hours to create a rich sauce with tender slivers of meat. Another famous dish that's not for the faint hearted is pasta with *pajata*, made with the entrails of young veal calves, considered a delicacy since they contain the mother's congealed milk.

Other offal delicacies to look out for include *trippa* (tripe), *coratella* (heart, lung and liver), *animelle* (sweetbreads), *testarella* (head), *lingua* (tongue) and *zampe* (trotters).

homemade cake, a light lunch or laid-back dinner. There's also brunch on Sundays.

Pizzeria Da Remo   Pizza €

(📞06 574 62 70; Piazza Santa Maria Liberatrice 44; pizzas from €5.50; ⊙7pm-1am Mon-Sat; 🚇Via Marmorata) For an authentic Roman experience, join the noisy crowds at this, one of the city's best-known and most popular pizzerias. It's a spartan-looking place, but the thin-crust Roman pizzas are the business, and there's a cheerful, boisterous vibe. Expect to queue after 8.30pm.

Li Rioni   Pizza €

(📞06 7045 0605; Via dei Santissimi Quattro Coronati 24; meals €15-20; ⊙ 7pm-midnight Thu-Tue, closed Aug; 🚇Via di San Giovanni in Laterano) Locals swear by Li Rioni, arriving for the second sitting around 9pm after the tourists have left. A classic neighbourhood

pizzeria, it buzzes most nights as diners squeeze into the kitschy interior – set up as a Roman street scene – and tuck into wood-fired thin-crust pizzas and crispy fried starters.

Trapizzino   Fast Food €

(www.trapizzino.it; Via Branca 88; trapizzini from €3.50; ⊙noon-1am Tue-Sun; 🚇Via Marmorata) This pocket-size joint is the birthplace of the *trapizzino*, a kind of hybrid sandwich made by stuffing a small cone of doughy bread with fillers like *polpette al sugo* (meatballs in tomato sauce) or *pollo alla cacciat*ore (stewed chicken). They're messy to eat but quite delicious.

Flavio al Velavevodetto   Trattoria €€

(📞06 574 41 94; www.ristorantevelavevodetto. it; Via di Monte Testaccio 97-99; meals €30-35; ⊙12.30-3pm & 7.45-11pm; 🚇Via Galvani) Housed in a rustic Pompeian-red villa, this welcoming eatery specialises in earthy, no-nonsense *cucina romana* (Roman cuisine). Expect *antipasti* of cheeses and cured meats, huge helpings of homemade pastas, and uncomplicated meat dishes.

Da Felice   Lazio Cuisine €€

(📞06 574 68 00; www.feliceatestaccio.it; Via Mastro Giorgio 29; meals €35-40; ⊙12.30-3pm & 7.30-10.30pm; 🚇Via Marmorata) Foodies swear by this historic stalwart, famous for its unwavering dedication to local culinary traditions. In contrast to the light-touch modern decor, the menu is pure old-school with a classic weekly timetable: *pasta e fagioli* (pasta and beans) on Tuesdays, *bollito di manzo* (boiled beef) on Thursdays, seafood on Fridays. Reservations essential.

Trattoria da Bucatino   Trattoria €€

(📞06 574 68 86; www.bucatino.com; Via Luca della Robbia 84; meals €30-35; ⊙noon-3pm & 7pm-midnight Tue-Sun; 🚇Via Marmorata) This genuine neighbourhood trattoria is hugely popular. It's far from refined with its dated decor and brusque service, but the typical Roman food is excellent – try its trademark *bucatini all'amatriciana* – and helpings are generous.

Il Bocconcino
Trattoria €€

(📱06 7707 9175; www.ilbocconcino.com; Via Ostilia 23; meals €35; ⏰12.30-3.30pm & 7.30-11.30pm Thu-Tue, closed Aug; 🚇Via Labicana) One of the better options in the touristy pocket near the Colosseum, this laid-back trattoria stands out for its authentic regional cooking and use of locally sourced seasonal ingredients. Daily specials are chalked up on blackboards or there's a regular menu of classic Roman pastas, meaty mains and imaginative desserts.

Aroma
Ristorante €€€

(📱06 9761 5109; www.aromarestaurant.it; Via Labicana 125; tasting menu €130; ⏰12.30-3pm & 7.30-11.30pm; 🚇Via Labicana) One for a special-occasion dinner, the rooftop restaurant of the Palazzo Manfredi hotel offers 'marry-me' views of the Colosseum and Michelin-starred food that rises to the occasion. Overseeing the kitchen is chef Giuseppe Di Iorio, whose brand of luxurious, forward-thinking Mediterranean cuisine has won widespread applause from critics and diners alike.

Checchino dal 1887
Lazio Cuisine €€€

(📱06 574 63 18; www.checchino-dal-1887.com; Via di Monte Testaccio 30; tasting menus €40-65; ⏰12.30-3pm & 8pm-midnight Tue-Sat; 🚇Via Galvani) A pig's whisker from the city's former slaughterhouse, Checchino is one of the grander restaurants specialising in the *quinto quarto* (fifth quarter – or insides of the animal). Signature dishes include *coda all vaccinara* (oxtail stew) and *rigatoni alla pajata* (pasta tubes with a sauce of tomato and veal intestines).

🍴 Villa Borghese & Northern Rome

Neve di Latte
Gelateria €

(Via Poletti 6; gelato €2.50-5; ⏰noon-10pm Sun-Thu, to 11pm Fri & Sat) Near the MAXXI gallery, this out-of-the-way gelateria is reckoned one of Rome's best. There are few exotic flavours, rather the onus is on the classics, all prepared with high-quality organic ingredients. The pistachio, made with nuts from

Trippa alla Roma

EZUMEIMAGES/GETTY IMAGES ©

Cheese display in a delicatessen's window

the Sicilian town of Bronte, is outstanding, as is the creme caramel.

Bar Pompi
Pastries €

(Via Cassia 8; tiramisu €3.50; ⏺7am-midnight Wed-Mon, 4pm-midnight Tue; 🚇Ponte Milvio) This renowned *pasticceria* serves Rome's most celebrated tiramisu. Alongside the classic coffee, liqueur and cocoa combination, there are several other versions including strawberry, pistachio, and banana and chocolate.

Caffè delle Arti
Cafe, Ristorante €€

(Map p256; ☎06 3265 1236; www.caffedelleart-iroma.com; Via Gramsci 73; meals €45; ⏺12.30-3.30pm daily & 7.30-11pm Tue-Sun; 🚇Piazza Thorvaldsen) The cafe-restaurant of the Galleria Nazionale d'Arte Moderna (p58) sits in neoclassical splendour in a tranquil corner of Villa Borghese. An elegant venue, it's at its best on sultry summer evenings when you can sit on the terrace and revel in the romantic atmosphere over coffee, cocktails or an al fresco dinner of classic Italian cuisine.

Metamorfosi
Ristorante €€€

(☎06 807 68 39; www.metamorfosiroma.it; Via Giovanni Antonelli 30-32; tasting menus €80-110, lunch menu €45; ⏺12.30-2.30pm & 8-10.30pm, closed Sat lunch & Sun; 🚇Via Giovanni Antonelli) Since opening in 2011, chef Roy Carceres' Michelin-starred restaurant has established itself as one of Rome's top dining tickets, offering innovative, contemporary cuisine, impeccable service, and a chic but informal setting. Various tasting menus are available, including a three-course lunch option.

Molto
Ristorante €€€

(☎06 808 29 00; www.moltoitaliano.it; Viale Parioli 122; meals €45-50; ⏺1-3pm & 8-11pm; 🚇Viale Parioli) Fashionable and quietly glamorous, Molto is a Parioli favourite. The discreet entrance gives onto an elegant, modern interior and open-air terrace, while the menu offers everything from simple, homemade pastas to more decadent truffle-flavoured dishes and succulent roast meats.

✗ Southern Rome

Pizza Ostiense
Pizza €

(Via Ostiense 56; ◷6.30pm-1am; Ⓜ️Pyramide) Run by folk formerly of the much-lauded classic Roman pizzeria Remo, in Testaccio, Pizza Ostiense offers similarly paper-thin, crispy bases and delicious fresh toppings and scrumptious *fritti* (fried things) in unfussy surroundings, with a friendly vibe.

Doppiozeroo
Italian €

(🖉06 5730 1961; www.doppiozeroo.com; Via Ostiense 68; ◷7am-2am Mon-Sat; Ⓜ️Piramide) This easy-going bar was once a bakery, hence the name ('double zero' is a type of flour). But today the sleek, modern interior attracts hungry, trendy Romans like bees to honey, especially for the cheap lunches (*primo/secondo* €4.50/6.50) and famously lavish, dinnertastic *aperitivo* between 6pm and 9pm.

Andreotti
Pastries €

(🖉06 575 07 73; Via Ostiense 54; ◷7.30am-9.30pm; 🚊Via Ostiense) Film director and Ostiense local Ferzan Ozpetek is such a fan of the pastries here he's known to cast them in his films. They're all stars, from the buttery *crostate* (tarts) to the piles of golden *sfogliatelle romane* (ricotta-filled pastries). You can also eat a cheap lunch or dinner here from the tasty *tavola calda*, with pasta dishes ringing in at €5.

Eataly
Italian €

(🖉06 9027 9201; www.eataly.net/it_en; Air Terminal Ostiense, Piazzale XII Ottobre 1492; ◷shop 10am-midnight, restaurants noon-11.30pm; Ⓜ️Piramide) Eataly is an enormous, mall-like complex, a glittering, gleaming, somewhat confusing department store, entirely devoted to Italian food. As well as foodstuffs from all over the country, books and cookery implements, the store is also home to 19 cafes and restaurants, including excellent pizzas, pasta dishes, ice cream and more.

Porto Fluviale
Trattoria, Pizza €€

(🖉06 574 31 99; www.portofluviale.com; Via del Porto Fluviale 22; meals €35; ◷10.30am-2am; Ⓜ️Piramide) A hip, buzzing restaurant in the industrial-chic vein, Porto Fluviale is a great space and a good place to go with families: it's lively, spacious and good value, offering pasta, pizza and *cicchetti* (tapas-style appetisers, eg artichoke and ham bruschetta) that are served until late.

Trattoria Priscilla
Trattoria €€

(🖉06 513 63 79; Via Appia Antica 68; meals €30; ◷1-3pm daily, 8-11pm Mon-Sat; 🚊Via Appia Antica) Set in a 16th-century former stable, this intimate family-run trattoria has been feeding hungry travellers along the Appian Way for more than a hundred years, serving up traditional *cucina Romana,* so think carbonara, *amatriciana* and *cacio e pepe.* The tiramisu wins plaudits.

Qui Non se More Mai
Italian €€

(🖉06 780 3922; Via Appia Antica 198; meals around €40; ◷12.30-3pm & 6.30-11.30pm Tue-Sat; 🚊Via Appia Antica) This small, charismatically rustic restaurant has an open fire for grilling, plus a small terrace for when the weather's good. The menu offers Roman classics such as pasta *amatriciana*, carbonara, *gricia, cacio e pepe,* and so on. Just the thing to set you up for the road ahead.

TREASURE HUNT

Begin your shopping adventure

Treasure Hunt

Rome boasts the usual cast of flagship chain stores and glitzy designer outlets, but what makes shopping here so special is its legion of small, independent shops: historic, family owned-delis, picture-framers, dusty furniture workshops, small-label fashion boutiques and artists' studios. Adding to the fun are the much-frequented neighbourhood markets selling everything from secondhand jeans to bumper produce from local farms.

Italy's reputation for quality is deserved and Rome is a top place to shop for designer clothes, shoes and leather goods. Foodie treats are another obvious choice and you'll find no end of heavenly delis, bakeries, pasticcerie (pastry shops) and chocolate shops. Homewares are another Italian speciality, and many shops focus on covetable stainless-steel kitchenware and sleek interior design.

In This Section

Useful Phrases

I'd like to buy... Vorrei comprare... (vo.*ray* kom.*pra*.re)

I'm just looking. Sto solo guardando. (sto *so*.lo gwar.*dan*.do)

Can I look at it? Posso dare un'occhiata? (po.so *da*.re oo.no.*kya*.ta)

How much is this? Quanto costa questo? (*kwan*.to *kos*.ta *kwe*.sto)

Vatican City, Borgo & Prati
Fill up on foodie treasures, accessories and vintage clothes (p158)

Villa Borghese & Northern Rome
Explore an antique market and a historic wine shop (p163)

Tridente, Trevi & the Quirinale
From high-fashion designer boutiques to flagship chain stores (p154)

Centro Storico
Boutiques, one-off designers, antiques, vintage threads, jewellery and swoon-worthy delis (p150)

Monti, Esquilino & San Lorenzo
Centre for independent fashion, homeware and vintage boutiques (p159)

Trastevere & Gianicolo
Gifts and one-off shops in one of Rome's prettiest neighbourhoods (p161)

San Giovanni & Testaccio
Browse a colourful food market and glorious delis (p163)

Opening Hours

Most city-centre shops 9am to 7.30pm (or 10am to 8pm) Monday to Saturday; some close Monday morning

Smaller shops 9am to 1pm and 3.30pm to 7.30pm (or 4pm to 8pm) Monday to Saturday

Sales

To grab a bargain, time your visit to coincide with the *saldi* (sales). Winter sales run from the first Saturday in January to mid-February, and summer sales from the first Saturday in July to early September.

The Best...

Experience Rome's best shopping

Handicrafts

Bottega di Marmoraro (p154) Commission a marble inscription to remind you of Rome.

Le Artigiane (p151) Maintaining Italy's artisanal traditions with a collection of handmade clothes, costume jewellery, ceramics, design objects and lamps.

Officina della Carta (p162) Beautiful hand-decorated notebooks, paper and cards.

Ibiz – Artigianato in Cuoio (p150) Wallets, bags and sandals in a variety of soft leathers.

Clothing

Luna & L'Altra (pictured above; p150) Fashion-heaven, with clothes by Comme des Garçons, Issey Miyake and Yohji Yamamoto.

Tina Sondergaard (p159) This Monti boutique adjusts retro-inspired dresses to fit perfectly.

daDADA 52 (p152) Cocktail dresses and summer frocks to make you stand out from the crowd (in a good way).

Bookshops

Feltrinelli International (p161) An excellent range of the latest releases in English, Spanish, French, German and Portuguese.

Almost Corner Bookshop (pictured above; p162) A crammed haven full of rip-roaring reads.

Open Door Bookshop (p162) Many happy moments browsing secondhand books in English, Italian, French and Spanish.

Libreria l'Argonauta (p163) Travel bookshop great for sparking dreams of your next trip.

Gifts

Vertecchi Art (p155) Classy stationers, selling different hues of paper, notebooks and gifts appropriate to the season.

Arion Esposizioni (p161) Art, architecture and children's books, plus design-conscious presents.

Fabriano (p155) Leather-bound diaries, funky notebooks and products embossed with street maps of Rome.

A S Roma Store (p152) Trastevere treasure-trove perfume store, with hundreds of choices from niche labels.

Ai Monasteri (p154) Exquisite herbal unguents made by monks, plus wines, liqueurs and biscuits.

Foodstuffs

Volpetti (p163) Bulging with delicious delicacies, and notably helpful staff.

Eataly (p143) Mall-scale food shop, filled with products from all over Italy, plus books, cooking utensils and more.

Salumeria Roscioli (p151) The name is a byword for foodie excellence, with mouthwatering Italian and foreign delicacies.

Pio La Torre (p152) Unpretentious, and every cent you spend helps in the fight against the mafia.

Shoes

Borini (p151) An unfussy shop filled to the brim with the latest women's footwear fashions.

Danielle (p155) A fast-changing collection of whatever is in right now, in a rainbow palette of colours, at affordable prices.

Barrilà Boutique (p155) With hundreds of different women's styles, it's a good chance to find the perfect shoe.

Giacomo Santini (p161) Pick up an exquisite, Fausto-designed bargain at this outlet shop.

Homewares

Spot (p159) A careful selection of beautiful midcentury furnishings.

Mercato Monti Urban Market (p159) Vintage homeware finds cram this weekend market.

C.U.C.I.N.A (p157) Gastronomic gadgets to enhance your culinary life.

★ Lonely Planet's Top Choices

Confetteria Moriondo & Gariglio (p150) A magical chocolate shop.

Vertecchi Art (p155) Art emporium with beautiful paper and notebooks.

Bottega di Marmoraro (p154) Have the motto of your choice carved into a marble slab at this delightful shop.

Pelletteria Nives (p155) Leather artisans make bags, wallets and more to your specifications.

🔒 Ancient Rome

Mercato di Circo Massimo
Food & Drink

(Map p252; www.mercatocircomassimo.it; Via di San Teodoro 74; ⊘9am-6pm Sat, to 4pm Sun, closed Sun Jul & all Aug; 🚇Via dei Cerchi) Rome's best and most popular farmers market is a colourful showcase for seasonal, zero-kilometre produce. As well as fresh fruit and veg, you can stock up on *pecorino Romano* cheese, milky mozzarella (known locally as *fior di latte*), olive oils, preserves, and *casareccio* bread from the nearby town of Genzano.

🔒 Centro Storico

Confetteria Moriondo & Gariglio
Food

(Map p250; Via del Piè di Marmo 21-22; ⊘9am-7.30pm Mon-Sat; 🚇Via del Corso) Roman poet Trilussa was so smitten with this historic chocolate shop – established by the Torinese confectioners to the royal house of Savoy – that he dedicated several sonnets to it. And we agree, it's a gem. Many of the bonbons and handmade chocolates laid out in ceremonial splendour in the glass cabinets are still prepared according to original 19th-century recipes.

Ibiz – Artigianato in Cuoio
Accessories

(Map p250; Via dei Chiavari 39; ⊘9.30am-7.30pm Mon-Sat; 🚇Corso Vittorio Emanuele II) In their diminutive workshop, Elisa Nepi and her father craft exquisite, well-priced leather goods, including wallets, bags, belts and sandals, in simple but classy designs and myriad colours. You can pick up a belt for about €35, while for a bag you should bank on at least €110.

Luna & L'Altra
Fashion

(Map p250; Piazza Pasquino 76; ⊘10am-2pm Tue-Sat, 3.30-7.30pm Mon-Sat; 🚇Corso Vittorio Emanuele II) An address for fashionistas with their fingers on the pulse, this is one of a number of independent boutiques on and around Via del Governo Vecchio. In its austere, gallery-like interior, clothes by Comme

Shoppers on Via del Corso, Centro Storico

LONELY PLANET/GETTY IMAGES ©

des Garçons, Issey Miyake, Yohji Yamamoto and others are exhibited in reverential style.

Le Artigiane — Clothing, Handicrafts

(Map p250; www.leartigiane.it; Via di Torre Argentina 72; ☺10am-7.30pm; ☐Largo di Torre Argentina) A space for local artisans to showcase their wares, this eclectic shop is the result of an ongoing project to sustain and promote Italy's artisanal traditions. It's a browser's dream, with an eclectic range of handmade clothes, costume jewellery, ceramics, design objects and lamps.

Salumeria Roscioli — Food

The rich scents of fine Italian produce, cured meats and cheeses intermingle in this top-class deli.

SBU — Fashion

(Map p250; www.sbu.it; Via di San Pantaleo 68-69; ☺10am-7.30pm Mon-Sat; ☐Corso Vittorio Emanuele II) The flagship store of hip fashion label SBU, aka Strategic Business Unit, occupies a 19th-century workshop near Piazza Navona, complete with cast-iron columns and wooden racks. Pride of place goes to the jeans, superbly cut from top-end Japanese denim, but you can also pick up shirts, jackets, hats, sweaters and T-shirts.

Borini — Shoes

(Map p250; Via dei Pettinari 86-87; ☺9am-1pm Tue-Sat, 3.30-7.30pm Mon-Sat; ☐Via Arenula) Don't be fooled by the discount, worka-day look — those in the know head to this seemingly down-at-heel shop for the latest footwear fashions. Women's styles, ranging from ballet flats to heeled boots, are displayed in the functional glass cabinets, alongside a small selection of men's leather shoes.

Arsenale — Fashion

(Map p250; www.patriziapieroni.it; Via del Pellegrino 172; ☺10am-7.30pm Tue-Sat, 3.30-7.30pm Mon; ☐Corso Vittorio Emanuele II) Arsenale, the atelier of Roman designer Patrizia Pieroni, is a watchword for original, high-end women's fashion. The virgin white interior creates a clean, contemporary

---

High Fashion

Big-name designer boutiques gleam in the grid of streets between Piazza di Spagna and Via del Corso. The great Italian and international names are represented here, as well as many lesser-known designers, selling clothes, shoes, accessories and dreams. The immaculately clad spine is Via dei Condotti, but there's also lots of high fashion in Via Borgognona, Via Frattina, Via della Vite and Via del Babuino.

Downsizing a euro or two, Via Nazionale, Via del Corso, Via dei Giubbonari and Via Cola di Rienzo are good for midrange clothing stores, with some enticing small boutiques set amid the chains.

---

showcase for beautifully cut clothes ranging from winter coats in warm, earthy tones to wispy, free-flowing summer dresses.

Rachele — Children's clothing

(Map p250; www.racheleartchildrenswear.it; Vicolo del Bollo 6; ☺10.30am-2pm & 3.30-7.30pm Tue-Sat; ☐Corso Vittorio Emanuele II) Mums looking to update their kids' (under 12s) wardrobe would do well to look up Rachele in her delightful shop just off Via del Pellegrino. With everything from hats and mitts to romper suits and jackets, all brightly coloured and all handmade, this sort of shop is a dying breed. Most items are around the €40 to €50 mark.

Tempi Moderni — Jewellery, Clothing

(Map p250; Via del Governo Vecchio 108; ☺9am-1.30pm & 3-7.30pm Mon-Sat; ☐Corso Vittorio Emanuele II) Klimt prints sit side by side with pop-art paintings and cartoon ties at this kooky curiosity shop on Via del Governo Vecchio. It's packed with vintage costume jewellery, Bakelite pieces from the '20s and '30s, art nouveau and art deco trinkets, 19th-century resin brooches and pieces by couturiers such as Chanel, Dior and Balenciaga.

Help Fight the Mafia

To look at it there's nothing special about **Pio La Torre** (Map p250; www.liberaterra.it; Via dei Prefetti 23; ⊙10.30am-7.30pm Tue-Sat, 10.30am-2.30pm Sun, 3.30-7.30pm Mon; 🚌Via del Corso), a small, unpretentious food store near Piazza del Parlamento. But shop here and you're making a small but concrete contribution to the fight against the mafia. All the gastronomic goodies on sale, including organic olive oils, pastas, flours, honeys and wine, have been produced on land confiscated from organised crime outfits in Calabria and Sicily. The shop is one of several across the country set up by Libera Terra, a grassroots movement of agricultural cooperatives working on terrain that was once owned by the mob.

I Colori di Dentro   Arts

(www.mgluffarelli.com; Via dei Banchi Vecchi 29; ⊙11am-7pm Mon-Sat; 🚌Corso Vittorio Emanuele II) Take home some Mediterranean sunshine. Artist Maria Grazia Luffarelli's paintings are a riotous celebration of Italian colours, with sunny yellow landscapes, blooming flowers, Roman cityscapes and comfortable-looking cats. You can buy original watercolours or prints, as well as postcards, T-shirts, notebooks and calendars.

A S Roma Store   Sports

(Map p250; Piazza Colonna 360; ⊙10am-7.30pm Mon-Sat, 10.30am-7pm Sun; 🚌Via del Corso) An official club store of A S Roma, one of Rome's two top-flight football teams. There's an extensive array of Roma-branded kit, including replica shirts, caps, T-shirts, scarves, hoodies, keyrings and a whole lot more. You can also buy match tickets here.

daDADA 52   Fashion

(Map p250; www.dadada.eu; Via dei Giubbonari 52; ⊙noon-8pm Mon, 11am-2pm & 3-8pm Tue-Sat, 11.30am-7.30pm Sun; 🚌Via Arenula) Girls with an eye for what works should make a beeline for this small boutique. Here you'll find a selection of eye-catching cocktail dresses that can be dressed up or down, print summer frocks, eclectic coats and colourful hats. There's a second **branch** (Map p256; ☎06 6813 9162; www.dadada.eu; Via del Corso 500; Ⓜ Flaminio, Spagna) at Via del Corso 500.

Officina Profumo Farmaceutica di Santa Maria Novella   Beauty

(Map p250; www.smnovella.it; Corso del Rinascimento 47; ⊙10am-7.30pm Mon-Sat; 🚌Corso del Rinascimento) This, the Roman branch of one of Italy's oldest pharmacies, stocks natural perfumes and cosmetics as well as herbal infusions, teas and potpourri, all shelved in wooden, glass-fronted cabinets under a Murano chandelier. The original pharmacy was founded in Florence in 1612 by the Dominican monks of Santa Maria Novella, and many of its cosmetics are based on 17th-century herbal recipes.

Nardecchia   Arts

(Map p250; Piazza Navona 25; ⊙10am-1pm Tue-Sat, 4.30-7.30pm Mon-Sat; 🚌Corso del Rinascimento) Famed for its antique prints, this historic Piazza Navona shop sells everything from 18th-century etchings by Giovanni Battista Piranesi to more affordable 19th-century panoramas. Bank on at least €150 for a small framed print.

Casali   Arts

(Via dei Coronari 115; ⊙10am-1pm Mon-Sat plus 3.30-7.30pm Sat; 🚌Corso del Rinascimento) On lovely Via dei Coronari, Casali deals in original and reproduction etchings and old prints, many delicately hand-coloured. The shop is small but the choice is not, ranging from 16th-century botanical manuscripts to postcard prints of Rome.

Le Tele di Carlotta   Handicrafts

(Map p250; Via dei Coronari 228; ⊙10.30am-1pm & 3.30-7pm Mon-Fri; 🚌Corso del Rinascimento) Search out this tiny sewing box of a shop for hand-embroidered napkins, cushion covers, bags and antique jewellery. If you're stopping long enough in Rome,

★ Artisans

Rome's shopping scene has a surprising number of artists and artisans who create their goods on the spot in hidden workshops. There are several places in Tridente where you can get a custom made bag, wallet or belt.

Clockwise from top: A S Roma Store; Market, Trastevere (p161); Frame crafter

you can have pieces embroidered to your specifications.

Aldo Fefè
Handicrafts

(Map p250; Via della Stelletta 20b; ⊘8am-7.30pm Mon-Sat; 🚊Corso del Rinascimento) This authentic artisanal workshop produces beautifully hand-painted paper as well as leather-bound notebooks (€32), picture frames and photo albums (from €15). You can also buy Florentine wrapping paper and calligraphic pens.

Bartolucci
Toys

(Map p250; www.bartolucci.com; Via dei Pastini 98; ⊘10am-10pm; 🚊Via del Corso) It's difficult to resist going into this magical toy shop where everything is carved out of wood. It's guarded by a cycling Pinocchio and a full-sized motorbike, and within are all manner of ticking clocks, rocking horses, planes and more Pinocchios than you'll have ever seen in your life.

Alberta Gloves
Accessories

(Map p250; Corso Vittorio Emanuele II 18; ⊘10am-6.30pm; 🚊Largo di Torre Argentina) From elbow-length silk gloves to tan-coloured driving mitts, this tiny family-run shop sells a wide range of handmade gloves for every conceivable occasion. Scarves and woolly hats too.

Ai Monasteri
Beauty

(Map p250; www.aimonasteri.it; Corso del Rinascimento 72; ⊘10.30am-7.30pm, closed Thu afternoon & Sun; 🚊Corso del Rinascimento) With balms for the body and food for the soul, this monastic apothecary stocks a range of herbal essences, lotions and cosmetics, all made by monks from across Italy, as well as wines, liqueurs and biscuits. There are even elixirs promising love, happiness, and eternal youth.

De Sanctis
Ceramics

(Map p250; www.desanctis1890.com; Piazza di Pietra 24; ⊘10am-1.30pm & 3-7.30pm Mon-Sat, closed Tue morning; 🚊Via del Corso) De Sanctis – in business since 1890 – is full of impressive Sicilian and Tuscan ceramics, with sunbursts of colour decorating

crockery, kitchenware and objets d'art. If your purchases are too heavy to carry, it ships worldwide.

Leone Limentani
Kitchenware

(Map p250; www.limentani.com; Via del Portico d'Ottavia 47; ⊘9am-1pm & 3.30-7pm Mon-Fri, 10am-8pm Sat; 🚊Via Arenula) Family-run for seven generations, this well-stocked basement store has a huge, rambling choice of kitchenware and tableware, expensive porcelain and knick-knacks, crockery, cutlery and crystal, many by top brands and all at bargain prices.

Loco
Shoes

(Map p250; Via dei Baullari 22; ⊘10.30am-7.30pm Tue-Sat, 3.30-7.30pm Mon; 🚊Corso Vittorio Emanuele II) Sneaker fetishists should hotfoot it to Loco for the very latest in big-statement trainers. It's a small shop, but full of attitude, with a jazzy collection of original sneakers (for boys and girls), boots and pumps by international and Italian designers. It also sells bags and costume jewellery.

Tartarughe
Fashion

(Map p250; www.letartarughe.eu; Via del Piè di Marmo 17; ⊘10am-7.30pm Tue-Sat, noon-7.30pm Mon; 🚊Via del Corso) Fashionable, versatile and elegant, Susanna Liso's seasonal designs adorn this relaxed, white-walled boutique. Her clothes, which include understated woollen coats, strikingly cut jackets, sweaters, and trousers, provide a vibrant modern update on classic styles. You'll also find a fine line in novel accessories.

🏛 Tridente, Trevi & the Quirinale

Bottega del Marmoraro
Arts

(Map p256; Via Margutta 53b; ⊘8am-7.30pm Mon-Sat; Ⓜ Flaminio) A particularly charismatic hole-in-the-wall shop lined with marble carvings, where you can get marble tablets engraved with any inscription you like (€15). Peer inside at lunchtime and you might see the cheerfully quizzical *mar-*

moraro, Enrico Fiorentini, cooking pasta for his lunch next to the open log fire.

Danielle   Shoes
(☎06 679 24 67; Via Frattina 85a; ⊙10.30am-7.30pm; MSpagna) If you're female and in need of an Italian shoe fix, this is an essential stop on your itinerary. It sells both classic and fashionable styles – foxy heels, boots and ballet pumps – at extremely reasonable prices. Shoes are soft leather and come in myriad colours.

Pelletteria Nives   Accessories
(☎333 3370831; Via delle Carrozze 16; ⊙9am-1pm & 4-8pm Mon-Sat; MSpagna) Take the rickety lift to this workshop, choose from the softest leathers, and you will shortly be the proud owner of a handmade, designer-style bag, wallet, belt or briefcase. Bags cost €200 to €350 and take around a week to make.

Vertecchi Art   Arts
(Via della.Croce 70; ⊙3.30-7.30pm Mon, 10am-7.30pm Tue-Sat; MSpagna) Ideal for last-minute gift buying, this large paperware and art shop has beautiful printed paper, cards and envelopes that will inspire you to bring back the art of letter writing, plus an amazing choice of notebooks, art stuff and trinkets.

Fabriano   Arts, Crafts
(Map p256; ☎06 3260 0361; www.fabriano boutique.com; Via del Babuino 173; ⊙10am-8pm; MFlaminio, Spagna) Fabriano makes stationery sexy, with deeply desirable leather-bound diaries, funky notebooks and products embossed with street maps of Rome. It's perfect for picking up a gift, with other items including beautifully made leather key rings (€10) and quirky paper jewellery by local designers.

Mercato delle Stampe   Market
(Largo della Fontanella di Borghese; ⊙7am-1pm Mon-Sat; Piazza Augusto Imperatore) The Mercato delle Stampe (Print Market) is well worth a look if you're a fan of vintage books and old prints. Squirrel through the permanent stalls and among the tired posters and

🛍 Delis & Markets

Rome's well-stocked delis and fresh-produce markets are a fabulous feature of the city's shopping-scape. Most neighbourhoods have a few local delis and their own daily food market, which typically operates from around 7am to 1.30pm Monday to Saturday. The most high profile of these is on **Campo de' Fiori** (Map p250; ⊙6am-2pm Mon-Sat; Corso Vittorio Emanuele II), but you'll also find plenty to peruse at **Piazza San Cosimato** (⊙7am-2pm Mon-Sat; Viale di Trastevere, Viale di Trastevere) in Trastevere and the Nuovo Mercato di Testaccio (p163). There are also some excellent farmers markets, such as the Mercato di Circo Massimo (p150), which provides a colourful weekend showcase for seasonal, zero-kilometre produce.

Rome's top delis include the sumptuously stocked Salumeria Roscioli (p151) and historic Volpetti (p163). For the full gamut of foodie purchases, Eataly (p143) is a mall-sized state-of-the-art food emporium with produce from all over Italy and several restaurants.

Nuovo Mercato di Testaccio (p163)
S LUBENOW/LOOK-FOTO/GETTY IMAGES ©

dusty back editions, and you might turn up some interesting music scores, architectural engravings or chromolithographs of Rome.

Barrilà Boutique   Shoes
(Map p256; Via del Babuino 34; ⊙10am-8pm; MFlaminio, Spagna) For classic, handmade Italian women's shoes that won't crack the credit card, head to Barrilà. This boutique

5 Must-Buy Mementos

Antique Print

Photos are fine but for a timeless depiction of Rome consider a historic etching or print from the Piazza Navona specialist Nardecchia (p152) or nearby Casali (p152).

Leather Bag

Nothing screams Roman style as much as a silky soft leather bag. There are several shops where you can get one made, including Pelletteria Nives (p155).

Rosary Beads

Rosary beads and other assorted religious paraphernalia, ranging from papal key rings to original hand-painted icons, can be found in the Vatican and Borgo area.

Espresso Maker

A design classic and easy-to-carry icon, a caffettiera will remind you of Rome every time you make a coffee. Try C.U.C.I.N.A.

Cheese & Chocolate

Buy *pecorino Romano* cheese at Volpetti (p163) and chocolate at Confetteria Moriondo & Gariglio (p150).

stocks myriad styles in soft leather. From the window they all look a bit traditional, but you're bound to find something you'll like in the jam-packed interior.

L'Olfattorio   Beauty
(Map p256; ☑06 361 23 25; Via di Ripetta 34; ⊙10.30am-7.30pm Mon-Sat, 11am-7pm Sun; ⓂFlaminio) This is like an *enoteca* (wine bar), but with perfume instead of drinks: scents are concocted by names such as Artisan Parfumeur, Diptyque, Les Parfums de Rosine and Coudray. The assistants will guide you through different combinations of scents to work out your ideal fragrance. Exclusive perfumes are available to buy. Smellings are free but you should book ahead.

Lucia Odescalchi   Jewellery
(Map p255; ☑06 6992 5506; Palazzo Odescalchi, Piazza dei Santissimi Apostoli 81; ⊙9.30am-2pm Mon-Fri; ⓂSpagna) If you're looking for a unique piece of statement jewellery that will make an outfit, this is the place to head. Housed in the evocative archives of the family *palazzo* (mansion), the avant-garde pieces often have an almost-medieval beauty, and run from incredible polished steel and chain mail to pieces created out of pearls and fossils. Beautiful. Prices start at around €140.

C.U.C.I.N.A.   Homewares
(☑06 679 12 75; Via Mario de' Fiori 65; ⊙3.30-7.30pm Mon, 10am-7.30pm Tue-Fri, 10.30am-7.30pm Sat; ⓂSpagna) If you need a foodie gadget, C.U.C.I.N.A. is the place. Make your own *cucina* (kitchen) look the part with the designerware from this famous shop, with myriad devices you'll decide you simply must have, from jelly moulds to garlic presses.

Furla   Accessories
(Map p255; ☑06 6920 0363; Piazza di Spagna 22; ⊙10am-8pm Mon-Sat, 10.30am-8pm Sun; ⓂSpagna) Simple, good-quality bags in soft leather and a brilliant array of colours is why the handbagging hordes keep flocking to Furla, where all sorts of accessories, from sunglasses to shoes, are made. There

are many other branches dotted across Rome.

Sermoneta   Accessories
(Map p255; ☑06 679 19 60; www.sermoneta gloves.com; Piazza di Spagna 61; ⊙9.30am-8pm Mon-Sat, 10am-7pm Sun; ⓂSpagna) Buying leather gloves in Rome is a rite of passage for some, and its most famous glove-seller is the place to do it. Choose from a kaleidoscopic range of quality leather and suede gloves lined with silk and cashmere. An expert assistant will size up your hand in a glance. Just don't expect them to crack a smile.

Fendi   Clothing
(☑06 69 66 61; Largo Goldoni 420; ⊙10am-7.30pm Mon-Sat, 11am-2pm & 3-7pm Sun; ⓂSpagna) A temple to subtly blinging accessories, this multistorey art deco building is the Fendi mother ship: this is the global headquarters, as the brand was born in Rome. Fendi is particularly famous for its products made of leather and (more controversially) fur.

Focacci   Food
(☑06 679 12 28; Via della Croce 43; ⊙8am-8pm; ⓂSpagna) One of several smashing delis along this pretty street, this is the place to buy cheese, cold cuts, smoked fish, caviar, pasta, olive oil and wine.

Bulgari   Jewellery
(☑06 679 38 76; Via dei Condotti 10; ⊙10am-5pm Tue-Sat, 11am-7pm Sun & Mon; ⓂSpagna) If you have to ask the price, you can't afford it. Sumptuous window displays mean you can admire the world's finest jewellery without spending a *centesimo*.

Fausto Santini   Shoes
(☑06 678 41 14; Via Frattina 120; ⊙11am-7.30pm Mon, 10am-7.30pm Tue-Sat, 11am-2pm & 3-7pm Sun; ⓂSpagna) Rome's best-known shoe designer, Fausto Santini is famous for his beguilingly simple, architectural shoe designs, with beautiful boots and shoes made from butter-soft leather. Colours are beautiful, the quality impeccable. Seek out

Ecclesiastical Threads

Even if you're not in the market for a bishop's mitre or a ceremonial cassock, Rome's religious outfitters harbour some good deals. South of the Pantheon, a string of ecclesiastical shops has clerics from all over the world trying out elaborate capes and classic dog collars. That might not be you, but if you're after a sober V-neck sweater, an icon or a pair of glorious cardinal's socks in poppy red or deep purple, head to Via dei Cestari.

the end-of-line discount shop (p161) if this looks out of your price range.

Tod's   Shoes
(📞06 6821 0066; Via della Fontanella di Borghese 56; 🚌Via del Corso) Tod's trademark is its rubber-studded loafers (the idea was to reduce those pesky driving scuffs), perfect weekend footwear for kicking back at your country estate.

Galleria Alberto Sordi   Shopping Centre
(Map p250; Piazza Colonna; ⏰10am-10pm; 🚌Via del Corso) This elegant stained-glass arcade appeared in Alberto Sordi's 1973 classic film, *Polvere di stelle,* and has since been renamed for Rome's favourite actor, who died in 2003. It's a serene place to browse stores such as Zara and Feltrinelli, and there's an airy cafe ideal for a quick coffee break.

Underground   Market
(Map p255; 📞06 3600 5345; Via Francesco Crispi 96, Ludovisi underground car park; ⏰3-8pm Sat & 10.30am-7.30pm Sun, 2nd weekend of the month Sep-Jun; Ⓜ Barberini) Monthly market held underground in a car park near Villa Borghese. There are more than 150 stalls selling everything from antiques and collectables to clothes and toys.

🏛 Vatican City, Borgo & Prati

Enoteca Costantini   Wine
(www.pierocostantini.it; Piazza Cavour 16; ⏰9am-1pm Tue-Sat, 4.30-8pm Mon-Sat; 🚌Piazza Cavour) If you're after a hard-to-find grappa or something special for your wine collection, this historic *enoteca* is the place to try. Opened in 1972, Piero Costantini's superbly stocked shop is a point of reference for aficionados across town with its 800-sq-metre basement cellar and a colossal collection of Italian and world wines and more than 1000 spirits.

Antica Manufattura Cappelli   Accessories
(📞06 3972 5679; www.antica-cappelleria. it; Via degli Scipioni 46; ⏰9am-7pm Mon-Fri; Ⓜ Ottaviano–San Pietro) A throwback to a more elegant age, the atelier-boutique of milliner Patrizia Fabri offers a wide range of beautifully crafted hats. Choose from the off-the-peg line of straw Panamas, vintage cloches, felt berets and tweed deerstalkers, or have one made to measure. Prices range from about €70 to €300 and ordered hats can be delivered within the day.

Rechicle   Vintage
(Piazza dell'Unità 21; ⏰11am-1.30pm Tue-Sat, 2.30-7.30pm Mon-Sat; 🚌Via Cola di Rienzo) Search out this discreet boutique behind the covered market on Piazza dell'Unità for secondhand styles and vintage fashions. Designer labels are in obvious evidence among the racks of women's clothes, shoes, bags and accessories displayed alongside the occasional vintage piece.

Castroni   Food & Drink
(www.castronicoladirienzo.com; Via Cola di Rienzo 196; ⏰7.45am-8pm Mon-Sat, 9.30am-8pm Sun; 🚌Via Cola di Rienzo) This is a real Aladdin's cave of gourmet treats. Towering, ceiling-high shelves groan under the weight of Italian wines and foodie specialities, classic foreign delicacies, and all manner of sweets and chocolates. Adding to the atmosphere are the coffee odours that waft up from the in-store bar.

Piazza dell' Unità   Market

(🚇Piazza del Risorgimento) Near the Vatican, perfect for stocking up for a picnic.

🛍 Monti, Esquilino & San Lorenzo

Mercato Monti Urban Market   Market

(Map p252; www.mercatomonti.com; Via Leonina 46; ⏱10am-8pm Sat & Sun; Ⓜ Cavour) Vintage clothes, accessories, one-off pieces by local designers, this market in the hip hood of Monti is well worth a rummage.

Tina Sondergaard   Clothing

(Map p255; 📱334 3850799; Via del Boschetto 1d; ⏱3-7.30pm Mon, 10.30am-7.30pm Tue-Sat, closed Aug; Ⓜ Cavour) Sublimely cut and whimsically retro-esque, these handmade threads are a hit with female fashion cognoscenti, including Italian rock star Carmen Consoli and the city's theatre and TV crowd. You can have adjustments made (included in the price), and dresses cost around €140.

Spot   Homewares

(Map p255; 📱338 9275739; Via del Boschetto; ⏱10.30am-7.30pm Mon-Sat; Ⓜ Cavour) This small shop has an impeccable collection of midcentury furnishings, plus glassware designed by the owners and papier mâché vases designed by their friends. It's frequented by the likes of Paolo Sorrentino (who directed *La Grande Belleza*).

La Bottega del Cioccolato   Food

(Map p252; 📱06 482 14 73; Via Leonina 82; ⏱9.30am-7.30pm Oct-Aug; Ⓜ Cavour) Run by the younger generation of Moriondo & Gariglio, this is a magical world of scarlet walls and old-fashioned glass cabinets set into black wood, with irresistible smells wafting in from the kitchen and rows of lovingly homemade chocolates on display.

Fabio Piccioni   Jewellery

(Map p252; 📱06 474 16 97; Via del Boschetto 148; ⏱10.30am-1pm Tue-Sat, 2-8pm Mon-Sat;

stalls selling everything from rare books...to Peruvian shawls and MP3 players

Porta Portese Market (p161)

★ **Top Five For Foodie Treats**

Salumeria Roscioli (p151)

Confetteria Moriondo & Gariglio (p150)

Volpetti (p163)

Eataly (p143)

Podere Vecciano (see below)

From left: Chocolates, Confetteria Moriondo & Gariglio (p150); Vinegar tasting, Volpetti (p163)

Ⓜ️Cavour) A sparkling Aladdin's cave of decadent, one-of-a-kind costume jewellery; artisan Fabio Piccioni recycles old trinkets to create remarkable art deco–inspired jewellery.

101 Clothing

(Via Urbana; ⏲10am-1.30pm & 2-8pm; Ⓜ️Cavour) The collection at this individual boutique might include gossamer-light jumpers, broad-brimmed hats, chain-mail earrings and silk dresses: it's always worth a look to discover a special something.

Podere Vecciano Food

(Map p252; 📞06 4891 3812; Via dei Serpenti 33; ⏲10am-8pm; Ⓜ️Cavour) Selling produce from its Tuscan farm, this shop is a great place to pick up presents, such as different varieties of pesto, honey and marmalade, selected wines, olive-oil-based cosmetics and beautiful olive wood chopping boards. There's even an olive tree growing in the middle of the shop.

Creje Clothing

(Map p255; 📞06 4890 5227; Via del Boschetto 5A; ⏲10am-2.30pm & 3-8pm; Ⓜ️Cavour) This

eclectic, inexpensive Monti boutique sells a mix of clothing sourced from exotic places, including Indian dresses, plus dramatic silver costume jewellery and soft leather bags.

Abito Clothing

(Map p255; 📞06 488 10 17; http://abito61. blogspot.co.uk; Via Panisperna 61; ⏲10.30am-8pm Mon-Sat, noon-8pm Sun; Ⓜ️Cavour) Wilma Silvestre designs elegant clothes with a difference. Choose from the draped, chic, laid-back styles on the rack, and you can have one made up just for you in a day or just a few hours – customise the fabric and the colour. There's usually one guest designer's clothes also being sold at the shop.

La Grande Officina Jewellery

(📞06 445 03 48; http://lagrandeofficinagioielli. blogspot.co.uk; Via dei Sabelli 165B; ⏲11am-7.30pm Tue-Fri, 11am-2pm Sat, 1-7.30pm Mon; 🚉Via Tiburtina) Under dusty workshop lamps, husband-and-wife team Giancarlo Genco and Daniela Ronchetti turn everything from old clock parts and Japanese fans into beautiful work-of-art jewellery. Head here for something truly unique.

CULTURA RM EXCLUSIVE/PHILIP LEE HARVEY/GETTY IMAGES ©

Arion Esposizioni
Books

(Map p255; ☑06 4891 3361; Via Milano 15-17; ☺10am-8pm Sun-Thu, to 10.30pm Fri & Sat; ⬛Via Nazionale) In cool, gleaming white rooms designed by Firouz Galdo, Arion Esposizioni – the bookshop attached to Palazzo delle Esposizioni – is just made for browsing. There are books on art, architecture and photography, DVDs, CDs, vinyl, children's books and gifts for the design lover in your life.

Giacomo Santini
Shoes

(Map p255; ☑06 488 09 34; Via Cavour 106; ☺3.30-7.30pm Mon, 10am-1pm & 3.30-7.30pm Tue-Sat; ⓂCavour) Close to the Basilica di Santa Maria Maggiore, this Fausto Santini outlet store is named after the accessory designer's father, Giacomo. It sells end-of-line and discounted Fausto Santini boots, shoes and bags, and has bargain signature architectural designs in butter-soft leather at a fraction of the retail price. Sizes are limited, however.

Feltrinelli International
Books

(Map p255; ☑06 482 78 78; Via VE Orlando 84; ☺9am-8pm Mon-Sat, 10.30am-1.30pm & 4-8pm

Sun; ⓂRepubblica) The international branch of Italy's ubiquitous bookseller has a splendid collection of books in English, Spanish, French, German and Portuguese. You'll find everything from recent best sellers to dictionaries, travel guides, DVDs and an excellent assortment of maps.

Nuovo Mercato Esquilino
Market

(Via Lamarmora; ☺5am-3pm Mon-Sat; ⓂVittorio Emanuele) Cheap, colourful food market, and the best place to find exotic herbs and spices.

🏛 Trastevere & Gianicolo

Porta Portese Market
Market

(Piazza Porta Portese; ☺6am-2pm Sun; ⬛Viale di Trastevere, ⬛Viale di Trastevere) To see another side of Rome, head to this mammoth flea market. With thousands of stalls selling everything from rare books and fell-off-a-lorry bikes to Peruvian shawls and MP3 players, it's crazily busy and a lot of fun. Keep your valuables safe and wear your haggling hat.

Boutiques & Vintage Clothes

The bohemian enclave of Monti is a hot-bed of hip shopping action. Via del Boschetto, Via Urbana and Via dei Serpenti are lined with independent-label clothing boutiques and small-scale artisanal jewellery makers. The area also boasts a number of vintage clothes shops, as well as a weekend vintage market, Mercato Monti Urban Market (p159).

Other good areas for cutting-edge designer boutiques and vintage clothes include Via del Governo Vecchio, a delightful cobbled street that runs from a small square just off Piazza Navona towards the river, Via del Pellegrino, and around Campo de' Fiori.

Vintage shop on Via del Governo Vecchio
JESSICA STEWART/CONTRIBUTOR/GETTY IMAGES ©

Roma-Store — Beauty

(📞06 581 87 89; Via della Lungaretta 63; ⊙10am-8pm; 🚊Viale di Trastevere, 🚊Viale di Trastevere) An enchanting perfume shop crammed full of deliciously enticing bottles of scent, including lots of small, lesser-known brands that will have perfume lovers practically fainting with joy.

Antica Caciara Trasteverina — Food & Drink

(Via San Francesco a Ripa 140; ⊙7am-2pm & 4-8pm Mon-Sat; 🚊Viale di Trastevere, 🚊Viale di Trastevere) The fresh ricotta is a prized possession at this century-old deli, and usually snapped up by lunch. If you're too late, take solace in the famous *pecorino Romano* or the *burrata pugliese* (a creamy cheese from

the Puglia region), or simply lust after the fragrant hams, bread, Sicilian anchovies and local wines.

Officina della Carta — Gifts

(📞06 589 55 57; Via Benedetta 26b; ⊙10.30am-7.30pm Mon-Sat; 🚊Piazza Trilussa) A perfect present pit stop, this tiny workshop produces attractive hand-painted paper-bound boxes, photo albums, recipe books, notepads, photo frames and diaries.

Almost Corner Bookshop — Books

(📞06 583 69 42; Via del Moro 45; ⊙10am-7.30pm Mon-Thu, 10am-8pm Fri & Sat, 11am-8pm Sun; 🚊Piazza Trilussa) This is how a bookshop should look: a crammed haven full of rip-roaring reads, with every millimetre of wall space containing English-language fiction and nonfiction (including children's) and travel guides.

Open Door Bookshop — Books

(Via della Lungaretta 23; ⊙10am-8pm Mon-Sat; 🚊Viale di Trastevere, 🚊Viale di Trastevere) A lovely crammed secondhand bookshop, this is a great place to browse and happen on a classic, with novels and nonfiction in English, Italian, French and Spanish.

La Cravatta su Misura — Accessories

(📞06 890 69 41; Via di Santa Cecilia 12; ⊙10am-7pm Mon-Sat; 🚊Viale di Trastevere, 🚊Viale di Trastevere) With ties draped over the wooden furniture, this inviting shop resembles the study of an absent-minded professor. But don't be fooled: these guys know their ties. Only the finest Italian silks and English wools are used in neckwear made to customers' specifications. At a push, a tie can be ready in a few hours.

Scala Quattordici Clothing — Clothing

(Villa della Scala 13-14; ⊙10am-1.30pm & 4-8pm Tue-Sat, 4-8pm Mon; 🚊Piazza Trilussa) Make yourself over à la Audrey Hepburn with these classically tailored clothes in beautiful fabrics – either made to measure or off the peg. Pricey (a frock will set you back €600 plus) but oh so worth it.

🛍 San Giovanni to Testaccio

Volpetti
Food & Drink

(www.volpetti.com; Via Marmorata 47; ⊗8am-2pm & 5-8.15pm Mon-Sat; 🚌Via Marmorata) This superstocked deli, considered by many the best in town, is a treasure trove of gourmet delicacies. Helpful staff will guide you through the extensive selection of smelly cheeses, homemade pastas, olive oils, vinegars, cured meats, vegie pies, wines and grappas. It also serves excellent sliced pizza.

Nuovo Mercato di Testaccio
Market

(entrances Via Galvani, Via Beniamino Franklin; ⊗6am-3pm Mon-Sat; 🚌Via Marmorata) Even if you don't need to buy anything, a trip to Testaccio's daily food market is fun. Occupying a modern, purpose-built site, it hums with activity as locals go about their daily shopping, picking, prodding and sniffing the brightly coloured produce and cheerfully shouting at all and sundry.

Calzature Boccanera
Shoes

(Via Luca della Robbia 36; ⊗9.30am-1.30pm Tue-Sat & 3.30-7.30pm Mon-Sat; 🚌Via Marmorata) From just-off-the-runway heels to classic driving shoes, high-end trainers and timeless lace-ups, this historic shoe shop stocks a wide range of footwear by top international brands, as well as bags, belts and leather accessories.

Soul Food
Music

(www.haterecords.com; Via di San Giovanni in Laterano 192; ⊗10.30am-1.30pm & 3.30-8pm Tue-Sat; 🚌Via di San Giovanni in Laterano) Run by Hate Records, Soul Food is a laid-back record store with an eclectic collection of vinyl that runs the musical gamut, from '60s garage and rockabilly to punk, indie, new wave, folk, funk and soul. You'll also find retro-design T-shirts, fanzines and other groupie clobber.

Via Sannio
Market

(⊗9am-1.30pm Mon-Sat; Ⓜ San Giovanni) This clothes market in the shadow of the Aureli-an Walls is awash with wardrobe staples. It has a good assortment of new and vintage clothes, bargain-price shoes, jeans and leather jackets.

🛍 Villa Borghese & Northern Rome

Libreria l'Argonauta
Books

(www.librerialargonauta.com; Via Reggio Emilia 89; ⊗10am-8pm Mon-Fri, 10am-1pm & 4-8pm Sat; 🚌Via Nizza) Near the Museo d'Arte Con-temporanea di Roma (MACRO) museum, this travel bookshop is a lovely place to browse. With its serene atmosphere and shelves of travel literature, guides, maps and photo tomes, it can easily spark day-dreams of far-off places.

Bulzoni
Wine

(www.enotecabulzoni.it; Viale Parioli 36; ⊗8.30am-2pm & 4.30-8.30pm; 🚌Viale Parioli) This historic wine shop has been supply-ing Parioli with wine since 1929. It has a formidable collection of Italian regional wines, as well as European and New World labels, and a carefully curated selection of champagnes, liqueurs, olive oils and gourmet delicacies.

Bagheera
Fashion

(www.bagheeraboutique.com; Piazza Euclide 30; ⊗9.30am-1pm Tue-Sat, 3.30-7.30pm Mon-Sat; 🚌Piazza Euclide) This modish boutique has long been a local go-to for the latest fash-ions. Alongside sandals and vampish high heels you'll find dresses by Dries Van Noten and a selection of bags and accessories by big-name international designers.

Anticaglie a Ponte Milvio
Market

(Via Capoprati; ⊗9am-8pm 1st & 2nd Sun of month, closed Aug; 🚌Ponte Milvio) The 2nd-century-BC Ponte Milvio forms the backdrop to this monthly antique market. On the first and second Sunday of every month up to 200 stalls spring up on the riverbank laden with antiques, objets d'art, vintage clothes, period furniture and all manner of collectable clobber.

BAR OPEN

Afternoon beers, evening wines and midnight cocktails

Bar Open

Often the best way to enjoy nightlife in Rome is to wander from restaurant to bar, getting happily lost down picturesque cobbled streets. There's simply no city with better backdrops for a drink: you can savour a Campari overlooking the Roman Forum or sample artisanal beer while watching the light bounce off baroque fountains.

Night-owl Romans tend to eat late, then drink at bars before heading off to a club at around 1am. Like most cities, Rome is a collection of districts, each with its own character, which is often completely different after dark. The centro storico *(historic centre) and Trastevere pull in a mix of locals and tourists as night falls, while Ostiense and Testaccio are the grittier clubbing districts.*

In This Section

Opening Hours

Cafes 7.30am to 8pm

Traditional bars 7.30am to 1am or 2am

Bars, pubs & enoteche (wine bars)
lunchtime or 6pm to 2am

Nightclubs 10pm to 4am

Villa Borghese & Northern Rome
From a cool aperitif bar to hip
alternative venues (p181)

Vatican City, Borgo & Prati
Low-key scene with a sprinkling
of quiet wine bars (p173)

Tridente, Trevi & the Quirinale
Historic cafes and swanky, good-
looking cocktail bars (p172)

Centro Storico
Bars and a few clubs, a mix of
touristy and sophisticated (p170)

Monti, Esquilino & San Lorenzo
Boho bars in Monti and
Pigneto, underground clubs
in San Lorenzo (p173)

Ancient Rome
A couple of popular retreats
near the Roman ruins (p170)

Trastevere & Gianicolo
Buzzing area riddled with
bars, pubs and cafes (p177)

San Giovanni & Testaccio
Nightowls swarm to Testaccio's
strip of poptastic clubs (p180)

Southern Rome
Serious clubbing territory with
cool venues in Ostiense's ex-
industrial venues (p183)

Costs

Expect to pay somewhere around the
following for a drink:
Espresso €0.80
Cappuccino €1.20
Glass of wine from €3
Beer €5

Tipping

Tipping in bars is not necessary,
although many people leave small
change, perhaps a €0.20 coin, if
standing at the bar.

Websites

Roma 2 Night (http://2night.it)
Zero (http://roma.zero.eu)

The Best...

Experience Rome's finest drinking establishments

Enoteche

Il Tiaso (p174) With a hip, living-room vibe, plentiful wines and live music.

Fafiuché (p174) A charming warm-orange space with wine and artisanal beers.

La Barrique (p174) Inviting Monti address, with great wines and accompanying meals.

Il Goccetto (p171) An old-school *vino e olio* (wine and oil) shop that makes for a great neighbourhood wine bar.

Alternative Venues

Lanificio 159 (p182) Cool underground venue that hosts live gigs and club nights.

Big Bang (p180) Reggae, dancehall, dub and techno in a graffitti-sprayed former slaughterhouse.

Big Star (p179) Backstreet Trastevere bar, with regular DJs and a laid-back crowd.

Yeah! Pigneto (p176) Cool bar hosting live gigs and DJs in Rome's most boho district.

Aperitivo

La Meschita (p180) Delicious nibbles in this tiny *enoteca* (wine bar) adjoining La Ferrara restaurant.

Momart (p182) Students and local professionals love its expansive array of pizza and other snacks.

Freni e Frizioni (p179) Perenially cool bar with lavish nightly buffet of snacks.

For a Lazy Drink

Ombre Rosse (p179) Lovely, relaxed Trastevere bar, with outside seating.

Stravinskij Bar (p172) Hotel de Russie's elegant bar, with its courtyard garden backed by Borghese gardens.

Yeah! Pigneto (p176) Boho bar that has plenty of places to sit and chat and DJs and regular live gigs.

Gay

Coming Out (pictured above; p181) A friendly gay bar near the Colosseum, open all day, with gigs, drag shows and karaoke later on.

L'Alibi (p181) Kitsch shows and house, techno and dance pumping up a mixed gay and straight crowd.

My Bar (p181) A mixed crowd by day, and gayer by night, in the shadow of the Colosseum.

See & Be Seen

Etablì (p171) Chic bar near Campo de'Fiori, filled with vintage French furniture and laid-back cool.

Salotto 42 (p172) A sitting-room-style bar, offering cocktails facing the ancient Roman Stock Exchange.

Co.So (p174) Opened by the Hotel de Russie's former mixologist, this is Pigneto's hippest haunt.

Rec 23 (p180) With NY style and locally inspired cocktails, this is the place to be seen in Testaccio.

★ Lonely Planet's Top Choices

Ai Tre Scalini (p173) Buzzing *enoteca* that feels as convivial as a pub.

Ma Che Siete Venuti a Fà (p179) Tiny pub that's the heart of Rome's artisanal-beer explosion.

Co.So (p174) A real buzz in this Pigneto hotspot, serving up out-there cocktails on bubble-wrap coasters.

Sciascia Caffè (p173) Classy joint serving the unparalleled *caffè eccellente,* a velvety smooth espresso in a chocolate-lined cup.

Barnum Cafe (p170) Cool vintage armchairs to sink into by day and dressed-up cocktails by night.

🍷 Ancient Rome

0,75   Bar
(Map p252; www.075roma.com; Via dei Cerchi
65; ◷11am-2am; 📶; 🚉Via dei Cerchi) This
welcoming bar on the Circo Massimo is
good for a lingering drink, an *aperitivo*
(6.30pm onwards) or a light meal (mains
€6 to €13.50, salads €5.50 to €7.50). It's a
friendly place with a laid-back vibe, an attractive exposed-brick look and cool tunes.

Cavour 313   Wine Bar
(Map p252; 📞06 678 54 96; www.cavour313.
it; Via Cavour 313; ◷12.30-2.45pm & 7.30pm-
12.30am, closed Sun summer; Ⓜ Cavour) Close
to the Forum, wood-panelled Cavour 313
attracts everyone from tourists to actors
and politicians. It serves a daily food menu
and a selection of salads, cold cuts and
cheeses (€8 to €12), but the headline act is
the wine. And with more than 1200 labels to

> *it's well worth trying a few
> local drops while you're in
> Rome*

choose from you're sure to find something
to tickle your palate.

🍷 Centro Storico

Barnum Cafe   Cafe
(Map p250; www.barnumcafe.com; Via del Pellegrino 87; ◷9am-10pm Mon, 8.30am-2am Tue-
Sat; 📶; 🚉Corso Vittorio Emanuele II) A relaxed,
friendly spot to check your email over a
freshly squeezed orange juice or spend
a pleasant hour reading a newspaper on
one of the tatty old armchairs in the white
bare-brick interior. Come evenings and the
scene is cocktails, smooth tunes and coolly
dressed-down locals.

Caffè Sant'Eustachio   Cafe
(Map p250; www.santeustachioilcaffe.it; Piazza
Sant'Eustachio 82; ◷8.30am-1am Sun-Thu, to
1.30am Fri, to 2am Sat; 🚉Corso del Rinascimento) This small, unassuming cafe, generally
three deep at the bar, is reckoned by many
to serve the best coffee in town. Created
by beating the first drops of espresso and
several teaspoons of sugar into a frothy

paste, then adding the rest of the coffee, it's superbly smooth and guaranteed to put some zing into your sightseeing.

La Casa del Caffè
Tazza d'Oro   Cafe
(Map p250; www.tazzadorocoffeeshop.com; Via degli Orfani 84-86; ☺7am-8pm Mon-Sat, 10.30am-7.30pm Sun; 🚇Via del Corso) A busy, stand-up cafe with burnished 1940s fittings, this is one of Rome's best coffee houses. Its espresso hits the mark nicely and there's a range of delicious coffee concoctions, including a cooling *granita di caffè*, a crushed-ice coffee drink served with whipped cream. There's also a small shop and, outside, a coffee vending machine for those out-of-hours caffeine emergencies.

Open Baladin   Bar
(Map p250; www.openbaladinroma.it; Via degli Specchi 6; ☺noon-2am; 🛜; 🚇Via Arenula) A hip, shabby-chic lounge bar near Campo de' Fiori, Open Baladin is a leading light in Rome's craft-beer scene, with more than 40 beers on tap and up to 100 bottled brews, many from Italian artisanal micro-breweries. There's also a decent food menu with *panini,* gourmet burgers and daily specials.

Etablì   Bar
(Map p250; ☎06 9761 6694; www.etabli.it; Vicolo delle Vacche 9a; ☺11am-2am, closed Mon in winter, Sun in summer; 🛜; 🚇Corso del Rinascimento) Housed in a lofty 16th-century *palazzo,* Etablì is a rustic-chic lounge-bar-restaurant where you can drop by for a morning coffee, have a light lunch or chat over an *aperitivo*. It's laid-back and good-looking, with original French-inspired country decor – think leather armchairs, rough wooden tables and a crackling fire-place. It also serves weekend brunch and full restaurant dinners (€45), and hosts the occasional jam session.

Circus   Bar
(Map p250; www.circusroma.it; Via della Vetrina 15; ☺10.30am-2am; 🛜; 🚇Corso del

🍷 Bars & Pubs

Bars range from regular Italian cafe-bars that have seemingly changed little over the centuries, to chic, contem-porarily styled places serving esoteric cocktails – such as Co.So (p174) and Salotto 42 (p172) – and laid-back, per-ennially popular haunts – such as Freni e Frizioni (p179) – that have a longevity rarely seen in other cities. Pubs are also popular, with several long-running Irish-style pubs filled with chattering Ro-mans, and more pub-like bars opening on the back of the artisanal beer trend.

Rinascimento) A great little bar, tucked around the corner from Piazza Navona. It's a relaxed place popular with out-of-town students who come here to catch up on the news – wi-fi is free and there are interna-tional newspapers to read – and hang out over a drink. The atmosphere hots up in the evening when cocktails and shots take over from tea and cappuccino.

No.Au   Bar
(Map p250; Piazza Montevecchio 16; ☺6pm-1am Tue-Thu, noon-1am Fri-Sun; 🚇Corso del Rinascimento) Opening onto a charming *centro storico* piazza, No.Au – pronounced know how – is a cool bistro-bar set-up. Like many fashionable bars, it's big on beer and offers a knowledgeable list of artisanal craft brews, as well as local wines and a small but select food menu.

Il Goccetto   Wine Bar
(Via dei Banchi Vecchi 14; ☺11.30am-2pm Tue & Sat, 6.30pm-midnight Mon-Sat, closed Aug; 🚇Corso Vittorio Emanuele II) This old-school *vino e olio* (wine and oil) shop has everything you could want in a neighbour-hood wine bar: a colourful cast of regulars, a cosy, bottle-lined interior, a selection of cheeses and cold cuts, and a serious, 800-strong wine list.

Clubbing & Centri Sociali

Rome has a range of clubs, with DJs spinning everything from lounge and jazz to dancehall and hip-hop. The scene is centred on Testaccio (main-stream clubs) and Ostiense (industrial, warehouse vive for serious clubbers), although you'll also find popular places in Trastevere and the *centro storico* (historics centre).

Clubs tend to get busy after midnight, or even after 2am. Admission is often free, but drinks are expensive. Cocktails can cost from €10 to €20, but you can drink much more cheaply in the studen-ty clubs of San Lorenzo, Pigneto and the *centri sociali* (social centres).

Rome's *centri sociali* were originally hubs of left-wing activism but many have now resurrected themselves as arts centres hosting live music and contemporary arts events. They offer Rome's most unusual, cheap and alternative nightlife options. Top spots include Brancaleone (p182) and Esc Atelier (p177).

You'll need to dress the part for the big clubs, some of which have a seem-ingly whimsical door policy, and men, whether single or in groups, will often find themselves turned away.

Jerry Thomas Project   Cocktail Bar

(☎06 9684 5937; www.thejerrythomasproject.it; Vicolo Cellini 30; ☺10pm-4am; ☒Corso Vittorio Emanuele II) A self-styled speakeasy with a 1920s look and a password to get in – check the website and call to book – this hidden bar is setting the standards for the cocktail trend currently sweeping Rome. Its hipster mixologists know their stuff and the retro decor lends the place a real Prohibi-tion-era feel.

L'Angolo Divino   Wine Bar

(Map p250; www.angolodivino.it; Via dei Bale-strari 12; ☺10.30am-3pm Tue-Sat, 5pm-1.30am daily; ☒Corso Vittorio Emanuele II) A hop and a skip from Campo de' Fiori, this is a warm, woody wine bar. It's an oasis of genteel calm, with a carefully selected wine list, mostly Italian but a few French and New World labels, and a small daily menu of hot and cold dishes such as creamy Andria *burrata* (cheese made from mozzarella and cream) with sun-dried tomatoes.

Salotto 42   Bar

(Map p250; www.salotto42.it; Piazza di Pietra 42; ☺10.30am-2am Tue-Sun; ☒Via del Corso) On a picturesque piazza, facing the columns of the Temple of Hadrian, this is a glamorous lounge bar, complete with subdued lighting, vintage 1950s armchairs, Murano lamps and a collection of heavyweight design books. Come for the daily lunch buffet or to hang out with the 'see-and-be-seen' crowd over an evening cocktail.

🍷 Tridente, Trevi & the Quirinale

La Scena   Bar

(Map p256; Via della Penna 22; ☺7am-1am; ⓂFla-minio) Part of the art deco Hotel Locarno, this bar has a faded Agatha Christie–era feel, and a greenery-shaded outdoor terrace bedecked in wrought-iron furniture. Cocktails cost €13 to €15, or you can par-take of afternoon tea from 3pm to 6pm and *aperitivo* from 7pm to 10pm.

Stravinskij Bar – Hotel de Russie   Bar

(Map p256; ☎06 328 88 70; Via del Babuino 9; ☺9am-1am; ⓂFlaminio) Can't afford to stay at the celeb-magnet Hotel de Russie? Then splash out on a drink at its swish bar. There are sofas inside, but best is a drink in the sunny courtyard, with sunshaded tables overlooked by terraced gardens. Impossibly romantic in the best dolce vita style, it's perfect for a cocktail (from €20) or beer (€13) and some posh snacks.

Canova   Bar

(Map p256; ☎06 361 22 31; Piazza del Popolo 16; ☺8am-midnight; ⓂFlaminio) While left-wing authors Italo Calvino and Alberto Moravia used to drink at Rosati, over the square, their right-wing counterparts came here. Today tourists are the main clientele, and the views are as good as ever

Micca Club   Club
(Map p255; ☑393 3236244; www.miccaclub.com; Via degli Avignonesi; MBarberini) No longer in its brick-arched cellar in southern Rome, but now close to Piazza Barberini, Micca Club now has a less arresting interior but still retains its vintage, quirky vibe. This is Rome's burlesque club, where you can sip cocktails while watching shimmying acts upping the kitsch factor. Reserving a table by phone is advised.

🍷 Vatican City, Borgo & Prati

Sciascia Caffè   Cafe
(Via Fabio Massimo 80/A; ⊙7.30am-6.30pm Mon-Sat; MOttaviano-San Pietro) The timeless elegance of this polished cafe is perfectly suited to the exquisite coffee it makes. There are various options but nothing can beat the *caffè eccellente*, a velvety smooth espresso served in a delicate cup that has been lined with melted chocolate. The result is nothing short of magnificent.

Makasar   Wine Bar, Teahouse
(www.makasar.it; Via Plauto 33; ⊙noon-midnight Tue-Thu, to 2am Fri & Sat, 5.30-11.30pm Sun; 🚇Piazza del Risorgimento) Recharge your batteries with a quiet drink at this oasis of bookish tranquillity. Pick your tipple from the nine-page tea menu or opt for an Italian wine and sit back in the casually stylish, softly lit interior. For something to eat, there's a small menu of salads, bruschette, baguettes and healthy hot dishes.

Passaguai   Wine Bar
(☑06 8745 1358; www.passaguai.it; Via Leto 1; ⊙10am-2am Mon-Fri, 6pm-2am Sat & Sun; 🛜; 🚇Piazza del Risorgimento) A cosy basement bar with tables in a vaulted interior and on a quiet side street, Passaguai feels pleasingly

🍸 Grattachecca

It's summertime, the living is easy, and Romans like nothing better than in the sultry evening heat than to amble down to the river and partake of some *grattachecca* (crushed ice covered in fruit and syrup). It's the ideal way to cool down and there are kiosks along the riverbank satisfying this very Roman need. Try Sora Mirella Caffè (grattachecce €3-6; ⊙11am-3am May-Sep), next to Ponte Cestio.

Mint *grattachecca*
STEFANO CAROCCI/GETTY IMAGES ©

off the radar. It's a great spot for a beer or glass of wine – there's an excellent choice of both – accompanied by cheese and cold cuts, or even a full meal from the limited menu. Free wi-fi.

🍷 Monti, Esquilino & San Lorenzo

Ai Tre Scalini   Wine Bar
(Map p252; Via Panisperna 251; ⊙12.30pm-1am; MCavour) The 'Three Steps' is always packed, with crowds spilling out into the street. Apart from a tasty choice of wines, it sells the damned fine Menabrea beer, brewed in northern Italy. You can also tuck into a heart-warming array of cheeses, salami and dishes such as *polpette al sugo* (meatballs with sauce; €7.50).

Il Tiaso   Bar
(☑06 4547 4625; www.iltiaso.com; Via Perugia 20; 🛜; 🚇Circonvallazione Casilina) Think living room with zebra-print chairs, walls of indie

art, Lou Reed biographies shelved between wine bottles, and 30-something owner Gabriele playing his latest New York Dolls album to neobeatnik chicks, corduroy professors and the odd neighbourhood dog. Well-priced wine, an intimate chilled vibe and regular live music.

Co.So — Bar

(Via Braccio da Montone 80; cocktails €10; ⊙7pm-3am Mon-Sat; 🚌Via Prenestina) The chicest bar in the Pigneto district, this tiny place, opened by Massimo D'Addezio, former master mixologist at Hotel de Russie, is buzzing and is hipster to the hilt, with its Carbonara Sour cocktail (with vodka infused with pork fat), bubble-wrap coasters, and popcorn and M&M bar snacks.

Birra Piu — Bar

(📞06 7061 3106; Via del Pigneto 105; beer €5; ⊙5pm-midnight Mon-Thu, 5pm-2am Fri & Sat, 7pm-midnight Sun; 🚌Circonvallazione Casilina) A small, relaxed bar, with a laid-back crowd draped over blonde-wood bar stools and tables. To a soundtrack of the Doors, Blur and so on, you can drink a wide variety of craft beers, with names such as 'Total Insanity'.

Fafiuché — Wine Bar

(Map p252; 📞06 699 09 68; www.fafiuche.it; Via della Madonna dei Monti 28; ⊙5.30pm-1am Mon-Sat; Ⓜ️Cavour) Fafiuché means 'light-hearted fun' in the Piedmontese dialect, and this place lives up to its name. The narrow, bottle-lined warm-orange space exudes charm: come here to enjoy wine and artisanal beers, eat delicious dishes originating from Puglia to Piedmont or buy delectable foodstuffs. *Aperitivo* is from 6.30pm to 9pm.

La Barrique — Wine Bar

(Map p255; Via del Boschetto 41b; ⊙12.30-3.30pm & 5.30pm-1am Mon-Sat; Ⓜ️Cavour) This appealing *enoteca*, with wooden furniture and whitewashed walls, is a classy yet informal place to hang out and sample excellent French, Italian and German wines; a choice of perfectly cooked, delicious main courses provide a great accompaniment, or you can stick to artisanal cheeses and cold cuts.

★ Enoteche

An *enoteca* was originally where the old boys from the neighbourhood would gather to drink rough local wine poured straight from the barrel. Times have changed: nowadays they tend to be sophisticated but still atmospheric places, offering Italian and international vintages, delicious cheeses and cold cuts.

Clockwise from top left: Via della Scala, Trastevere (p179): Trastevere cafe; Frascati Superiore wine (p177); Irish-style pub

Wine on display

Al Vino al Vino   Wine Bar

(Map p252; Via dei Serpenti 19; ⊘6pm-1am, shop open all day; MCavour) A rustic *enoteca* that's a favourite with the locals, mixing ceramic tabletops and contemporary paintings, this is an attractive spot to linger over a fine collection of wines, particularly *passiti* (sweet wines). The other speciality is *distillati* – grappa, whisky and so on – and there are snacks to help it all go down, including some Sicilian delicacies.

Bohemien   Bar

(Map p252; Via degli Zingari 36; ⊘6pm-2am Wed-Sun; MCavour) ⊘ This little bar lives up to its name; it feels like something you might stumble on in Left Bank Paris. It's small, with mismatched chairs and tables and an eclectic crowd drinking wine by the glass, and tea and coffee.

Yeah! Pigneto   Bar

(⊘06 6480 1456; www.yeahpigneto.com; Via Giovanni de Agostini 41; small beer €3, aperitivo €7; ⊘7pm-2am Mon-Fri, 8pm-2am Sat & Sun) We say si! to Yeah! Pigneto. A relaxed boho-feeling bar with DJs playing jazz and the walls covered in collages and classic album covers, this is a good place for lingering over not-too-expensive beer. Regular live gigs.

Locanda Atlantide   Club

(⊘06 4470 4540; www.locandatlantide.it; Via dei Lucani 22b; free or €3-5; ⊘9pm-2am Oct-Jun; MVia Tiburtina, ⊘Scalo San Lorenzo) Come, tickle Rome's grungy underbelly. Descend through a door in a graffiti-covered wall into this cavernous basement dive, packed to the rafters with studenty, alternative crowds and featuring everything from prog-folk to DJ-spun electro music. It's good to know that punk is not dead.

Gente di San Lorenzo   Bar

(⊘06 445 44 25; Via degli Aurunci 42; ⊘7am-2am; ⊘Via dei Reti) On the corner of San Lorenzo's Piazza dell'Immacolata, which gets thronged with students on balmy nights, this is a relaxed place for a drink and snack or meal. The interior is airy, with warm wooden floors and brick arches, and there are some outdoor tables as well as regular DJs and occasional live music.

Esc Atelier Club

(www.escatelier.net; Via dei Volsci 159; ⊙varies; 🚇Via Tiburtina, 🚋Via dei Reti) This left-wing alternative arts centre hosts live gigs and club nights: expect electronica DJ sets featuring live sax, discussions, exhibitions, political events and more. Admission and drinks are cheap.

Ice Club Bar

(Map p252; www.iceclubroma.it; Via della Madonna dei Monti 18; ⊙6pm-2am; 🚇Colosseo) Novelty value is what the Ice Club is all about. Pay €15 (you get a free vodka cocktail served in a glass made of ice), put on a thermal cloak and mittens, and enter the bar, in which everything is made of ice (temperature: −5°C). Most people won't chill here for long – the record is held by a Russian (four hours).

Vicious Club Club

(📞06 7061 4349; www.viciousclub.com; Via Achille Grandi 3a; admission varies; ⊙10pm-4.30am Tue & Thu-Sat, to 4am Sun; 🚇Roma Laziali) Vicious is a gay-friendly club that welcomes all to dance and chatter to a soundtrack of electro, no wave, deep techno, glam indie, and deep house. It's small enough to feel intimate; try Alchemy every Saturday.

Vini e Olii Bar

(Via del Pigneto 18; 🚇Circonvallazione Casilina) Forget the other bars that line Pigneto's main pedestrianised drag, with their scattered outside tables and styled interiors. This is where the locals head, turning their noses up at newer interlopers. This traditional 'wine and oil' shop sells cheap beer and wine (bottles from €7.50), and you can snack on platefuls of antipasti and *porchetta* (pork roasted in herbs). It's outside seating only.

Bar Zest at the Radisson Blu Es Bar

(Via Filippo Turati 171; ⊙9am-1am; 🚇Via Cavour) In need of a cocktail in the Termini district? Pop up to the 7th-floor bar at the slinkily designed Radisson Blu Es. Waiters are cute, chairs are by Jasper Morrison, views

Regional Lazio Wines

Wines produced in the surrounding region of Lazio may not be household names yet, but it's well worth trying a few local drops while you're in Rome. Although whites dominate Lazio's production – 95% of the region's Denominazione di origine controllata (DOC; the second of Italy's four quality classifications) wines are white – there are a few notable reds as well. To sample Lazio wines, Palatium (p130) and Terre e Domus (p124) are good places to go.

Most of the house white in Rome will be from the Castelli Romani area to the southeast of Rome, centred on Frascati and Marino. New production techniques have led to a lighter, drier wine that is beginning to be taken seriously. Frascati Superiore is now an excellent tipple, Castel de Paolis' Vigna Adriana wins plaudits, while the emphatically named Est! Est!! Est!!!, produced by the renowned wine house Falesco, based in Montefiascone on the volcanic banks of Lago Bolsena, is increasingly drinkable.

Falesco also produces the excellent Montiano, blended from Merlot grapes. Colacicchi's Torre Ercolana from Anagni is another opulent red, which blends local Cesanese di Affile with cabernet sauvignon and merlot. Velvety, complex and fruity, this is a world-class wine.

are through plate glass and there's a sexy rooftop pool to look at.

🍷 Trastevere & Gianicolo

Ma Che Siete Venuti a Fà Pub

(www.football-pub.com; Via Benedetta 25; ⊙11am-2am; 🚇Piazza Trilussa) Named after a football chant, which translates politely as 'What did you come here for?', this pint-sized Trastevere pub is a beer-buff's paradise, packing in at least 13 international

Rome in a Glass

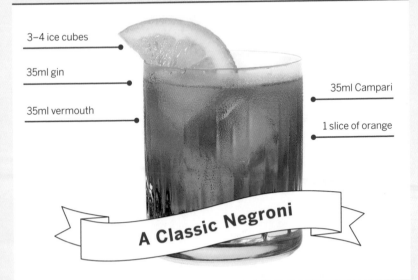

3–4 ice cubes

35ml gin

35ml vermouth

35ml Campari

1 slice of orange

A Classic Negroni

Make a Negroni

o Tip the ice cubes into a short whisky glass and pour on the gin, vermouth and Campari.

o Stir quickly with a cocktail spoon before topping with the orange slice. *Salute!*

Story Behind the Cocktail

Equal parts gin, vermouth and Campari, the ruby-red negroni is one of Rome's great cocktails. According to drinking lore, it was created in Florence in 1919, after Count Camillo Negroni asked a bartender to fortify his Americano by adding gin in place of soda water. Modern variations include the fizzier, lighter *negroni sbagliato*, made with *prosecco* (a type of sparkling wine) instead of gin.

★ Top 3 Bars for Negronis

Barnum Cafe (p170)

Stravinskij Bar – Hotel De Russie (p172)

Jerry Thomas Project (p172)

Friends at a bar
LEONARDO PATRIZI/GETTY IMAGES ©

craft beers on tap and even more by the bottle.

Bar San Calisto — Cafe

(📞06 589 56 78; Piazza San Calisto 3-5; ⏱6am-1.45am Mon-Sat; 🚊Viale di Trastevere, 🚊Viale di Trastevere) Those in the know head to the down-at-heel 'Sanca' for its basic, stuck-in-time atmosphere and cheap prices (beer €1.50). It attracts everyone from intellectuals to keeping-it-real Romans, alcoholics and American students. It's famous for its chocolate – hot with cream in winter, ice cream in summer. Try the *sambuca con la mosca* ('with flies' – raw coffee beans). Expect occasional late-night jam sessions.

Da Biagio — Wine Bar

(www.dabiagio.it; Via della Scala 64; ⏱10am-1.30pm & 5pm-midnight; 🚊Piazza Sonnino) With the sign 'Vini & Olio' scrawled above the door, this is a hole-in-the-wall Trastevere institution, lined by bottles of grappa and wine-for-sale, but also offering wine and spirits by the glass, shots and beer on tap. The owner is a funny guy, and has been serving up tipples since 1972. In the evening, drinkers spill out on the cobbled Trastevere street.

Freni e Frizioni — Bar

(Map p250; 📞06 4549 7499; www.freniefrizioni.com; Via del Politeama 4-6; ⏱6.30pm-2am; 🚊Piazza Trilussa) This perennially cool Trastevere bar is housed in a former mechanic's workshop – hence its name (Brakes and Clutches). It draws a young *spritz*-loving crowd that swells onto the small piazza outside to sip well-priced cocktails (from €7) and to snack on the daily *aperitivo* (€6 to €10, 7pm to 10pm).

Ombre Rosse — Bar

(📞06 588 41 55; Piazza Sant'Egidio 12; ⏱8am-2am Mon-Sat, 11am-2am Sun; 🚊Piazza Trilussa) A seminal Trastevere hang-out; grab a table on the terrace and watch the world go by amid a clientele ranging from elderly Italian wide boys to wide-eyed tourists. Tunes are slinky and there's live music (jazz, blues, world) on Thursday evenings from September to April.

🍷🍸 Cocktails & Digestives

Cocktail bars are the current buzz in Rome, some featuring special local creations such as the Carbonara Sour at Co.So (p174), which has vodka infused with pork fat in a homage to the classic Roman pasta sauce.

Popular aperitifs are based on bitter alcoholic liqueurs, such Campari soda or Aperol *spritz*, which mixes Aperol with *prosecco*. Crodino is a herbal, medicinal-tasting nonalcoholic aperitif. Italians love to finish off a meal with a digestif. The best of these aren't shop bought, so if it's '*fatta in casa*' (homemade), give it a try.

Crodino
ALAN BENSON/GETTY IMAGES ©

Big Star — Bar

(Via Goffredo Mameli 25; ⏱6pm-2am; 🚊Viale de Trastevere, 🚊Viale de Trastevere) Off the beaten Trastevere track, this is a cool backstreet bar set away from the main action, with an alternative feel and the drink prices scrawled up on a blackboard. It's a small yet airy interior, where you can drink a wide range of beers and cocktails while listening to the hipster DJs, with a laid-back, appealing vibe.

Bar Stuzzichini — Bar

(Piazzale Giuseppe Garibaldi; ⏱7.30am-1am or 2am; 🚊Passeggiata del Gianicolo) This little kiosk nestles on the top of Gianicolo, and serves up coffees and drinks, including cocktails. There are a few tables to perch at and the views are unmatchable. On New Year's Eve it opens all night.

Coffee

Drinking an espresso standing at a bar shoulder to shoulder with the locals is a quintessential Roman experience. But to enjoy it you'll need to know what to order.

For an espresso (a shot of strong black coffee), ask for *un caffè;* if you want it with a drop of hot or cold milk, order *un caffè macchiato* ('stained' coffee). Long black coffee (as in a watered-down version) is known as *caffè lungo* (an espresso with more water) or *caffè all'american* (a filter coffee).

Then, of course, there's the cappuccino (served warm rather than hot), a staple of many Roman breakfasts. Italians drink cappuccino only during the morning and never after meals.

In summer, *cappuccino freddo* (iced coffee with milk, usually already sugared), *caffè freddo* (iced espresso) and *granita di caffè* (frozen coffee, usually with cream) top the charts.

A *caffè latte* is a milkier version of the cappuccino with less froth; a *latte macchiato* is even milkier (warmed milk 'stained' with a spot of coffee).

La Mescita   Wine Bar

(Map p250; ☑06 5833 3920; Piazza Trilussa 41; ☺5pm-midnight Sun-Thu, to 1am Fri & Sat; ⬚Piazza Trilussa) This tiny bar inside the entrance to upmarket restaurant Enoteca Ferrara serves delectable *aperitivo* and has a wide range of wines by the glass, from €7. Fancy an intimate tête-à-tête, with fine wines and yummy snacks? This is your place.

Il Baretto   Bar

(☑06 5836 5422; Via Garibaldi 27; ☺6am-2am Mon-Sat, 5pm-2am Sun; ⬚Piazza Sonnino, ⬚Piazza Sonnino) Venture a little way up the Gianicolo, up a steep flight of steps from Trastevere. Go on, it's worth it: you'll dis-cover this well-kept-secret cocktail bar. The basslines are meaty, the bar staff hip, and the interior mixes vintage with pop art.

Bar le Cinque   Bar

(Vicolo del Cinque 5; ☺6.30am-2am Mon-Sat; ⬚Piazza Sonnino) There's no sign outside, and it looks like a rundown ordinary bar, but this is a long-standing Trastevere favourite and always has a small crowd clustered around outside; they're here for the pivotal location, easygoing vibe and cheap drinks.

San Giovanni & Testaccio

Rec 23   Bar

(☑06 8746 2147; www.rec23.com; Piazza dell'Emporio 2; ☺6.30pm-2am daily & 12.30-3.30pm Sat & Sun; ⬚Via Marmorata) All plate glass and exposed brick, this popular, NY-inspired venue caters to all moods, serving aperitifs, restaurant meals and a weekend brunch. Arrive thirsty to take on the Testaccio Mule, one of a long list of cocktails, or get to grips with the selection of Scottish whiskies and Latin American rums. It also hosts regular live gigs.

Big Bang   Club

(www.bigbangroma.org; Via di Monte Testaccio 22; ☺10pm-4.30am Fri & Sat; ⬚Via Galvani) For one of the capital's best reggae parties, head to the Bababoomtime Friday-night session at Big Bang. The club, housed in Rome's graffiti-sprayed former slaughter-house, draws a casual, music-loving crowd who know their reggae, dancehall, dub and techno.

L'Oasi della Birra   Bar

(☑06 574 61 22; Piazza Testaccio 41; ☺4.30pm-2am; ⬚Via Marmorata) In a local bottle shop, this cramped cellar bar is exactly what it says it is – an Oasis of Beer. With up to 500 labels, from Teutonic heavyweights to boutique brews, as well as wines, cheeses, cold cuts and the like, it's ideally set up for elbow-to-elbow quaffing.

Coming Out   Bar
(www.comingout.it; Via di San Giovanni in Laterano 8; ⊙7am-2am; ⊡Via Labicana) On warm
evenings, with lively crowds on the street
and the Colosseum as a backdrop, there
are few finer places to sip than this friendly,
gay bar. It's open all day but at its best in
the evening when the the the atmosphere hots
up and the gigs, drag shows and karaoke
nights get under way.

Il Pentagrappolo   Wine Bar
(Via Celimontana 21b; ⊙noon-3pm & 6pm-1am
Tue-Fri, 6pm-1am Sat & Sun; Ⓜ Colosseo) This
vaulted, softly lit bar is the perfect antidote
to sightseeing overload. Join the mellow
crowd for an evening of wine and jazz courtesy of the frequent live gigs. There's also
lunch and a daily *aperitif*.

L'Alibi   Club
(Via di Monte Testaccio 44; ⊙11.30pm-5am
Thu-Sun; ⊡Via Galvani) A historic gay club,
L'Alibi does high camp with style, putting
on kitsch shows and playing house, techno
and dance to a mixed gay and straight
crowd. It's spread over three floors and if

the sweaty atmosphere on the dance floors
gets too much, head up to the spacious
summer terrace. Saturday's Tommy Night
is the hot date right now.

My Bar   Bar
(Via di San Giovanni in Laterano 12; ⊙9am-2am;
⊡Via Labicana) On the nearest thing that
Rome has to a gay street, this cafe near the
Colosseum serves mainly tourists during
the day and a gay clientele in the evenings.
DJs and live music fuel the fun.

🍷 Villa Borghese & Northern Rome

Momart   Bar
(www.momartcafe.it; Viale XXI Aprile 19;
⊙noon-2am Mon-Fri, 6pm-2am Sat & Sun; ⊡Via
XXI Aprile) A spacious modern bar in the
university district near Via Nomentana, Momart serves one of Rome's most popular

drinking an espresso standing
at a bar is a quintessential
Roman experience

Barista preparing coffee

KATHRIN ZIEGLER/GETTY IMAGES

aperitifs. A mixed crowd of students and local professionals flocks here to fill up on the pizza-led buffet and kick back over cocktails on the pavement terrace.

Brancaleone   Club

(www.brancaleone.eu; Via Levanna 11; ⊘hours vary, typically 10.30pm-late; ☐Via Nomentana) From its anti-establishment roots as a *centro sociale* (social centre), Brancaleone has grown to become one of Rome's top clubs, drawing blockbuster DJs and a young clubbing crowd. Rap, hip-hop, drum and bass, and electronica feature heavily, and there's a regular calendar of events and one-off evenings. The club is in the outlying Montesacro district.

Lanificio 159   Club

(www.lanificio159.com; Via Pietralata 159a; ⊘hours vary, typically 11pm-4am; ☐Via Val Brembana) Occupying an ex–wool factory in Rome's northeastern suburbs, this cool underground venue hosts live gigs and hot clubbing action, led by top Roman crews

and international DJs. The club is part of a larger complex which stages more reserved events such as Sunday markets, exhibitions and aperitifs.

Chioschetto di Ponte Milvio   Bar

(Ponte Milvio 44; ⊘6pm-2am summer only; ☐Ponte Milvio) A local landmark, this green kiosk next to the Ponte Milvio bridge is perennially popular with the young crowd from Rome's wealthy northern suburbs. It might look like a shack – it is a shack – but the mojitos are the business and it does an excellent thirst-quenching *grattachecca* (shaved ice flavoured with fruit syrup).

Piper Club   Club

(www.piperclub.it; Via Tagliamento 9; ⊘11pm-5am Fri & Sat; ☐Viale Regina Margherita) To Rome what Studio 54 was to New York, Piper has been a nightlife fixture for 50 years, and it just keeps on going. Fridays it hosts themed parties, everything from Latin nights to '90s house celebrations, while on Saturdays resident DJs drive the rhythms.

🍷 Southern Rome

Porto Fluviale   Bar

(📞06 574 31 99; www.portofluviale.com; Via del Porto Fluviale 22; ⏰10.30am-2am; ⓂPiramide) A large bar in a converted factory, this has an ex-industrial look – dark-green walls and a brickwork floor – and is a relaxing, appealing place for morning coffee, *aperitivo* or an evening drink to a soundtrack of plinky jazz. In line with Rome's current love of artisanal brews, it serves its own Porto Fluviale craft beer (medium €5.50).

Goa   Club

(📞06 574 82 77; www.goaclub.com; Via Libetta 13; ⏰11.30pm-4.30am Thu-Sat; ⓂGarbatella) Goa is Rome's serious superclub, with international names, ethnic styling, a fashion-forward crowd, podium dancers and heavies on the door.

Neo Club   Club

(Via degli Argonauti 18; ⏰11pm-4am Fri & Sat; ⓂGarbatella) This small, dark two-level club has an underground feel and is one of the funkiest choices in the zone, featuring a dancetastic mishmash of breakbeat, techno and old-skool house.

La Saponeria   Club

(📞06 574 69 99; Via degli Argonauti 20; ⏰11pm-4.30am Tue-Sun Oct-May; ⓂGarbatella) Formerly a soap factory, nowadays La Saponeria is a cool space that's all exposed brick and white walls and brain-twisting light shows. It lathers up the punters with guest DJs spinning everything from nu-house to nu-funk, minimal techno, dance, hip-hop and 1950s retro.

🍺🍸 Craft Beer

In recent years beer drinking has really taken off in Italy, and especially in Rome, with specialised bars and restaurants offering microbrewed beers. Local favourites include Birradamare in Fiumicino, Porto Fluviale in Ostiense, and Birra Del Borgo in Rieti (on the border between Lazio and Abruzzo), which opened local beer haunts **Bir & Fud** (Via Benedetta 23; meals €25; ⏰7.30pm-midnight, to 2am Fri & Sat; ❄; 🚇Piazza Trilussa) and Open Baladin (p171). Local beers reflect the seasonality that's so important in Rome – for example, look for winter beers made from chestnuts.

Other important addresses on the artisanal beer trail include Porto Fluviale, Ma Che Siete Venuti a Fà (p179) and Birra Piu (p174).

ONEMOREIMAGE/GETTY IMAGES ©

Rashomon   Club

(www.rashomonclub.com; Via degli Argonauti 16; ⏰11pm-4am Fri & Sat Oct-May; ⓂGarbatella) Rashomon is sweaty, not posey, and where to head when you want to dance your ass off. Shake it to a music-lovers' feast of the sound of the underground, especially house, techno and electronica.

SHOWTIME

Opera, jazz, theatre and more

Showtime

Watching the world go by in Rome is often entertainment enough, but there's plenty more to having a good time in Rome than people-watching. The city's music scene is a hive of activity with gigs and concerts of all musical genres drawing knowledgeable and enthusiastic audiences. Theatres put on everything from Shakespearian drama to avant-garde dance, while cinemas screen art-house flicks and arts festivals turn the city into a stage, particularly in summer when al fresco performances play out against backdrops of spectacular Roman ruins.

So whether you're an opera buff or a rapper, a cinephile or a theatregoer, you're sure to find something to suit your taste.

In This Section

Tickets

Tickets for concerts, live music and theatrical performances are widely available across the city. Hotels can often reserve tickets for guests, or you can contact the venue or organisation directly. Otherwise you can try the following:

Hellò Ticket (www.helloticket.it)

Orbis (Map p255; Piazza dell'Esquilino 37)

Opera performers in Giuseppe Verdi's *Nabucco*, Terme di Caracalla (p98)

The Best...

Classical Venues

Auditorium Parco della Musica (p192) Top international musicians and multiple concert halls.

Teatro dell'Opera di Roma (p189) Red-velvet and gilt interior for Rome's opera and dance companies.

Terme di Caracalla (p98) Wonderful outdoor setting for Rome's opera and ballet companies.

Auditorium Conciliazione (p189) Classical and contemporary concerts, cabarets, dance, theatre, film and exhibitions.

Teatro Olimpico (p192) Home to the Accademia Filarmonica Romana.

Jazz

Alexanderplatz (p189) Rome's premier jazz club stages international and local musicians.

Charity Café (p190) An intimate space, hosting regular live gigs.

Big Mama (p190) An atmospheric Trastevere venue for jazz, blues, funk, soul and R & B.

Gregory's (p188) Popular with local musicians, a smooth venue close to the Spanish Steps.

Fonclea (p189) Pub venue regularly hosting live jazz, moving riverside in the summer.

☆ Centro Storico

Teatro Argentina Theatre
(Map p250; ☎06 684 00 03 11; www.teatrodi
roma.net; Largo di Torre Argentina 52; tickets
€16-29; 🚇Largo di Torre Argentina) Founded in
1732, Rome's top theatre is one of the two
official homes of the Teatro di Roma (the
other is the Teatro India in the southern
suburbs). Rossini's *Barber of Seville*
premiered here in 1816; today it stages a
wide-ranging program of drama (mostly in
Italian), high-profile dance performances
and classical-music concerts.

Isola del Cinema Cinema
(www.isoladelcinema.com) Independent films
in the romantic outdoor setting of the Isola
Tiberina in July and August. This runs in
conjunction with the riverside Lungo il
Tevere festival.

Teatro dell'Orologio Theatre
(☎06 687 55 50; www.teatroorologio.com; Via
dei Filippini 17a; 🚇Corso Vittorio Emanuele II) A
well-known experimental theatre, the three-
stage Orologio offers a varied program of

contemporary and classic works, including
occasional performances in English.

☆ Tridente, Trevi & the Quirinale

Gregory's Live Music
(Map p255; ☎06 679 63 86; www.gregorysjazz.
com; Via Gregoriana 54d; ⊗7pm-2am Tue-Sun
Sep-Jun; 🚇Barberini, Spagna) If Gregory's
were a tone of voice, it'd be husky: unwind
in the downstairs bar, then unwind some
more on squashy sofas upstairs to some
slinky live jazz and swing, with quality local
performers, who also like to hang out here.

Teatro Quirino Theatre
(Map p255; ☎06 679 45 85; www.teatroquirino.
it; Via delle Vergini 7; 🚇Via del Tritone) Within
splashing distance of the Trevi Fountain,
this grand 19th-century theatre produces
the odd new work and a stream of well-
known classics – expect to see works
(in Italian) by Arthur Miller, Tennessee

Teatro Argentina

ALLE ARTI DI MELPOMENE
D EUTERPE E DI TERSICORE

Williams, Shakespeare, Seneca and Luigi Pirandello.

Teatro Sistina Theatre
(Map p255; ☎06 420 07 11; www.ilsistina.com; Via Sistina 129; Ⓜ Barberini) Big-budget theatre spectaculars, musicals, concerts and comic star turns are the staples of the Sistina's ever-conservative, ever-popular repertoire.

☆ Vatican City, Borgo & Prati

Alexanderplatz Jazz
(☎06 3972 1867; www.alexanderplatzjazzclub.com; Via Ostia 9; ⊙8.30pm-2am, concerts 9.45pm; Ⓜ Ottaviano-San Pietro) Small, intimate and underground, Rome's most celebrated jazz club draws top Italian and international performers and a respectful cosmopolitan crowd. Book a table for the best stage views or if you want to dine to the tunes. Check the website for upcoming gigs.

Auditorium Conciliazione Live Performance
(☎06 3281 0333; www.auditoriumconciliazione.it; Via della Conciliazione 4; 🚌Piazza Pia) On the main approach road to St Peter's Basilica, this large auditorium plays host to a wide range of events – classical and contemporary concerts, cabarets, dance spectacles, theatre productions, film screenings and exhibitions.

Fonclea Live Music
(☎06 689 63 02; www.fonclea.it; Via Crescenzio 82a; ⊙7pm-2am Sep-May; 🚌Piazza del Risorgimento) Fonclea is a great little pub venue, serving up nightly gigs by bands playing everything from jazz and soul to funk, rock and Latin (concerts start at around 9.30pm). Get in the mood with a drink during happy hour (7pm to 8.30pm daily). From June to August, the pub ups sticks and moves to a site by the Tiber.

Jazz, Rock & Rap

Jazz, introduced by US troops during WWII, grew in popularity during the postwar period and took off in the 1960s. Since then, it has gone from strength to strength and the city now boasts some fabulous jazz clubs, including Alexanderplatz, Big Mama (p190) and the Casa del Jazz (p192).

Major music concerts are staged at the Auditorium Parco della Musica as well as arenas and stadiums, such as the Stadio Olimpico (p198) and the racetrack on Via Appia Nuova, the Ippodromo La Capannelle.

The *centri sociali*, alternative arts centres set up in venues across Rome, are also good places to catch a gig, especially Brancaleone (p182) in northern Rome, with music policies encompassing hip-hop, electro, dubstep, reggae and dancehall.

Alexanderplatz

☆ Monti, Esquilino & San Lorenzo

Teatro dell'Opera di Roma Opera
(Map p255; ☎06 481 70 03; www.operaroma.it; Piazza Beniamino Gigli; ballet €12-80, opera €17-150; ⊙9am-5pm Tue-Sat, to 1.30pm Sun; Ⓜ Repubblica) Rome's premier opera house boasts a plush and gilt interior, a Fascist 1920s exterior and an impressive history: it premiered Puccini's *Tosca*, and Maria Callas once sang here. Opera and ballet

Opera & Classical Music

Rome's abundance of beautiful settings makes it a superb place to catch a concert. Many international stars play at the Auditorium Parco della Musica (p192), a state-of-the-art, Renzo Piano–designed complex. However, there are often creative uses of other spaces, and in recent years there have been major gigs on the ancient racetrack **Circo Massimo** (Circus Maximus; Map p252; Via del Circo Massimo; MCirco Massimo).

Music in Rome is not just about the Auditorium Parco della Musica (p192). There are concerts by the Accademia Filarmonica Romana at the Teatro Olimpico (p192); the Auditorium Conciliazione (p189), Rome's premier classical-music venue before the newer Auditorium was opened; and the Istituzione Universitaria dei Concerti, holds concerts in the Aula Magna of La Sapienza University.

Classical-music performances – often free – are regularly held in churches, especially around Easter, Christmas and the New Year.

Rome's opera house, the Teatro dell'Opera di Roma (p189), is a magnificent, grandiose venue, but productions can be a bit hit-and-miss. It's also home to Rome's official Corps de Ballet and has a ballet season running in tandem with its opera performances. Both ballet and opera move outdoors for the summer season to the ancient Terme di Caracalla (p98), an even more spectacular setting.

performances are staged between September and June.

Blackmarket — Live Music

(Map p255; www.black-market.it; Via Panisperna 101; ⊗5.30pm-2am; MCavour) A bit outside the main Monti hub, this charming, living-room-style bar filled with eclectic vintage furniture is a small but rambling place, great for sitting back on mismatched armchairs for a leisurely, convivial drink. It hosts regular acoustic indie and folk gigs, which feel a bit like having a band in your living room.

Charity Café — Live Music

(Map p255; ☏328 8452915; www.charitycafe.it; Via Panisperna 68; ⊗7pm-2am; MCavour) Think narrow space, spindly tables, dim lighting and a laid-back vibe: this is a place to snuggle down and listen to some slinky live jazz. Civilised, relaxed, untouristy and very Monti. Gigs usually take place from 10pm, with live music and *aperitivo* on Sundays. There's open mic from 7pm on Monday and Tuesday.

Istituzione Universitaria dei Concerti — Live Music

(IUC; ☏06 361 00 51; www.concertiiuc.it; Piazzale Aldo Moro 5; MCastro Pretorio) The IUC organises a season of concerts in the Aula Magna of La Sapienza University, including many visiting international artists and orchestras. Performances cover a wide range of musical genres, including baroque, classical, contemporary and jazz.

Teatro Ambra Jovinelli — Theatre

(☏06 8308 2884; www.ambrajovinelli.org; Via G Pepe 43-47; MVittorio Emanuele) A home from home for many famous Italian comics, the Ambra Jovinelli is a historic venue for alternative comedians and satirists. Between government-bashing, the theatre hosts productions of classics, musicals, opera, new works and the odd concert.

☆ Trastevere & Gianicolo

Big Mama — Blues

(☏06 581 25 51; www.bigmama.it; Vicolo di San Francesco a Ripa 18; ⊗9pm-1.30am, shows 10.30pm, closed Jun-Sep; ▣Viale di Trastevere, ▣Viale di Trastevere) Head to this cramped Trastevere basement for a mellow night of Eternal City blues. A long-standing venue,

JASON KNOTT/ALAMY STOCK PHOTO ©

Teatro dell'Opera di Roma (p189)

it also stages jazz, funk, soul and R & B, as well as popular Italian cover bands.

Lettere Caffè Gallery   Live Music

(☏06 9727 0991; www.letterecaffe.org; Vicolo di San Francesco a Ripa 100/101; ☺7pm-2am, closed mid-Aug–mid-Sep; ☒Viale di Trastevere, ☒Viale di Trastevere) Like books? Poetry? Blues and jazz? Then you'll love this place – a clutter of bar stools and books, where there are regular live gigs, poetry slams, comedy and gay nights, plus DJ sets playing indie and new wave.

Alcazar Cinema   Cinema

(☏06 588 00 99; Via Merry del Val 14; ☒Viale di Trastevere, ☒Viale di Trastevere) This old-style cinema with plush red seats occasionally shows films in their original language with Italian subtitles.

Nuovo Sacher   Cinema

(☏06 581 81 16; www.sacherfilm.eu; Largo Ascianghi 1; ☒Viale di Trastevere, ☒Viale di Trastevere) Owned by cult Roman film director Nanni Moretti, this small, red-velvet-seated cinema is the place to catch the latest European art-house offering, with regular screenings of films in their original language.

Teatro Vascello   Theatre

(☏06 588 10 21; www.teatrovascello.it; Via Giacinto Carini 72, Monteverde; ☒Via Giacinto Carini) Left-field in vibe and location, this independent, fringe theatre stages interesting, cutting-edge new work, including avant-garde dance, multimedia events and works by emerging playwrights.

☆ San Giovanni & Testaccio

ConteStaccio   Live Music

(www.contestaccio.com; Via di Monte Testaccio 65b; ☺7pm-4am Tue-Sun; ☒Via Galvani) With an under-the-stars terrace and cool, arched interior, ConteStaccio is one of the top venues on the Testaccio clubbing strip. It's something of a multipurpose outfit, with a cocktail bar, a pizzeria and a restaurant but, is best known for its daily concerts. Gigs by emerging groups set the tone, spanning indie, rock, acoustic, funk and electronic.

☆ Villa Borghese & Northern Rome

Auditorium Parco della Musica   Concert Venue
(📞06 8024 1281; www.auditorium.com; Viale Pietro de Coubertin 30; 🚌Viale Tiziano) The hub of Rome's thriving cultural scene, the Renzo Piano-designed Auditorium is the capital's premier concert venue and one of Europe's most popular arts centres. Its three concert halls offer superb acoustics, and, together with a 3000-seat open-air arena, stage everything from classical-music concerts to jazz gigs, public lectures, and film screenings.

The Auditorium is also home to Rome's world-class Orchestra dell' Accademia Nazionale di Santa Cecilia (www.santace cilia.it).

Teatro Olimpico   Theatre
(📞06 326 59 91; www.teatroolimpico.it; Piazza Gentile da Fabriano 17; 🚌Piazza Mancini, 🚌Piazza Mancini) The Teatro Olimpico is home to the Accademia Filarmonica Romana (www.filarmonicaromana.org), a classical-music organisation whose past members have included Rossini, Donizetti and Verdi. The theatre offers a varied program of classical and chamber music, opera, ballet, one-man shows and comedies.

Silvano Toti Globe Theatre   Theatre
(Map p256; 📞06 06 08; www.globetheatrero ma.com; Largo Aqua Felix, Villa Borghese; tickets €10-23; 🚌Piazzale Brasile) Like London's Globe Theatre but with better weather, Villa Borghese's open-air Elizabethan theatre serves up Shakespeare (performances mostly in Italian) from July through to September.

☆ Southern Rome

La Casa del Jazz   Jazz
(📞06 70 47 31; www.casajazz.it; Viale di Porta Ardeatina 55; admission varies; ⊙gigs around 8-9pm; Ⓜ Piramide) In the middle of a 2500-sq-metre park in the southern suburbs, the Casa del Jazz is housed in a three-storey 1920s villa that once belonged

Auditorium Parco della Musica

to a Mafia boss. When he was caught, the Comune di Roma (Rome Council) converted it into a jazz-fuelled complex, with a 150-seat auditorium, rehearsal rooms, a cafe and a restaurant. Some events are free.

Caffè Letterario
Live Music

(☑06 5730 2842, 340 3067460; www. caffeletterarioroma.it; Via Ostiense 83, 95; ☺10am-2am Tue-Fri, 4pm-2am Sat & Sun; ☐Via Ostiense) Caffè Letterario is an intellectual hang-out housed in the funky converted, post-industrial space of a former garage. It combines designer looks, a bookshop, a gallery, performance space and a lounge bar. There are regular gigs from 10pm to midnight, ranging from soul and jazz to Indian dance.

XS Live
Live Music

(☑06 5730 5102; www.xsliveroma.com; Via Libetta 13; ☺11.30pm-4am Thu-Sun Sep-May; Ⓜ️Garbatella) A rocking live-music and club venue, hosting regular gigs. Big names playing here in recent times range from Peter Doherty to Jefferson Starship, and club nights range from Cool Britanni-themed trips to '80s odysseys.

Teatro India
Theatre

(☑06 8400 0311; www.teatrodiroma.net; Lungotevere dei Papareschi; tickets €10-30; ☐Via Enrico Fermi) Inaugurated in 1999 in the postindustrial landscape of Rome's southern suburbs, the India is the younger sister of Teatro Argentina. It's a stark modern

Theatre

Rome has a thriving local theatre scene, with theatres including both traditional places and smaller experimental venues. Performances are usually in Italian.

Particularly wonderful are the summer festivals that make use of Rome's archaeological scenery. Performances take place in settings such as Ostia Antica's Roman theatre and the Teatro di Marcello. In summer the **Miracle Players** (☑06 7039 3427; www.miracleplay ers.org) perform classic English drama or historical comedy in English next to the Roman Forum and other open-air locations. Performances are usually free.

Teatro di Marcello
KEN WELSH/GETTY IMAGES ©

space in a converted industrial building, a fitting setting for its cutting-edge program, with a calendar of international and Italian works.

ACTIVE ROME

From football to cooking courses

Active Rome

The Romans have long been passionate about sport. Ever since crowds flocked to the Colosseum to support their favourite gladiators and to the Circo Massimo to cheer on chariot riders, the locals have enjoyed a good performance. Rome's modern-day Colosseum is the Stadio Olimpico, where footballing rivalries are played out in front of thousands of fans and major-league rock stars strut their stuff.

If you prefer your pursuits more hands-on, there is a whole range of courses you can take, ranging from cooking in historic palazzi (mansions) to wine tasting and language learning. Tours are also a popular activity and a good way of covering a lot of ground in a short time.

In This Section

Sports Seasons

Football is the big sport in Rome with the season running from September to May. Rugby can be seen on weekends in February and March, while tennis fans can enjoy world-class games at the Italian Open Tennis Tournament in May.

SOLOROMA/ALAMY STOCK PHOTO ©

Foro Italico (p198)

The Best...

Sports Venues

Foro Italico (p198) Magnificent Fascist-era sports complex.

Stadio Olimpico (p198) Rome's 70,000-seat football stadium, part of the fascist-era Foro Italico.

Piazza di Siena (p58) Lovely racecourse in the heart of the Villa Borghese park.

Courses

Roman Kitchen (p200) Learn about the intricacies of Italian cuisine with a hands-on cooking course.

Vino Roma (p200) Sniff, sip and spit your way through Italian vintages on a wine course.

Art Studio Café (p201) Put your creativity to the test, learning the ancient art of mosaic-making.

Torre di Babele Centro di Lingua e Cultura Italiana (p201) Learn to speak the language in like-minded company.

⚡ Spectator Sports

Stadio Olimpico   Stadium
(📞 06 3685 7520; Viale dei Gladiatori 2, Foro Italico) A trip to Rome's impressive Stadio Olimpico offers an unforgettable insight into Rome's sporting heart. Throughout the football season (September to May) there's a game on most Sundays. Tickets cost from around €16, depending on the match, and can be bought at Lottomatica (lottery centres), the stadium, ticket agencies, www.listicket.it, or one of the many Roma or Lazio stores around the city. Note that ticket purchase regulations are far stricter than they used to be. Tickets have to bear the holder's name and passport or ID number, and you must present a photo ID at the turnstiles when entering the stadium.

Foro Italico   Stadium
(📞 800 622662; www.foroitalicoticketing.it; Viale del Foro Italico) The Fascist-era Foro Italico was built between 1928 and 1938 and originally named the Foro Mussolini. Foro Italico hosts the Italian Open, one of the most important events on the European tennis circuit, attracting the world's top players to the clay courts. Tickets can usually be bought at the Foro Italico each day of the tournament, except for the final days, which are sold out weeks in advance.

Stadio Flaminio   Stadium
(📞 06 3685 7309; www.federugby.it; Viale Maresciallo Pilsudski) Large concerts take place at Stadio Flaminio, a sports stadium.

⚡ Tours

Taking a tour is a good way to see a lot in a short time or investigating a sight in depth. There are several outfits running hop-on hop-off bus tours, typically costing about €20 per person. Both the Colosseum and Vatican Museums offer official guided tours, but for a more personalised service you'll be better off with a private guide.

A Friend in Rome   Tour
(📞 340 501 92 01; www.afriendinrome.it) Silvia Prosperi organises private tailor-made tours (on foot, by bike or scooter) to suit

Cyclists on Piazza della Chiesa Nuova, Centro Storico

MAREMAGNUM/GETTY IMAGES ©

your interests. She covers the Vatican and main historic centre as well as areas outside the capital. Rates are €50 per hour, with a minimum of three hours for most tours. She can also arrange kid-friendly tours, cooking classes, vintage-car tours and more.

Roman Guy   Tour
(http://theromanguy.com) A professional set-up that organises a wide range of group and private tours. Packages, led by English-speaking experts, include early-bird visits to the Vatican Museums (US$84), foodie tours of Trastevere and the Jewish Ghetto (US$84), and a bar-hop through the historic centre's cocktail bars.

Dark Rome   Tour
(📞06 8336 0561; www.darkrome.com) Runs a range of themed tours, costing from €25 to €150, including skip-the-line visits to the Colosseum and Vatican Museums, and semiprivate visits to the Sistine Chapel. Other popular choices include a Crypts and Catacombs tour, which takes in Rome's buried treasures, and a day trip to Pompeii.

Through Eternity
Cultural Association   Walking Tour
(📞06 700 93 36; www.througheternity.com) A reliable operator offering private and group tours led by English-speaking experts. Popular packages include a twilight tour of Rome's piazzas and fountains (€39, 2½ hours), a skip-the-line visit to the Vatican Museums by day/night (€56/66, 3½ hours) and a foodie tour of Testaccio (€80, four hours).

Arcult   Walking Tour
(📞339 650 31 72; www.arcult.it) Run by architects, Arcult offers excellent customisable group tours focusing on Rome's contemporary architecture. Prices depend on the itinerary.

Roma Cristiana   Walking Tour
(📞06 69 89 61; www.operaromanapellegrinaggi.org) Runs various tours, including guided visits to the Vatican Museums (adult/

🏀 Football

Throughout the football season there's a game most Sundays at the Stadio Olimpico involving one of the city's two Serie A (Italy's premier league) teams: **Roma**, known as the *giallorossi* (yellow and reds; www.asroma.it), or **Lazio**, the *biancazzuri* (white and blues; www.sslazio.it).

The Rome derby is one of the football season's highest-profile games. The rivalry between Roma and Lazio is fierce and little love is lost between the fans. If you go to the stadium, make sure you get it right – Roma fans flock to the Curva Sud (Southern Stand), while Lazio supporters stand in the Curva Nord (Northern Stand). If you want to sit on the fence, head to the Tribuna Tevere or Tribuna Monte Mario.

To get to the Olimpico, take metro line A to Ottaviano–San Pietro and then bus 32.

A new Roma stadium is currently being built at Tor di Valle, due to be completed in time for the 2017/18 season.

A S Roma fans
MARCO IACOBUCCI EPP/SHUTTERSTOCK ©

reduced €35/25) and two-hour tours of St Peter's Basilica (€14).

Top Bike Rental
& Tours   Bicycle Tour
(📞06 488 28 93; www.topbikerental.com; Via Labicana 49; ⊙10am-7pm) Offers a series of bike tours throughout the city, including a four-hour 16km exploration of the city

🏀 Six Nations Rugby

Italy's rugby team, the Azzurri (the Blues), entered the Six Nations tournament in 2000, and has been the competition underdog ever since. However, it has scored some big wins in recent years, with shock wins over France in 2011 and 2013, and Scotland in 2015. But in 2016 normal business was resumed and the side finished with the wooden spoon.

Despite poor results, home games, which are played at the Stadio Olimpico, draw huge crowds of Azzurri fans and high-spirited away supporters.

Six Nations rugby game, Stadio Olimpico (p198)
PACIFIC PRESS/GETTY IMAGES ©

centre (€45) and an all-day 30km ride through Via Appia Antica and environs (€79). Out-of-town tours take in Castel Gandolfo, Civita di Bagnoregio and Orvieto.

Bici & Baci   Tour
(Map p255; ☑06 482 84 43; www.bicibaci.com; Via del Viminale 5; ⏰8am-7pm) Bici & Baci runs daily bike tours of central Rome, taking in the historic centre, Campidoglio and the Colosseum, as well as tours on vintage Vespas and in classic Fiat 500 cars. Reckon on €49 for the bike tour, €145 for the Vespa ride, and €290 for the four-hour guided drive.

Rome Boat Experience   Boat Tour
(☑06 8956 7745; www.romeboatexperience.com; adult/reduced €18/12) From April to October, hop-on, hop-off boats cruise along the Tiber. From May to October, there are

also dinner cruises (€62, two hours) every Friday and Saturday, and a daily wine-bar cruise (€25, 1½ hours) from Monday to Thursday. Embarkation points are at Molo Sant'Angelo and Isola Tiberina.

Open Bus Cristiana   Bus Tour
(www.operaromanapellegrinaggi.org; single tour €15, 24/48hr ticket €20/48; ⏰9am-6pm) The Vatican-sponsored Opera Romana Pellegrinaggi runs a hop-on, hop-off bus departing from Via della Conciliazione and Termini. Stops are situated near to main sights including St Peter's Basilica, Piazza Navona, the Trevi Fountain and the Colosseum. Tickets are available on board or at the meeting point just off St Peter's Sq.

🏃 Courses

Roman Kitchen   Cooking Course
(Map p250; ☑06 678 57 59; www.italiangourmet.com; per day €200) Cookery writer Diane Seed (*The Top One Hundred Pasta Sauces*) runs cooking courses from her kitchen in Palazzo Doria Pamphilj. There are one-day, two-day, three-day and weeklong courses costing €200 per day and €1000 per week.

Vino Roma   Course
(☑328 4874497; www.vinoroma.com; Via in Selci 84/G; 2hr tastings per person €50) With beautifully appointed 1000-year-old cellars and a chic tasting studio, Vino Roma guides novices and experts in tasting wine, under the knowledgeable stewardship of sommelier Hande Leimer and his expert team. Tastings are in English, but German, Japanese, Italian and Turkish sessions are available on special request. It also offers a wine-and-cheese dinner (€60), with snacks, cheeses and cold cuts to accompany the wines, as well as bespoke three-hour food tours. Book online.

Città di Gusto   Cooking Course
(☑06 5511 2264; www.gamberorosso.it; Via Fermi 161) Demonstrations, workshops, lessons and courses are held at this foodie complex.

MARIJAPEREZ/GETTY IMAGES ©

Art Studio Café
Art Course

(☑06 3260 9104; www.artstudiocafe.it; Via dei Gracchi 187a) This cafe, exhibition space and mosaic school offers a range of classes. Learn how to cut and glaze enamel tesserae, how to mix colours and how best to mount your final composition. One-day sessions start at €50.

Torre di Babele Centro di Lingua e Cultura Italiana
Language Course

(☑06 4425 2578; www.torredibabele.com; Via Cosenza 7) As well as language lessons, you can take courses on cooking, art, architecture and several other subjects.

Divulgazione Lingua Italiana
Language Course

(☑06 446 25 93; www.dilit.it; Via Marghera 22) School offering a range of language and cultural courses.

🏃 Spas

Hotel De Russie Wellness Zone
Spa

(Map p256; ☑06 3288 8820; www.hotelderussie.it; Via del Babuino 9; ⊙6.30am-10pm; ⓜFlaminio) This glamorous and gorgeous day spa is in one of Rome's best hotels, and allows admission to the gym and steam room. Treatments are also available, including shiatsu and deep-tissue massage (a 50-minute massage costs around €95).

Kami Spa
Spa

(Map p255; ☑06 42010039; www.kamispa.com; Via Degli Avignonesi 11-12; massage €120-160; ⓜBarberini) A chic, soothing spa not far from the Trevi Fountain, this is a great place to recharge your batteries if you want to fork out for the luxurious prices.

REST YOUR HEAD

Top tips for the best accommodation

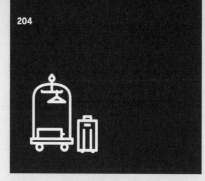

Rest Your Head

With a wide range of hotels, pensioni *(pensions) B&Bs, hostels and convents, Rome has accommodation to please everyone, from the fussiest prince to the most impecunious nun. At the top end of the market, opulent five-star hotels occupy stately historic palazzi (mansions) and chic boutique guesthouses boast discreet luxury. Family-run B&Bs and pensioni offer character and a warm welcome while religious houses cater to pilgrims and budget-minded travellers. Hostel goers can choose between party-loving hang-outs or quieter, more restrained digs.*

But while there's plenty of choice, rates are universally high in Rome and you'll need to book early to get the best deal.

In This Section

Tipping

Tipping is not necessary, but up to €5 for porter, housekeeping or room service in a top-end hotel is fine.

Luxurious hotel room, Trevi

Reservations

○ Always try to book ahead, especially for the major religious festivals.

○ Ask for a *camera matrimoniale* for a room with a double bed or a *camera doppia* for twin beds.

Checking In & Out

○ When you check in you'll need to present your passport or ID card.

○ Checkout is usually between 10am and noon. In hostels it's around 9am.

○ Some guesthouses and B&Bs require you to arrange a time to check in.

🛏 Accommodation Types

Pensioni & Hotels

The bulk of Rome's accommodation consists of *pensioni* (pensions) and *alberghi* (hotels).

A *pensione* is a small, family-run hotel, often in a converted apartment. Rooms are usually fairly simple, though most come with a private bathroom.

Hotels are rated from one to five stars, though this rating relates to facilities only and gives no indication of value, comfort, atmosphere or friendliness. Most hotels in Rome's historic centre tend to be three-star and up. As a rule, a three-star room will come with a hairdryer, a minibar (or fridge), a safe, air-con and wi-fi. Some may also have satellite TV.

A common complaint in Rome is that hotel rooms are small. This is especially true in the *centro storico* and Trastevere, where many hotels are housed in centuries-old *palazzi* (mansions). Similarly, a spacious lift is a rare find, particularly in older *palazzi*,

and you'll seldom find one that can accommodate more than one average-sized person with luggage.

Breakfast in cheaper hotels is rarely worth setting the alarm for, so if you have the option, save a few bob and pop into a bar for a coffee and *cornetto* (croissant).

B&Bs & Guesthouses

Alongside traditional B&Bs, Rome has many boutique-style guesthouses offering chic, upmarket accommodation at midrange to top-end prices. Breakfast in a Roman B&B usually consists of bread rolls, croissants, yoghurt, ham and cheese.

Hostels

Rome's hostels cater to everyone from backpackers to budget-minded families. Many offer traditional dorms as well as smart hotel-style rooms (singles, doubles, even family rooms) with private bathrooms. Curfews are a thing of the past and some places even have 24-hour receptions. Many hostels don't accept prior reservations for

Views over Rome on a from a hotel rooftop

ILPO MUSTO/ALMY STOCK PHOTO ©

dorm beds, so arrive after 10am and it's first come, first served.

Religious Accommodation

Unsurprisingly, Rome is well furnished with religious institutions, many of which offer cheap(-ish) rooms for the night. Bear in mind, though, that many have strict curfews and that the accommodation, while spotlessly clean, tends to be short on frills. Also, while there are a number of centrally located options, many convents are situated out of the centre, typically in the districts north and west of the Vatican. Book well in advance.

Rental Accommodation

For longer stays, renting an apartment will generally work out cheaper than an extended hotel sojourn. Bank on about €900 per month for a studio apartment or one-bedroom flat. For longer stays, you'll probably have to pay bills plus a building maintenance charge.

🛏 Seasons & Rates

Rome doesn't have a low season as such but rates are at their lowest from November to March (excluding Christmas and New Year) and from mid-July through August. Expect to pay top whack in spring (April to June) and autumn (September and October) and over the main holiday periods (Christmas, New Year and Easter).

Most midrange and top-end hotels accept credit cards. Budget places might, but it's always best to check in advance.

Hotel Tax

Everyone overnighting in Rome has to pay a room-occupancy tax on top of their regular accommodation bill. This amounts to the following:

- €3 per person per night in one- and two-star hotels.

- €3.50 in B&Bs and room rentals.

- €4/6/7 in three-/four-/five-star hotels.

🧳 Online Rentals

Holiday rentals are booming in Rome right now thanks to online outfits like AirBnb and VRBO.

These sites offer a vast range of options, from single rooms in private houses to fully equipped apartments. They are often good value and will almost certainly save you money, especially in expensive areas such as the historic centre or Trastevere. Alternatively, they give the chance to get away from the touristy hot spots and see another side to the city – characterful neighbourhoods include Testaccio and Garbatella. Just make sure to research the location when you book and, if necessary, work out how you're going to get there (public transport, lift from the property owner etc).

Always make sure to check the property's reviews for things like noise (an issue in central locations) and privacy. You'll also need to check whether Rome's obligatory hotel tax is included in the rate or has to be paid separately.

Table settings on a hotel rooftop
PAOLO CORDELLI/GETTY IMAGES ©

The tax is applicable for a maximum of 10 consecutive nights. Prices in reviews do not include the tax.

🛏 Getting There

Most tourist areas are a bus ride or metro journey away from Stazione Termini. If you come by car, be warned that much of the city centre is a ZTL (limited traffic zone)

PAOLO CORDELLI/GETTY IMAGES ©

and off limits to unauthorised traffic. Note also that there is a terrible lack of on-site parking facilities in the city centre, although your hotel should be able to direct you to a private garage. Street parking is not recommended.

🛏 Useful Websites

Lonely Planet (www.lonelyplanet.com/italy/rome/hotels) Author-reviewed accommodation options and online booking.

060608 (www.060608.it/en/accoglienza/dormire) Official Comune di Roma site with accommodation lists; details not always up to date.

B&B Association of Rome (www.b-b.rm.it) Lists B&Bs and short-term apartment rentals.

B&B Italia (www.bbitalia.it) Rome's longest-established B&B network.

Rome As You Feel (www.romeasyoufeel.com) Apartment rentals, from cheap studio flats to luxury apartments.

Where to Stay

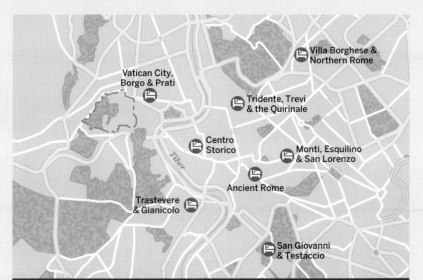

Neighbourhood	Atmosphere
Ancient Rome	Close to major sights such as Colosseum, Roman Forum and Capitoline Museums; quiet at night; not cheap; restaurants are touristy.
Centro Storico	Atmospheric area with everything on your doorstep: Pantheon, Piazza Navona, restaurants, bars, shops; most expensive part of town; can be noisy.
Tridente, Trevi & the Quirinale	Good for Spanish Steps, Trevi Fountain and designer shopping; excellent midrange to top-end options; good transport links; subdued after dark.
Monti, Esquilino & San Lorenzo	Lots of budget accommodation around Stazione Termini; top eating in Monti and good nightlife in San Lorenzo; good transport links; some dodgy streets near Termini.
San Giovanni & Testaccio	Authentic atmosphere with good eating and drinking options; Aventino is a quiet, romantic area; Testaccio is a top food and nightlife district; not many big sights.
Trastevere & Gianicolo	Gorgeous, atmospheric area; party vibe with hundreds of bars, cafes and restaurants; some interesting sights; expensive; noisy, particularly on summer nights.
Vatican City, Borgo & Prati	Near St Peter's Basilica; decent range of accommodation; some excellent shops and restaurants; on the metro; not much nightlife; sells out quickly for religious holidays.
Villa Borghese & Northern Rome	Largely residential area good for the Auditorium and Stadio Olimpico; some top museums; generally quiet after dark.

Tempio di Saturno, Roman Forum (p80)

In Focus

Rome Today

In late 2014, Rome was shocked as details emerged of deep-rooted corruption in city hall and links to organised crime. This, coming after a year of spending cuts and economic uncertainty, was a bitter pill for the city's residents to swallow. On the plus side, restoration work concluded on several high-profile monuments and Pope Francis continues to win over fans in the Vatican.

Above: Colosseum interior WIBOWO RUSLI/GETTY IMAGES ©

Scandal Rocks Rome

Rome is no stranger to controversy, but even hardened observers were shocked by the Mafia Capitale scandal that rocked the city in late 2014. The controversy centred on a criminal gang that had infiltrated city hall and was making millions by milking funds earmarked for immigration centres and camps for the city's Roma population. Thirty-seven people were arrested and up to 100 politicians and public officials, including former mayor Gianni Alemanno, were placed under police investigation. The Romans, not unused to the colourful behaviour of their elected officials, were appalled and a feeling of genuine outrage swept the city.

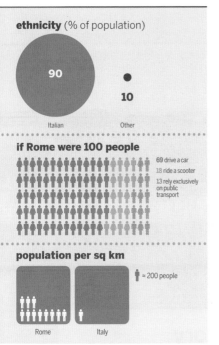

ethnicity (% of population)

90
Italian

10
Other

if Rome were 100 people

69 drive a car
18 ride a scooter
13 rely exclusively on public transport

population per sq km

♦ ≈ 200 people

Rome

Italy

Restoration & Street Art

Rome's recent economic straits have put an enormous strain on the city's capacity to maintain its historical monuments. But walk around town today and you'll see several high-profile monuments gleaming in the wake of recent makeovers.

Despite the very public nature of these restoration projects, most of them were actually financed by private money. In the past few years Rome's cultural administrators have been actively courting private investment to help shore up municipal budgets. And while this has attracted heated debate, it has proved successful: the Colosseum clean-up was sponsored by Tod's; the Fendi fashion house footed the bill for work on the Trevi Fountain; and Bulgari has pledged €1.5 million towards an overhaul of the Spanish Steps.

Away from the spotlight, street art has exploded onto the scene in recent times, and giant murals have become a feature of some of the city's lesser-known neighbourhoods.

Pope Francis & the Jubilee

Over on the west bank of the Tiber, the Vatican continues to capture the world's attention. In April 2014 an estimated 800,000 people flocked to St Peter's to witness the dual canonisation of Popes John Paul II and John XXIII. Overseeing events was Pope Francis, the popular Argentinian pontiff whose papacy has done much to resurrect the Church's image in the wake of Benedict XVI's troubled tenure.

The city celebrated a Jubilee, or Holy Year, in 2016. During a Jubilee, the Church offers a plenary indulgence to Catholics who visit one of Rome's patriarchal basilicas and observe certain religious conditions.

Tourism Thrives

As well as wooing Catholics back to the fold, Pope Francis has had a positive effect on tourism, and in 2014 he was credited with inspiring a 28% increase in the number of Argentinian visitors to the city. Surprisingly, Rome's recent tribulations haven't adversely affected tourism, which continues to go from strength to strength – arrivals in 2014 were up on previous years, confirming the recent upward trend.

History

Rome's history spans three millennia, from the classical myths of vengeful gods to the follies of Roman emperors, from Renaissance excess to swaggering 20th-century fascism. Emperors, popes and dictators have come and gone, playing out their ambitions and conspiring for their place in history. Everywhere you go in this remarkable city, you're surrounded by the past.

Above: St Peter's Basilica (p46) and the River Tiber RILINDH/ GETTY IMAGES ©

753 BC	**509 BC**	**15 March 44 BC**
According to legend, Romulus kills his twin brother Remus and founds Rome on the Palatino.	The Roman Republic is founded, paving the way for Rome's rise to European domination.	On the Ides of March, Julius Caesar is stabbed to death in the Teatro di Pompeo (on modern-day Largo di Torre Argentina).

The Myth of Ancient Rome

As much a mythical construct as a historical reality, ancient Rome's image has been carefully nurtured throughout history.

Rome's original myth makers were the first emperors. Eager to reinforce the city's status as *caput mundi* (capital of the world), they turned to writers such as Virgil, Ovid and Livy to create an official Roman history. These authors, while adept at weaving epic narratives, were less interested in the rigours of historical research and frequently presented myth as reality. In the *Aeneid*, Virgil brazenly draws on Greek legends and stories to tell the tale of Aeneas, a Trojan prince who arrives in Italy and establishes Rome's founding dynasty.

Ancient Rome's rulers were sophisticated masters of spin; under their tutelage, art, architecture and elaborate public ceremony were employed to perpetuate the image of Rome as an invincible and divinely sanctioned power.

AD 67	285	476
St Peter and St Paul become martyrs as Nero massacres Rome's Christians in a ploy to win popularity after the great fire of AD 64.	Diocletian splits the Roman Empire in two. The eastern half later joins the Byzantine Empire; the western half falls to the barbarians.	The fall of Romulus Augustulus marks the end of the Western Empire.

Ruins along Via Appia Antica

DAVID SOANES PHOTOGRAPHY/GETTY IMAGES ©

Legacy of an Empire

Rising out of the bloodstained remnants of the Roman Republic, the Roman Empire was the Western world's first great superpower. At its zenith under Emperor Trajan (r AD 98–117), it extended from Britannia in the north to North Africa in the south, from Hispania (Spain) in the west to Palestina (Palestine) and Syria in the east. Rome itself had more than 1.5 million inhabitants. Decline eventually set in during the 3rd century and by the latter half of the 5th century Rome was in barbarian hands.

In AD 285 the emperor Diocletian, prompted by widespread disquiet across the empire, split the empire into eastern and western halves – the west centred on Rome and the east on Byzantium (later called Constantinople) – in a move that was to have far-reaching consequences for centuries. In the west, the fall of the Western Roman Empire in AD 476 paved the way for the emergence of the Holy Roman Empire and the Papal States, while in the east, Roman (later Byzantine) rule continued until 1453 when the empire was finally conquered by rampaging Ottoman armies.

Christianity & Papal Power

For much of its history Rome has been ruled by the pope, and today the Vatican still wields immense influence over the city.

Emergence of Christianity

Christianity swept in from the Roman province of Judaea in the 1st century AD. Its early days were marred by persecution, most notably under Nero (r 54–68), but it slowly caught on, thanks to its popular message of heavenly reward.

However, it was the conversion of Emperor Constantine (r 306–37) that really set Christianity on the path to European domination. In 313 Constantine issued the Edict of Milan, officially legalising Christianity, and in 378, Theodosius (r 379–95) made Christianity Rome's state religion. By this time, the Church had developed a sophisticated organisa-

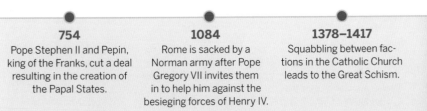

754	1084	1378–1417
Pope Stephen II and Pepin, king of the Franks, cut a deal resulting in the creation of the Papal States.	Rome is sacked by a Norman army after Pope Gregory VII invites them in to help him against the besieging forces of Henry IV.	Squabbling between factions in the Catholic Church leads to the Great Schism.

tional structure based on five major sees: Rome, Constantinople, Alexandria, Antioch and Jerusalem. At the outset, each bishopric carried equal weight, but in subsequent years Rome emerged as the senior party. The reasons for this were partly political – Rome was the wealthy capital of the Roman Empire – and partly religious – early Christian doctrine held that St Peter, founder of the Roman Church, had been sanctioned by Christ to lead the universal Church.

Papal Control

But while Rome had control of Christianity, the Church had yet to conquer Rome. This it did in the dark days that followed the fall of the Roman Empire by skilfully stepping into the power vacuum created by the demise of imperial power. And although no one person can take credit for this, Pope Gregory the Great (r 590–604) did more than most to lay the groundwork. A leader of considerable foresight, he won many friends by supplying free bread to Rome's starving citizens and restoring the city's water supply. He also stood up to the menacing Lombards, who presented a very real threat to the city.

It was this threat that pushed the papacy into an alliance with the Frankish kings, resulting in the creation of the two great powers of medieval Europe: the Papal States and the Holy Roman Empire. In Rome, the battle between these two superpowers translated into endless feuding between the city's baronial families and frequent attempts by the French to claim the papacy for their own. This political and military fighting eventually culminated in the papacy transferring to the French city of Avignon between 1309 and 1377, and the Great Schism (1378–1417), a period in which the Catholic world was headed by two popes, one in Rome and one in Avignon.

As both religious and temporal leaders, Rome's popes wielded influence well beyond their military capacity. For much of the medieval period, the Church held a virtual monopoly on Europe's reading material (mostly religious scripts written in Latin) and was the authority on virtually every aspect of human knowledge.

Romulus & Remus

The most famous of Rome's many legends is the story of Romulus and Remus, the mythical twins who are said to have founded Rome on 21 April 753 BC.

Romulus and Remus were born to the vestal virgin Rhea Silva after she'd been seduced by Mars. At their birth they were sentenced to death by their great-uncle Amulius, who had stolen the throne of Alba Longa from his brother, Rhea Silva's father, Numitor. The sentence was never carried out, and the twins were abandoned in a basket on the banks of the river Tiber. They were saved by a she-wolf and raised by a shepherd, Faustulus. Years later, the twins decided to build a city on the site where they'd originally been saved. They didn't know where this was, so they asked the omens. Remus, on the Aventine Hill, saw six vultures; his brother over on the Palatine saw 12. Romulus began building, which outraged his brother. They argued and Romulus killed Remus, going on to found his city.

1527	1626	1798
Pope Clement VII hides in Castel Sant'Angelo as Rome is sacked by troops loyal to Charles V, king of Spain and Holy Roman Emperor.	St Peter's Basilica is completed after 150 years' construction. The basilica remains the largest church in the world until 1997.	Napoleon marches into Rome. A republic is announced, but it doesn't last long and in 1801 Pope Pius VII returns to Rome.

Stanze di Raffaello, Vatican Museums

APIC/CONTRIBUTOR/GETTY IMAGES ©

Modern Influence

Almost 1000 years on and the Church is still a major influence on modern Italian life. In recent years, Vatican intervention in political and social debate has provoked fierce divisions within Italy. This relationship between the Church and Italy's modern political establishment is a fact of life that dates to the establishment of the Italian Republic in 1946. For much of the First Republic (1946–94), the Vatican was closely associated with Democrazia Cristiana (DC; Christian Democrat Party), Italy's most powerful party and an ardent opponent of communism. At the same time, the Church, keen to weed communism out of the political landscape, played its part by threatening to excommunicate anyone who voted for Italy's Partito Comunista Italiano (PCI; Communist Party). Today, no one political party has a monopoly on Church favour, and politicians across the spectrum tread warily around Catholic sensibilities.

Renaissance: A New Beginning

Bridging the gap between the Middle Ages and the modern age, the Renaissance (Rinascimento in Italian) was a far-reaching intellectual, artistic and cultural movement. It emerged in 14th-century Florence but quickly spread to Rome, where it gave rise to one of the greatest makeovers the city had ever seen.

Humanism & Rebuilding

The movement's intellectual cornerstone was humanism, a philosophy that focused on the central role of humanity within the universe, a major break from the medieval world view, which placed God at the centre of everything. It was not anti-religious though. One of the most celebrated humanist scholars of the 15th century was Pope Nicholas V (r 1447–84), who is considered the harbinger of the Roman Renaissance.

When Nicholas became pope in 1447, Rome was not in a good state. Centuries of medieval feuding had reduced the city to a semi-deserted battleground. In political terms, the

1870	1922	1929
Nine years after Italian unification, Rome's city walls are breached at Porta Pia and Pope Pius IX cedes the city to Italy.	Some 40,000 fascists march on Rome. King Vittorio Emanuele III invites the 39-year-old Mussolini to form a government.	The Lateran Treaty is signed, creating the state of Vatican City. To celebrate, Via della Conciliazione is bulldozed through the medieval Borgo.

papacy was recovering from the trauma of the Great Schism and attempting to face down Muslim encroachment in the east.

Against this background, Nicholas decided to rebuild Rome as a showcase of Church power, setting off an enormous program that would see the Sistine Chapel and St Peter's built.

Sack of Rome & Protestant Protest

But outside Rome an ill wind was blowing. The main source of trouble was the long-standing conflict between the Holy Roman Empire, led by the Spanish Charles V, and the Italian city-states. This simmering tension came to a head in 1527 when Rome was invaded by Charles' marauding army and ransacked as Pope Clement VII (r 1523–34) hid in Castel Sant'Angelo. The sack of Rome, regarded by most historians as the nail in the coffin of the Roman Renaissance, was a hugely traumatic event. It left the papacy reeling and gave rise to the view that the Church had been greatly weakened by its own moral shortcomings. That the Church was corrupt was well known, and it was with considerable public support that Martin Luther pinned his famous 95 Theses to a church door in Wittenberg in 1517, thus sparking off the Protestant Reformation.

Counter-Reformation

The Catholic reaction to the Reformation was all-out. The Counter-Reformation was marked by a second wave of artistic and architectural activity, as the Church once again turned to bricks and mortar to restore its authority. But in contrast to the Renaissance, the Counter-Reformation was a period of persecution and official intolerance. With the full blessing of Pope Paul III, Ignatius Loyola founded the Jesuits in 1540, and two years later the Holy Office was set up as the Church's final appeals court for trials prosecuted by the Inquisition. In 1559 the Church published the *Index Librorum Prohibitorum* (Index of Prohibited Books) and began to persecute intellectuals and freethinkers.

Despite, or perhaps because of, the Church's policy of zero tolerance, the Counter-Reformation was largely successful in re-establishing papal prestige. From being a rural backwater with a population of around 20,000 in the mid-15th century, Rome had grown to become one of Europe's great 17th-century cities, home to Christendom's most spectacular churches and a population of 100,000 people.

The First Tourists

While Rome has a long past as a pilgrimage site, its history as a modern tourist destination can be traced back to the late 1700s and the fashion for the Grand Tour. The 18th-century version of a gap year, the Tour was considered an educational rite of passage for wealthy young men from northern Europe, and Britain in particular.

1946
The Italian republic is born after a vote to abolish the monarchy.

1948
On 1 January 1948 the Italian constitution becomes law.

1957
The Treaty of Rome is signed in the Capitoline Museums and establishes the European Economic Community.

Natale di Roma parade

★ **Best Historical Celebrations**

Carnevale (p7)

Natale di Roma (p9)

Festa de' Noantri (p12)

Re-enactment of Caesar's death (p8)

Festa della Repubblica (p11)

Rome, enjoying a rare period of peace, was perfectly set up for this English invasion. The city was basking in the aftermath of the 17th-century baroque building boom, and a craze for all things classical was sweeping Europe. Rome's papal authorities were also crying out for money after their excesses had left the city coffers bare, reducing much of the population to abject poverty.

Thousands came, including Goethe, who stopped off to write his travelogue *Italian Journey* (1817), as well as Byron, Shelley and Keats, who all fuelled their romantic sensibilities in the city's vibrant streets.

Artistically, rococo was the rage of the moment. The Spanish Steps, built between 1723 and 1726, proved a major hit with tourists, as did the exuberant Trevi Fountain.

Ghosts of Fascism

Rome's fascist history is a deeply sensitive subject, and in recent years historians on both sides of the political spectrum have accused each other of recasting the past to suit their views.

Mussolini

Benito Mussolini was born in 1883 in Forlì, a small town in Emilia-Romagna. As a young man he was an active member of the Italian Socialist Party, rising through the ranks to become editor of the party's official newspaper. However, service in WWI and Italy's subsequent descent into chaos led to a change of heart and in 1919 he founded the Italian Fascist Party.

In 1921 Mussolini was elected to the Chamber of Deputies. His parliamentary support was limited, but on 28 October 1922 he marched on Rome with 40,000 black-shirted followers. The march was largely symbolic but it had the desired effect, and King Vittorio Emanuele III, fearful of a civil war between the fascists and socialists, invited Mussolini to form a government. By the end of 1925 he had seized complete control of Italy. In order to silence the Church he signed the Lateran Treaty in 1929, which made Catholicism the state

1960	1978	2005
Rome hosts the Games of the XVII Olympiad.	Former prime minister Aldo Moro is kidnapped and shot by a cell of the extreme left-wing Brigate Rosse (Red Brigades).	Pope John Paul II dies after 27 years on the papal throne. He is replaced by his long-standing ally Josef Ratzinger (Benedict XVI).

religion and recognised the sovereignty of the Vatican State.

Abroad, Mussolini invaded Abyssinia (now Ethiopia) in 1935 and sided with Hitler in 1936. In 1940, from the balcony of Palazzo Venezia, he announced Italy's entry into WWII to a vast, cheering crowd. The good humour didn't last, as Rome suffered, first at the hands of its own fascist regime, then, after Mussolini was ousted in 1943, at the hands of the Nazis. Rome was finally liberated from German occupation on 4 June 1944.

Postwar Period

Defeat in WWII didn't kill off Italian fascism, and in 1946 hardline Mussolini supporters founded the Movimento Sociale Italiano (MSI; Italian Social Movement). For close on 50 years this overtly fascist party participated in mainstream Italian politics, while on the other side of the spectrum the Partito Comunista Italiano (PCI; Italian Communist Party) grew into Western Europe's largest communist party. The MSI was finally dissolved in 1994.

Outside the political mainstream, fascism (along with communism) was a driving force of the domestic terrorism that rocked Rome and Italy during the *anni di piombo* (years of lead), between the late 1960s and the early '80s.

Jubilee Years

As seat of the Catholic Church, Rome was already one of the main pilgrim destinations in the Middle Ages, when, in 1300, Pope Boniface VIII proclaimed the first ever Holy Year (Jubilee). Promising full forgiveness for anyone who made the pilgrimage to St Peter's Basilica and the Basilica di San Giovanni in Laterano, his appeal to the faithful proved a resounding success. Hundreds of thousands answered his call and the Church basked in popular glory.

Some 700 years later and the Holy Year tradition is still going strong. A Jubilee was held in 2000, attracting up to 24 million visitors, and another, more low-key affair, in 2016.

2013
Pope Benedict XVI becomes the first pope to resign since 1415. Argentinian cardinal Jorge Mario Bergoglio is elected as Pope Francis.

2014
Ex-mayor Gianni Alemanno and 100 politicians and public officials are investigated as the Mafia Capitale scandal rocks Rome.

2015–16
Pope Francis declares a Jubilee Year to run from 8 December 2015 to 20 November 2016.

The Arts

Rome's turbulent history and magical cityscape have long provided inspiration for painters, sculptors, film makers, writers and musicians. The classical works of Roman antiquity fuelled the imagination of Renaissance artists; Counter-Reformation persecution led to baroque art and street satire; and the trauma of Mussolini and WWII found expression in neorealist cinema.

Above: Sarcofago degli Sposi (Sarcophagus of the Betrothed; p58)

Painting & Sculpture

Home to some of the Western world's most recognisable art, Rome is a visual feast. Its churches alone contain more masterpieces than many small countries, and the city's galleries are laden with works by world-famous artists.

Etruscan Groundwork

The Etruscans placed great importance on their funerary rites and they developed sepulchral decoration into a highly sophisticated art form. An important example is the *Sarcofago degli Sposi* (Sarcophagus of the Betrothed) in the Museo Nazionale Etrusco di

Villa Giulia. They were also noted for their bronze work, an example of which is the iconic *Lupa Capitolina* in the Capitoline Museums.

Roman Developments

In terms of decorative art, the Roman use of mosaics and wall paintings was derived from Etruscan funerary decoration. Typical themes included landscapes, still lifes, geometric patterns and depictions of gods. In the Museo Nazionale Romano: Palazzo Massimo alle Terme, you'll find some spectacular wall mosaics and 1st century BC frescoes.

Sculpture was an important element of Roman art, and was largely influenced by Greek styles. Early Roman sculptures were often made by Greek artists or were copies of Greek works. They were largely concerned with visions of male beauty – classic examples are the *Apollo Belvedere* and the *Laocoön* in the Museo Pio-Clementino of the Vatican Museums.

From the time of Augustus (r 27 BC–AD 14), Roman art became increasingly propagandistic. A new style of narrative art developed which often took the form of relief decoration – the Ara Pacis is a stunning example.

Early Christian Art

Some of Rome's earliest preserved Christian artworks are the faint biblical frescoes in the Catacombe di San Sebastiano on Via Appia Antica.

With the legalisation of Christianity in the 4th century, these images began to move into the public arena, appearing in churches such as the Basilica di Santa Maria Maggiore.

Eastern influences became much more pronounced between the 7th and 9th centuries, when Byzantine styles swept in from the East – you can see such brighter, golden works in the Basilica di Santa Maria in Trastevere.

The Renaissance

The Renaissance arrived in Rome in the latter half of the 15th century, and was to have a profound impact on the city, as the top artists of the day were summoned to decorate the many new buildings going up around town.

Rome's most celebrated works of Renaissance art are Michelangelo's paintings in the Sistine Chapel – his cinematic ceiling frescoes, painted between 1508 and 1512, and the *Giudizio Universale* (Last Judgment), which he worked on between 1536 and 1541.

Central to the Last Judgment and much Renaissance art was the human form. This led artists to develop a far greater appreciation of perspective. But while early Renaissance painters made great strides in formulating rules of perspective, they still struggled to paint harmonious arrangements of figures. And it was this that Raffaello Sanzio (Raphael; 1483–1520) tackled in his great masterpiece *La Scuola di Atene* (The School of Athens; 1510–11) in the Vatican Museums.

Counter-Reformation & the Baroque

The baroque burst onto Rome's art scene in the early 17th century. Combining a dramatic sense of dynamism with highly charged emotion, it was enthusiastically appropriated by the Catholic Church, which used it as a propaganda tool in its persecution of Counter-Reformation heresy. The powerful popes of the day eagerly championed the likes of Caravaggio, Gian Lorenzo Bernini, Domenichino, Pietro da Cortona and Alessandro Algardi.

Not surprisingly, much baroque art has a religious theme and you'll often find depictions of martyrdoms, ecstasies and miracles.

La dolce vita poster

★ Best Rome Films

Roma città aperta (1945)

Roman Holiday (1953)

La dolce vita (1960)

The Talented Mr Ripley (1999)

La grande belleza (2013)

One of its premier exponents was Milan-born Caravaggio (1573–1610), whose realistic interpretations of religious subjects often outraged his patrons. In contrast, the exquisite sculptural works of Gian Lorenzo Bernini (1598–1680) proved an instant hit.

Literature

Rome has a rich literary tradition, encompassing everything from ancient satires to contemporary thrillers.

Classics

Famous for his blistering oratory, Marcus Tullius Cicero (106–43 BC) was the Roman Republic's preeminent author. His contemporary, Catullus (c 84–54 BC) cut a very different figure with his epigrams and erotic verse.

On becoming emperor, Augustus (aka Octavian) encouraged the arts, and Virgil (70–19 BC), Ovid, Horace and Tibullus all enjoyed freedom to write.

Rome As Inspiration

Rome has provided inspiration for legions of foreign authors.

In the 18th century, historians and grand tourists poured into Rome from northern Europe. The German author Goethe captures the elation of discovering ancient Rome in his travelogue *Italian Journey* (1817). The city was also favoured by the Romantic poets: John Keats, Lord Byron, Percy Bysshe Shelley, Mary Shelley and other writers all spent time here.

In more recent fiction, Rome has provided a setting for many a blockbuster, including Dan Brown's thriller *Angels and Demons* (2001).

Writing Today

Born in Rome in 1966, Niccolò Ammaniti is the best known of the city's crop of contemporary authors. In 2007 he won the Premio Strega, Italy's top literary prize, for his novel *Come Dio comanda* (As God Commands), although he's probably best known for *Io non ho paura* (I'm Not Scared; 2001)

Cinema

Rome has a long cinematic tradition, spanning the works of the postwar neorealists and film-makers as diverse as Federico Fellini, Sergio Leone, Nanni Moretti, and Paolo Sorrentino, the Oscar-winning director of *La grande belleza* (The Great Beauty).

The 1940s was Roman cinema's Golden Age, when Roberto Rossellini (1906–77) produced a trio of neorealist masterpieces, most notably *Roma città aperta* (Rome Open City; 1945). Also important was Vittorio de Sica's 1948 *Ladri di biciclette* (Bicycle Thieves).

Federico Fellini (1920–94) took the creative baton from the neorealists, producing his era-defining hit *La dolce vita* in 1960. The films of Pier Paolo Pasolini (1922–75) are similarly demanding in their depiction of Rome's gritty underbelly in the postwar period.

Idiosyncratic and whimsical, Nanni Moretti continues to make films that fall into no mainstream tradition, such as *Habemus Papam*, his 2011 portrayal of a pope having a crisis of faith.

Recently, the big news in cinema circles has been the return of international film-making to Rome. In 2015 Daniel Craig charged around town filming the latest 007 outing, *Spectre,* while Ben Stiller was camping it up for *Zoolander 2*. Down in the city's southern reaches, a remake of *Ben-Hur* was filmed at the Cinecittà film studios, the very same place where the original sword-and-sandal epic was shot in 1959.

Neoclassicism

Emerging in the late 18th and early 19th centuries, neoclassicism signalled a departure from the emotional abandon of the baroque and a return to the clean, sober lines of classical art. Its major exponent was the sculptor Antonio Canova (1757–1822), whose study of Paolina Bonaparte Borghese as *Venere Vincitrice* (Venus Victrix) in the Museo e Galleria Borghese is typical of the mildly erotic style for which he became known.

Music

Despite years of austerity-led cutbacks, Rome's music scene is bearing up well. International orchestras perform to sell-out audiences, jazz greats jam in steamy clubs, and rappers rage in underground venues.

Jazz has long been a mainstay of Rome's music scene, while recent years have seen the emergence of a vibrant rap and hip-hop culture. Opera is served up at the Teatro dell'Opera and, in summer, at the spectacular Terme di Caracalla.

Architecture

From ancient ruins and Renaissance basilicas to baroque churches and hulking fascist palazzi *(palaces), Rome's architectural legacy is unparalleled. Michelangelo, Bramante, Borromini and Bernini, as well as more recently contemporary stars Renzo Piano and Zaha Hadid, are among the architects who have stamped their genius on Rome's remarkable cityscape.*

Chiesa di Sant'Agnese in Agone (p66) KAGENMI/GETTY IMAGES ©

The Ancients

Architecture was central to the success of the ancient Romans. In building their great capital, they were among the first people to use architecture to tackle problems of infrastructure, urban management and communication. For the first time, architects and engineers designed houses, roads, aqueducts and shopping centres alongside temples, tombs and imperial palaces. To do this, the Romans advanced methods devised by the Etruscans and Greeks, developing construction techniques and building materials that allowed them to build on a massive and hitherto unseen scale.

Etruscan Roots

By the 7th century BC the Etruscans were the dominant force on the Italian peninsula, with important centres at Tarquinia, Caere (Cerveteri) and Veii (Veio). But they built with wood and brick, which didn't last, and much of what we now know about the Etruscans derives from their impressive cemeteries. These were constructed outside the city walls and harboured richly decorated stone vaults covered by mounds of earth.

Roman Developments

When Rome was founded in 753 BC (or earlier if recent archaeological findings are to be believed), the Etruscans were at the height of their power and Greek colonists were establishing control over southern Italy. Against this background, Roman architects borrowed heavily from Greek and Etruscan traditions, gradually developing their own styles and techniques.

Ancient Roman architecture was monumental in form and often propagandistic in nature. Huge amphitheatres, aqueducts and temples joined muscular and awe-inspiring basilicas, arches and thermal baths in trumpeting the skill and vision of the city's early rulers and the nameless architects who worked for them.

Temples

Early Republican-era temples were based on Etruscan designs, but over time the Romans turned to the Greeks for their inspiration. But whereas Greek temples had steps and colonnades on all sides, the classic Roman temple had a high podium with steps leading up to a deep porch.

The Roman use of columns was also Greek in origin, even if the Romans favoured the more slender Ionic and Corinthian columns over the plain Doric pillars – to see how these differ study the exterior of the Colosseum, which incorporates all three styles.

Aqueducts & Sewers

One of the Romans' crowning architectural achievements was the development of a water supply infrastructure.

To meet the city's water demand, the Romans constructed a complex system of aqueducts to bring water in from the hills of central Italy and distribute it around town. The first aqueduct to serve Rome was the 16.5km Aqua Appia, which became fully operational in 312 BC. Over the next 700 years or so, up to 800km of aqueducts were built in the city, a network capable of supplying up to 1 million cu metres of water a day.

At the other end of the water cycle, waste water was drained away via an underground sewerage system known as the Cloaca Maxima (Great Sewer) and emptied downstream into the river Tiber.

Residential Housing

While Rome's emperors and aristocrats lived in luxury on the Palatino (Palatine Hill), the city's poor huddled together in large residential blocks called *insulae*. These poorly built structures were sometimes up to six or seven storeys high, accommodating hundreds of people in dark, unhealthy conditions. Near the foot of the steps that lead up to the Chiesa di Santa Maria in Aracoeli, you can still see a section of what was once a typical city-centre *insula*.

Pantheon interior

Concrete & Monumental Architecture

Grandiose structures such as the Colosseum, Pantheon and the Forums are not only reminders of the sophistication and scale of ancient Rome – just as they were originally designed to be – but also monuments to the vision of the city's ancient architects.

One of the key breakthroughs the Romans made was the invention of concrete in the 1st century BC. Made by mixing volcanic ash with lime and an aggregate, often tufa rock or brick rubble, concrete was quick to make, easy to use and cheap. It allowed the Romans to develop vaulted roofing, which they used to span the Pantheon's ceiling and the huge vaults at the Terme di Caracalla.

Early Christian

The most startling reminders of early Christian activity are the catacombs, a series of subterranean burial grounds built under Rome's ancient roads. Christian belief in the resurrection meant that the Christians could not cremate their dead, as was the custom in Roman times, and with burial forbidden inside the city walls they were forced to go outside the city.

The Christians began to abandon the catacombs in the 4th century and increasingly opted to be buried in the churches being built in the city. The most notable of the many churches that Constantine commissioned is the Basilica di San Giovanni in Laterano, the model on which many subsequent basilicas were based. Other period showstoppers include the Basilica di Santa Maria in Trastevere and the Basilica di Santa Maria Maggiore.

A second wave of church-building hit Rome in the period between the 8th and 12th centuries. As the early papacy battled for survival against the threatening Lombards, its leaders took to construction to leave some sort of historic imprint, resulting in churches such as the Chiesa di Santa Maria in Cosmedin, home of the Bocca della Verità (Mouth of Truth).

The Renaissance

Many claim it was the election of Pope Nicholas V in 1447 that sparked the Renaissance in Rome. Nicholas believed that as head of the Christian world Rome had a duty to impress, a theory that was endorsed by his successors, and it was at the behest of the great papal dynasties – the Barberini, Farnese and Pamphilj – that the leading artists of the day were summoned to Rome.

Bramante & the High Renaissance

It was under Julius II (1503–13) that the Roman Renaissance reached its peak, thanks largely to a classically minded architect from Milan, Donato Bramante (1444–1514).

Considered the high priest of Renaissance architecture, Bramante arrived in Rome in 1499 and developed a hugely influential classical style. His 1502 Tempietto is a masterpiece of elegance. In 1506 Julius commissioned him to start work on the job that would finally finish him off – the rebuilding of St Peter's Basilica. The fall of Constantinople's Aya Sofya (Church of the Hagia Sofia) to Islam in the mid-14th century had pricked Nicholas V into ordering an earlier revamp, but the work had never been completed and it wasn't until Julius took the bull by the horns that progress was made. However, Bramante died in 1514 and he never got to see how his original Greek-cross design was developed.

St Peter's Basilica occupied most of the other notable architects of the High Renaissance, including Michelangelo (1475–1564) who took over in 1547 and created the basilica's crowning dome. Modelled on Brunelleschi's cupola for the Duomo in Florence, this is considered the artist's finest architectural achievement and one of the most important works of the Roman Renaissance.

Rococo Frills

In the early days of the 18th century, as baroque fashions began to fade and neoclassicism waited to make its 19th-century entrance, the rococo burst into theatrical life. Drawing on the excesses of the baroque, it was a short-lived fad but one that left a memorable mark.

The Spanish Steps (p100), built between 1723 and 1726 by Francesco de Sanctis, provided a focal point for the many Grand Tourists who were busy discovering Rome's classical past. A short walk to the southwest, Piazza Sant'Ignazio was designed by Filippo Raguzzini (1680–1771) to provide a suitably melodramatic setting for the Chiesa di Sant'Ignazio di Loyola, Rome's second most important Jesuit church.

Most spectacular of all, however, was the Trevi Fountain (p86), one of the city's most exuberant and enduringly popular monuments. It was designed in 1732 by Nicola Salvi (1697–1751) and completed three decades later.

The Baroque

The Catholic Church became increasingly powerful in the 16th century. But with power came corruption and calls for reform. These culminated in the far-reaching Protestant Reformation, which prompted the Counter-Reformation (1560–1648), a vicious campaign to get people back into the Catholic fold. Art and architecture emerged as an effective form of propaganda. Stylistically, baroque architecture aims for a dramatic sense of dynamism, an effect that it often achieves by combining spatial complexity with clever lighting and a flamboyant use of decorative painting and sculpture.

The end of the 16th century and the papacy of Sixtus V (1585–90) marked the beginning of major urban-planning schemes that saw Domenico Fontana (1543–1607) and other architects create a network of major thoroughfares to connect parts of the sprawling medieval city.

Bernini vs Borromini

No two people did more to fashion the face of Rome than the two great figures of the Roman baroque – Gian Lorenzo Bernini (1598–1680) and Francesco Borromini (1599–1667). Naples-born Bernini, confident and suave, is best known for his work in the Vatican where he designed St Peter's Square and was chief architect at St Peter's Basilica from 1629.

Under the patronage of the Barberini pope Urban VIII, Bernini was given free rein to transform the city, and his churches, *palazzi,* piazzas and fountains remain landmarks to

★ Best Baroque

St Peter's Square (p49)

Fontana dei Quattro Fiumi (p66)

Chiesa di Sant'Agnese in Agone (p66)

this day. However, his fortunes nose-dived when the pope died in 1644. Urban's successor, Innocent X, wanted as little contact as possible with the favourites of his hated predecessor, and instead turned to Borromini.

Borromini, a solitary, peculiar man from Lombardy, created buildings involving complex shapes and exotic geometry such as the Chiesa di Sant'Agnese in Agone on Piazza Navona.

Rationalism & Fascism

Rome entered the 20th century in good shape. During the late 19th century it had been treated to one of its periodic makeovers, after being made capital in 1870. Piazzas were built, including Piazza Vittorio Emanuele II and neoclassical Piazza della Repubblica. To celebrate unification and pander to the ruling Savoy family, the ostentatious Vittoriano monument was built (1885–1911).

The 1920s saw the emergence of architectural rationalism. Its main Italian proponents, Gruppo Sette, combined classicism with modernism, which tied in perfectly with Mussolini's vision of fascism as the modern bearer of ancient Rome's imperialist ambitions. Mussolini's most famous architectural legacy is Rome's southern EUR district, built for the Esposizione Universale di Roma in 1942.

Modern Rome

The 21st century has witnessed a flurry of architectural activity in Rome as a clutch of starchitects have worked on projects in the city. Renzo Piano worked on the acclaimed Auditorium; American Richard Meier built the controversial pavilion for the 1st century AD Ara Pacis; and Anglo-Iraqi Zaha Hadid won plaudits for the Museo Nazionale delle Arti del XXI Secolo (MAXXI). Out in EUR, work continues on a striking conference centre, known as the Nuvola (Cloud), designed by Massimiliano Fuksas.

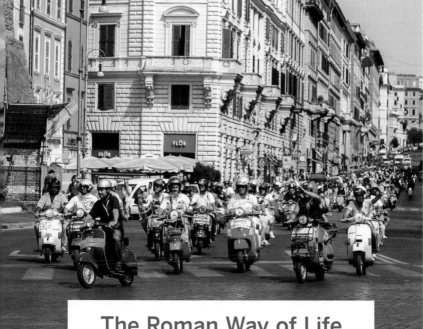

The Roman Way of Life

As a visitor, it's often difficult to see beyond Rome's spectacular veneer to the large, modern city that lies beneath. But how do the Romans live in their city? Where do they work? Who do they live with?

Vespa riders SIMON MONTGOMERY/ROBERTHARDING/GETTY IMAGES ©

Day in the Life

Rome's Mr Average, Signor Rossi, lives in a small, two-bedroom apartment and works in a government ministry.

His morning routine is somewhat the same as city dwellers the world over: a quick espresso followed by a short bus ride to the nearest metro station. On the way he'll stop at an *edicola* (kiosk) to pick up his daily newspaper (*Il Messaggero*) – a quick scan of the headlines reveals few surprises: Matteo Renzi promoting his latest reforms; the usual political shenanigans in city hall; Roma and Lazio match reports.

His work, like many in the swollen state bureaucracy, is secure and with a much sought-after *contratto a tempo indeterminato* (permanent contract) he doesn't have to worry about losing it. In contrast, younger colleagues work in constant fear that their temporary contracts won't be renewed.

Basilica di San Clemente

★ Best Churches

St Peter's Basilica (p46)

Chiesa di Santa Maria del Popolo (p88)

Basilica di San Clemente (p96)

Basilica di San Giovanni in Laterano (p90)

Lunch, usually a snack or *pizza al taglio* (pizza by the slice) from a nearby takeaway, is followed by a quick coffee in the usual bar.

Clocking-off time in most ministries is typically from 5pm onwards and by about 7pm the evening rush hour is in full swing.

Home Life & the Family

Romans, like most Italians, live in apartments. These are often small – 75 sq metres to 100 sq metres is typical – and expensive. House prices in central Rome are among the highest in the country and many first-time buyers are forced to move to distant suburbs.

It's still the rule rather than the exception for young Romans to stay at home until they marry, which they typically do at around 30.

Religion

Rome is packed with churches. And with the Vatican in the centre of town, the Church is an important point of reference. Yet the role of religion in modern Roman society is an ambiguous one. On the one hand, most people consider themselves Catholic, but on the other, church attendance is in freefall, particularly among the young.

St Peter's Basilica interior

Survival Guide

Directory A–Z

Customs Regulations

If you're arriving from a non-EU country you can import, duty free, 200 cigarettes, 1L of spirits (or 2L fortified wine), 4L wine, 60ml perfume, 16L beer, and goods, including electronic devices, up to a value of €300/430 (travelling by land/air or sea); anything over this value must be declared on arrival and the duty paid.

Non-EU residents can reclaim value-added tax (VAT) on expensive purchases on leaving the EU.

Electricity

230V/50Hz

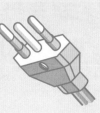

230V/50Hz

Emergency

Ambulance	☎118
Fire	☎115
Police	☎112, ☎113

Health

Nationals of the EU are entitled to reduced-cost, sometimes free, medical care with a European Health Insurance Card (EHIC), available from your home health authority; non-EU citizens should take out medical insurance.

For emergency treatment, you can go to the *pronto soccorso* (casualty) section of an *ospedale* (public hospital). For less serious ailments call the **Guardia**

Medica (☎06 8840113; Via Mantova 44; ⏱24hr).

More convenient, if you have insurance and can afford to pay up front, would be to call a private doctor for a home visit. Try the **International Medical Centre** (☎06 488 23 71; Via Firenze 47; GP call-out & treatment fee €140, 8pm-9am & weekends €200; ⏱24hr).

Pharmacies

Marked by a green cross, *farmacie* (pharmacies) open from 8.30am to 1pm and 4pm to 7.30pm Monday to Friday and on Saturday mornings. Outside these hours they open on a rotational basis, and all are legally required to post a list of places open in the vicinity.

Internet Access

You'll find several internet cafes in the area around Termini station. Most hotels have wi-fi these days, though with signals of varying quality.

Wi-fi access is available in much of central Rome courtesy of Roma Wireless (www.romawireless.com). It's free (for two hours a day) but you'll need to register the first time you use it, and to do that you'll need an Italian mobile-phone number. An easier option is to head to a cafe or bar offering free wi-fi.

Legal Matters

The most likely reason for a brush with the law is to report a theft. If you do have something stolen and you want to claim it on insurance, you must make a statement to the police, as insurance companies won't pay up without official proof of a crime.

The Italian police is divided into three main bodies: the *polizia,* who wear navy-blue jackets; the *carabinieri,* in a black uniform with a red stripe; and the grey-clad *guardia di finanza* (fiscal police). If you run into trouble, you're most likely to end up dealing with the *polizia* or *carabinieri.*

LGBT Travellers

Hardly San Fran on the Med, Rome nevertheless has a thriving, if low-key, gay scene. Close to the Colosseum, San Giovanni in Laterano has several bars dotted along it, including **Coming Out** (p181) and **My Bar** (p181).

Homosexuality is legal (over the age of 16) and even widely accepted, but Italy is notably conservative in its attitudes. In early 2016, however, the Italian parliament voted to recognise same-sex civil unions.

The main gay cultural and political organisation,

Roma Pass

A comprehensive discount card, the Roma Pass comes in two forms:

Classic Roma Pass (€36; valid for three days) Provides free admission to two museums or sites, as well as reduced entry to extra sites, unlimited city transport, and discounted entry to other exhibitions and events.

48-Hour Roma Pass (€28; valid for 48 hours) Gives free admission to one museum or site and then as per the classic pass.

Circolo Mario Mieli di Cultura Omosessuale (☑800 110611; www.mariomieli.org; Via Efeso 2a), organises debates, cultural events and social functions, including Gay Pride.

The national organisation for lesbians, **Coordinamento Lesbiche Italiano** (www.clrbp.it; Via San Francesco di Sales 1b), holds regular conferences and literary evenings.

Money

Italy's currency is the euro. The seven euro notes come in denominations of €500, €200, €100, €50, €20, €10 and €5. The euro coins are in denominations of €2 and €1, and 50, 20, 10, five, two and one cents.

ATMs

ATMs (*bancomat* in Italian) are widely available and most will accept cards tied into the Visa, MasterCard, Cirrus and Maestro systems. The daily limit for cash withdrawal is €250. Let your bank know when you

are going abroad, in case they block your card when payments from unusual locations appear.

Remember that every time you withdraw cash, your home bank charges you a foreign exchange fee (usually around 1% to 3%) as well as a transaction charge of around 1%.

Changing Money

You can change money in banks, at post offices or at a *cambio* (exchange office). There are exchange booths at Stazione Termini and at Fiumicino and Ciampino airports. In the centre, there are numerous bureaux de change, including **American Express** (☑06 6 76 41; Piazza di Spagna 38; ⏰9am-5.30pm Mon-Fri, 9am-12.30pm Sat).

Credit Cards

Credit cards are widely accepted but it's still a good idea to carry a cash backup. Virtually all midrange and top-end hotels accept cards, as do most restaurants and large shops. You can also use them to obtain cash advances at some banks. Some of the cheaper

Watch Your Valuables

Pickpockets follow the tourists, so watch out around the Colosseum, Piazza di Spagna, St Peter's Square and Stazione Termini. Be particularly vigilant around the bus stops on Via Marsala where thieves prey on travellers fresh in from Ciampino Airport. Crowded public transport is another hot spot – the 64 Vatican bus is notorious.

pensioni (guesthouses), trattorias and pizzerias accept nothing but cash.

Major cards such as Visa, MasterCard, Eurocard, Cirrus and Eurocheques are widely accepted. Amex is also recognised, although it's less common than Visa or MasterCard.

Opening Hours

Banks 8.30am to 1.30pm and 2.45pm to 4.30pm Monday to Friday

Bars & Cafes 7.30am to 8pm, sometimes until 1am or 2am

Clubs 10pm to 4am

Restaurants noon to 3pm and 7.30pm to 11pm (later in summer)

Shops 9am to 7.30pm or 10am to 8pm Monday to Saturday, some 11am to 7pm Sunday; smaller shops 9am to 1pm and 3.30pm to 7.30pm (or 4pm to 8pm) Monday to Saturday

Public Holidays

Most Romans take their annual holiday in August. Many businesses and shops close for at least part of the month, particularly around Ferragosto on 15 August.

Public holidays include the following:

Capodanno (New Year's Day) 1 January

Epifania (Epiphany) 6 January

Pasquetta (Easter Monday) March/April

Giorno della Liberazione (Liberation Day) 25 April

Festa del Lavoro (Labour Day) 1 May

Festa della Repubblica (Republic Day) 2 June

Festa dei Santi Pietro e Paolo (Feast of St Peter & St Paul) 29 June

Ferragosto (Feast of the Assumption) 15 August

Festa di Ognisanti (All Saints' Day) 1 November

Festa dell'Immacolata Concezione (Feast of the Immaculate Conception) 8 December

Natale (Christmas Day) 25 December

Festa di Santo Stefano (Boxing Day) 26 December

Safe Travel

Rome is not a dangerous city, but petty crime is a problem. Road safety is also an issue, so don't take it for granted that cars and scooters will stop at pedestrian crossings, or even at red lights.

Telephone

Domestic Calls

Rome's area code is ☎06. Area codes are an integral part of all Italian phone numbers and must be dialled even when calling locally. Mobile-phone numbers are nine or 10 digits long and begin with a three-digit prefix starting with a 3.

International Calls

To call abroad from Italy dial ☎00, then the country and area codes, followed by the telephone number.

You can Skype from most internet cafes.

Mobile Phones

Italian mobile phones operate on the GSM 900/1800 network, which is compatible with the rest of Europe and Australia but not always with the North American GSM or CDMA systems – check with your service provider.

If you can unlock your phone, it can cost as little as €10 to activate a *prepagato* (prepaid) SIM card in Italy. TIM (Telecom Italia Mobile; www.tim.it), Wind (www.wind.it) and Vodafone (www.vodafone.it) all offer SIM cards and have retail outlets across town. Note that by Italian law all SIM cards must be registered, so make sure you have a passport or

ID card with you when you buy one.

Time

Italy is in a single time zone, one hour ahead of GMT. Daylight-saving time, when clocks move forward one hour, starts on the last Sunday in March. Clocks are put back an hour on the last Sunday in October.

Italy operates on a 24-hour clock.

Toilets

There are toilets at the Colosseum, St Peter's Square, Castel Sant'Angelo and Stazione Termini (€1). Alternatively, nip into a cafe or bar, all of which are required by law to have a toilet.

Tourist Information

For phone enquiries, the Comune di Roma runs a free multilingual tourist information line (📞06 06 08).

There are tourist information points at **Fiumicino** (Terminal 3, International Arrivals; ⊙8am-7.30pm) and **Ciampino** (International Arrivals, baggage claim area; ⊙9am-6.30pm) airports, and at locations across the city:

Piazza delle Cinque Lune (⊙9.30am-7.15pm)
Stazione Termini (⊙8am-7.45pm)
Fori Imperiali (Via dei Fori Imperiali; ⊙9.30am-7pm)
Via Marco Minghetti (Via Marco Minghetti; ⊙9.30am-7.15pm)
Via Nazionale (Via Nazionale; ⊙9.30am-7.15pm)

For information about the Vatican, contact the **Centro Servizi Pellegrini e Turisti** (📞06 6988 1662; St Peter's Sq; ⊙8.30am-6pm Mon-Sat).

Useful websites include:
060608 (www.060608.it) Comprehensive information on sites, upcoming events, transport etc.
Roma Turismo (www.turismoroma.it) Rome's official tourist website with listings and up-to-date information.

Travellers with Disabilities

Cobbled streets, blocked pavements, tiny lifts and relentless traffic make Rome a difficult city for travellers with disabilities.

On metro line B all stations have wheelchair access except for Circo Massimo, Colosseo, Cavour and EUR Magliana; on line A only Cipro–Musei Vaticani and Valle Aurelia have lifts. Bus 590 covers the same route as metro line A and is wheelchair accessible. Newer buses and trams have disabled access; it's indicated on bus stops which routes are wheelchair accessible.

Contact ADR Assistance (www.adrassistance.it) for assistance at Fiumicino or Ciampino airports.

Some taxis are equipped to carry passengers in wheelchairs; ask for a taxi for a *sedia a rotelle* (wheelchair).

Visas

EU citizens do not need a visa to enter Italy. Nationals of some other countries, including Australia, Canada, Israel, Japan, New Zealand,

Practicalities

Media Vatican Radio (www.radiovaticana.org; 93.3 FM and 105 FM in Rome) is broadcast in Italian, English and other languages; RAI-1, RAI-2 and RAI-3 (www.rai.it) is the national broadcaster, running state TV and radio; and Canale 5 (www.mediaset.it/canale5), Italia 1 (www.mediaset.it/italia1), Rete 4 (www.mediaset.it/rete4) and La 7 (www.la7.it) are the main commercial stations.

Smoking Banned in enclosed public spaces, which includes restaurants, bars, shops and public transport. It's also been recently banned in Villa Borghese and all other public parks.

Weights and measures Italy uses the metric system.

Switzerland and the USA, do not need a visa for stays of up to 90 days.

Italy is one of the 15 signatories of the Schengen Convention, an agreement whereby participating countries abolished customs checks at common borders. The standard tourist visa for non-European visitors to a Schengen country is valid for 90 days; for more information see www. schengenvisainfo.com/ tourist-schengen-visa.

Women Travellers

Sexual harassment can be an issue in Rome; if you get groped, a loud 'che schifo!' (how disgusting!) will draw attention to the incident. Otherwise, women should take the usual precautions as they would in any large city, and, as in most places, avoid wandering around alone late at night, especially in the area around Termini.

Transport

Arriving in Rome

Most people arrive in Rome by plane, landing at one of its two airports: Leonardo da Vinci, better known as Fiumicino; or Ciampino, the hub for European low-cost carrier Ryanair. Flights from New York take around nine hours; from London 2¾ hours; from Sydney at least 22 hours.

As an alternative to short-haul flights, trains serve Rome's main station, Stazione Termini, from a number of European destinations, including Paris (about 15 hours), as well as cities across Italy.

Ferries serve Civitavecchia, some 80km north of the city, from a number of Mediterranean ports.

Flights, cars and tours can be booked online at lonelyplanet.com/bookings.

Leonardo da Vinci Airport

Rome's main international airport, **Leonardo da Vinci** (Fiumicino; 06 6 59 51; www. adr.it/fiumicino), is 30km west of the city. It's divided into four terminals: Terminals 1, 2 and 3 are for domestic and international flights; Terminal 5 is for American and Israeli airlines flying to the US and Israel.

Terminals 1, 2 and 3 are within easy walking distance of each other in the main airport building; Terminal 5 is accessible by shuttle bus from Terminal 3.

The easiest way to get into town is by train, but there are also buses and private shuttle services.

Train

Leonardo Express (one way €14) Runs to/from Stazione Termini. Departures from the airport every 30 minutes between 6.23am and 11.23pm; from Termini between 5.35am and 10.35pm. Journey time is 30 minutes.

FL1 (one way €8) Connects to Trastevere, Ostiense and Tiburtina stations, but not Termini. Departures from the airport every 15 minutes (half-hourly on Sunday and public holidays) between 5.57am and 10.42pm; from Tiburtina every 15 minutes between 5.46am and 7.31pm, then half-hourly until 10.02pm.

Bus

SIT (06 591 68 26; www. sitbusshuttle.it; one way €6) Regular departures from the airport to Stazione Termini (Via Marsala) from 8.30am to 11.50pm; from Termini between 5am and 8.30pm. All buses stop at the Vatican en route. Tickets are available on the bus. Journey time is approximately one hour.

Cotral (www.cotralspa.it; one way €5, if bought on the bus €7) Runs to/from Fiumicino from Stazione Tiburtina via Termini. Eight daily departures including night services from the airport at 1.15am, 2.15am, 3.30am and 5am, and from Tiburtina at 12.30am, 1.15am, 2.30am and 3.45am. Journey time is one hour.

Terravision (www.terravision.eu; one way €6, online €4) Regular services from the airport to Stazione Termini (Via Marsala) between 5.35am and 11pm; from Termini between 4.40am and 9.50pm. Allow about an hour for the journey.

Private Shuttle

Airport Connection Services
(📞06 2111 6248; www.airport-connection.it) Transfers to/from the city centre start at €35 per person.

Airport Shuttle (www.airport-shuttle.it) Transfers to/from your hotel for €13 per person for up to four passengers, then €5 for each additional passenger up to a maximum of eight.

Taxi

The set fare to/from the city centre is €48, which is valid for up to four passengers including luggage. Journey time is approximately 45 minutes to an hour depending on traffic.

Ciampino Airport

Ciampino (📞06 6 59 51; www.adr.it/ciampino), 15km southeast of the city centre, is used by Ryanair. It's not a big airport but there's a steady flow of traffic and at peak times it can get extremely busy.

To get into town, the best option is to take one of the dedicated bus services.

Bus

Terravision (www.terravision. eu; one way €6, online €4) Twice hourly departures to/from Stazione Termini (Via Marsala). From the airport, services run between 8.15am and 12.15am; from Via Marsala, between 4.30am and 9.20pm. Buy tickets at Terracafè in front of the Via Marsala bus stop. Journey time is 40 minutes.

SIT (📞06 591 68 26; www.sit-busshuttle.com; from/to airport

€4/6) Regular departures from the airport to Stazione Termini (Via Marsala) between 7.45am and 11.15pm; from Termini between 4.30am and 9.30pm. Get tickets on the bus. Journey time is 45 minutes.

Atral (www.atral-lazio.com) Runs buses to/from Anagnina metro station (€1.20) and Ciampino train station (€1.20), where you can get a train to Termini (€1.30).

Private Shuttle

Airport Shuttle (www. airportshuttle.it) Transfers to/ from your hotel for €25 for one person, then €5 for each additional passenger up to a maximum of eight.

Taxi

The set rate to/from the airport is €30. Journey time is approximately 30 minutes depending on traffic.

Termini Train Station

Almost all trains arrive at and depart from **Stazione Termini** (Piazza dei Cinque-

---

cento; 🅼 Termini), Rome's main train station and principal transport hub. There are regular connections to other European countries, all major Italian cities, and many smaller towns.

Train information is available from the Customer Service area on the main concourse to the left of the ticket desks. Alternatively, check www.trenitalia.com or phone 📞892021.

From Termini, you can connect with the metro or take a bus from Piazza dei Cinquecento out front. Taxis are outside the main entrance/exit.

Civitavecchia Port

The nearest port to Rome is at Civitavecchia, about 80km north of town. Ferries sail here from destinations across the Mediterranean, including Sicily and Sardinia. Check www.traghettiweb.it for route details and prices, and to book.

From Civitavecchia there are half-hourly trains to

Stazione Termini (€5 to €15, 40 minutes to 1¼ hours). Civitavecchia's station is about 700m from the entrance to the port.

Getting Around

Rome is a sprawling city, but the historic centre is relatively compact and it's quite possible to explore much of it on foot. The city's public transport system includes buses, trams, a metro and a suburban train system. Tickets, which come in various forms, are valid for all forms of transport.

Metro

o Rome has two main metro lines, A (orange) and B (blue), which cross at Stazione Termini. A branch line, 'B1', serves the northern suburbs, and a line C runs through the southeastern outskirts, but you're unlikely to use these.

o Trains run between 5.30am and 11.30pm (to 1.30am on Friday and Saturday).

o Take line A for the Trevi Fountain (Barberini), Spanish Steps (Spagna) and St Peter's (Ottaviano–San Pietro).

o Take line B for the Colosseum (Colosseo).

Bus & Tram

The main bus station is in front of Stazione Termini on Piazza dei Cinquecento, where there's an **information booth** (⊘7.30am-8pm). Other important hubs are at Largo di Torre Argentina and Piazza Venezia.

Buses generally run from about 5.30am until midnight, with limited services throughout the night.

Rome's night bus service comprises more than 25 lines, many of which pass Termini and/or Piazza Venezia. Buses are marked with an 'n' before the number and bus stops have a blue owl symbol. Departures are usually every 15 to 30 minutes between about 1am and 5am, but can be much slower.

The most useful routes:
n1 Follows the route of metro line A.

n2 Follows the route of metro line B.

n7 Piazzale Clodio, Piazza Cavour, Via Zanardelli, Corso del Rinascimento, Corso Vittorio Emanuele II, Largo di Torre Argentina, Piazza Venezia, Via Nazionale and Stazione Termini.

Taxi

o Official licensed taxis are white with an ID number and 'Roma Capitale' on the sides.

o Always go with the metered fare, never an arranged price (the set fares to/from the airports are exceptions).

o Official rates are posted in taxis.

o You can hail a taxi, but it's often easier to wait at a rank or phone for one. There are taxi ranks at the airports, Stazione Termini, Piazza della Repubblica, Piazza Barberini, Piazza di Spagna, the Pantheon, the Colosseum, Largo di Torre Argentina, Piazza Belli, Piazza Pio XII and Piazza del Risorgimento.

o Note that when you call for a cab, the meter is switched on straight away

---

Public Transport Tickets

Public transport tickets are valid on all of Rome's bus, tram and metro lines, except for routes to Leonardo da Vinci (Fiumicino) airport. Children under 10 travel free.

Buy tickets at *tabacchaio*, newsstands and from vending machines at main bus stops and metro stations. Tickets must be purchased before you start your journey and validated in the machines on buses, at the entrance gates to the metro, or at train stations. If you travel without a ticket you risk an on-the-spot €50 fine.

Tickets come in various forms:
BIT (*biglietto integrato a tempo;* a single ticket valid for 100 minutes and one metro ride) €1.50

Roma 24h (valid for 24 hours) €7

Roma 48h (valid for 48 hours) €12.50

Roma 72h (valid for 72 hours) €18

CIS (*carta integrata settimanale;* a weekly ticket) €24

and you pay for the cost of the journey from wherever the driver receives the call.

La Capitale (☎ 06 49 94)
Pronto Taxi (☎ 06 66 45)
Radio 3570 (☎ 06 35 70; www.3570.it)

Car & Motorcycle

Driving around Rome is not recommended. Riding a scooter or motorbike is faster and makes parking easier, but Rome is no place for learners, so if you're not an experienced rider give it a miss. Hiring a car for a day trip out of town is worth considering.

Most of Rome's historic centre is closed to unauthorised traffic from 6.30am to 6pm Monday to Friday, from 2pm to 6pm (10am to 7pm in some places) Saturday, and from 11pm to 3am Friday and Saturday. Evening restrictions also apply in Trastevere, San Lorenzo, Monti and Testaccio, typically from 9.30pm or 11pm to 3am on Friday and Saturday.

All streets accessing the 'Limited Traffic Zone' (ZTL) are monitored by electronic-access detection devices. If you're staying in this zone, contact your hotel. For further information, check www.agenziamobilita.roma.it.

Driving Licence

All EU driving licences are recognised in Italy. Holders of non-EU licences should get an International Driving Permit (IDP) to accompany their national licence. Apply to your national motoring association.

A licence is required to ride a scooter – a car licence will do for bikes up to 125cc; for anything over 125cc you'll need a motorcycle licence.

A good source of information is the **Automobile Club d'Italia** (ACI; www.aci.it), Italy's national motoring organisation.

Hire

To hire a car you'll require a driving licence (plus IDP if necessary) and credit card. Age restrictions vary but generally you'll need to be 21 or over.

Car hire is available at both Rome's airports and Stazione Termini.

Avis (☎ 199 100 133; www.avisautonoleggio.it)
Europcar (☎ 199 30 70 30; www.europcar.it)
Hertz (☎ 02 6943 0019; www.hertz.it)
Maggiore National (☎ 199 151 120; www.maggiore.it)

To hire a scooter, prices range from about €30 to €120 depending on the size of the vehicle. Reliable operators:

Bici & Baci (☎ 06 482 84 43; www.bicibaci.com; Via del Viminale 5; ⊙8am-7pm)
Eco Move Rent (☎ 06 4470 4518; www.ecomoverent.com; Via Varese 48-50; ⊙8.30am-7.30pm)

Parking

Blue lines denote pay-and-display parking – get tickets from meters (coins only) and *tabacchaio* (tobacconist's shops).

Expect to pay up to €1.20 per hour between 8am and 8pm (11pm in some places). After 8pm (or 11pm) parking is free until 8am the next morning.

Traffic wardens are vigilant and fines are not uncommon. If your car gets towed away, call ☎06 6769 2303.

Useful car parks:
Piazzale dei Partigiani (per hr €0.77; ⊙7am-11pm)
Stazione Termini (Piazza dei Cinquecento; per hr/day €2.20/18; ⊙6am-1am)
Villa Borghese (Viale del Galoppatoio 33; per hr/day €2.20/18; ⊙24hr)

Train

Apart from connections to Leonardo da Vinci airport, you'll probably only need the overground rail network if you head out of town.

○ Train information is available from the customer service area on the main concourse. Alternatively, check www.trenitalia.com or phone ☎892021.

○ Buy tickets on the main station concourse, from automated ticket machines, or from an authorised travel agency – look for an FS or *biglietti treni* sign in the window.

○ Rome's second train station is Stazione Tiburtina, four stops from Termini on metro line B. Of the capital's eight other train stations, the most important are Stazione Roma-Ostiense and Stazione Trastevere.

Language

Italian pronunciation isn't difficult as most sounds are also found in English. The pronunciation of some consonants depends on which vowel follows, but if you read our pronunciation guides below as if they were English, you'll be understood just fine. Just remember to pronounce double consonants as a longer, more forceful sound than single ones. The stressed syllables in words are in italics in our pronunciation guides.

To enhance your trip with a phrasebook, visit **lonelyplanet.com**. Lonely Planet iPhone phrasebooks are available through the Apple App store.

Basics

Hello.
Buongiorno./Ciao. (pol/inf)   bwon-*jor*-no/chow

How are you?
Come sta?   ko-me sta

I'm fine, thanks.
Bene, grazie.   be-ne *gra*-tsye

Excuse me.
Mi scusi.   mee skoo-zee

Yes./No.
Sì./No.   see/no

Please. (when asking)
Per favore.   per fa-*vo*-re

Thank you.
Grazie.   *gra*-tsye

Goodbye.
Arrivederci./Ciao. (pol/inf)   a-ree-ve-*der*-chee/chow

Do you speak English?
Parla inglese?   *par*-la een-*gle*-ze

I don't understand.
Non capisco.   non ka-*pee*-sko

How much is this?
Quanto costa?   *kwan*-to ko-sta

Accommodation

I'd like to book a room.
Vorrei prenotare   vo-*ray* pre-no-*ta*-re
una camera.   *oo*-na *ka*-me-ra

How much is it per night?
Quanto costa per   *kwan*-to *kos*-ta per
una notte?   *oo*-na *no*-te

Eating & Drinking

I'd like ..., please.
Vorrei ..., per favore.   vo-*ray* ... per fa-*vo*-re

What would you recommend?
Cosa mi consiglia?   *ko*-za mee kon-*see*-lya

That was delicious!
Era squisito!   e-ra skwee-*zee*-to

Bring the bill/check, please.
Mi porta il conto,   mee *por*-ta eel *kon*-to
per favore.   per fa-*vo*-re

I'm allergic (to peanuts).
Sono allergico/a   *so*-no a-*ler*-jee-ko/a
(alle arachidi). (m/f)   (a-le a-*ra*-kee-dee)

I don't eat ...
Non mangio ...   non *man*-jo ...

fish	*pesce*	*pe*-she
meat	*carne*	*kar*-ne
poultry	*pollame*	po-*la*-me

Emergencies

I'm ill.
Mi sento male.   mee *sen*-to *ma*-le

Help!
Aiuto!   a-*yoo*-to

Call a doctor!
Chiami un medico!   *kya*-mee oon *me*-dee-ko

Call the police!
Chiami la polizia!   *kya*-mee la po-lee-*tsee*-a

Directions

I'm looking for (a/the) ...
Cerco ...   *cher*-ko ...

bank	
la banca	la *ban*-ka
... embassy	
la ambasciata de ...	la am-ba-*sha*-ta de ...
market	
il mercato	eel mer-*ka*-to
museum	
il museo	eel moo-*ze*-o
restaurant	
un ristorante	oon rees-to-*ran*-te
toilet	
un gabinetto	oon ga-bee-*ne*-to
tourist office	
l'ufficio del turismo	loo-*fee*-cho del too-*reez*-mo

Behind the Scenes

Acknowledgements

Climate map data adapted from Peel
MC, Finlayson BL & McMahon TA (2007)
'Updated World Map of the Koppen-
Geiger Climate Classification', *Hydrology
and Earth System Sciences*, 11, 163344

Illustrations pp84–5 by Javier Martinez
Zarracina

This Book

This book was curated by Duncan Garwood and researched and written by Duncan and Abigail Blasi.
This guidebook was commissioned in Lonely Planet's Melbourne office, and produced by the following:
Destination Editor Anna Tyler
Series Designer Katherine Marsh
Cartographic Series Designer Wayne Murphy
Associate Product Director Liz Heynes
Senior Product Editor Catherine Naghten
Product Editor Kathryn Rowan
Senior Cartographer Anthony Phelan
Book Designers Virginia Moreno, Wibowo Rusli
Assisting Editors Victoria Harrison, Gabrielle Innes, Charlotte Orr, Gabrielle Stefanos
Cover Researchers Campbell McKenzie and Naomi Parker
Thanks to Indra Kilfoyle, Anne Mason, Kate Mathews, Jenna Myers, Kirsten Rawlings, Alison Ridgway, Dianne Schallmeiner, Luna Soo, Angela Tinson

Send Us Your Feedback

We love to hear from travellers – your comments keep us on our toes and help make our books better. Our well-travelled team reads every word on what you loved or loathed about this book. Although we cannot reply individually to postal submissions, we always guarantee that your feedback goes straight to the appropriate authors, in time for the next edition. Each person who sends us information is thanked in the next edition, the most useful submissions are rewarded with a selection of digital PDF chapters.

Visit lonelyplanet.com/contact to submit your updates and suggestions or to ask for help. Our award-winning website also features inspirational travel stories, news and discussions.

Note: We may edit, reproduce and incorporate your comments in Lonely Planet products such as guidebooks, websites and digital products, so let us know if you don't want your comments reproduced or your name acknowledged. For a copy of our privacy policy visit lonelyplanet.com/privacy.

Index

STACIA_S/SHUTTERSTOCK ©

Rome Maps

Centro Storico

◉ Sights

1 Area Archeologica del Teatro di Marcello e del Portico d'Ottavia....................................E8
2 Basilica di Santa Maria Sopra Minerva..E4
3 Campo de' Fiori....................................B5
4 Chiesa del Gesù E5
5 Chiesa di San Luigi dei Francesi..............C3
6 Chiesa di Sant'Agnese in Agone..............B3
7 Chiesa di Sant'Ignazio di Loyola.............E3
8 Colonna di Marco Aurelio F2
9 Fontana dei Quattro Fiumi......................B3
10 Fontana del Moro...................................B4
11 Fontana del Nettuno..............................B3
12 Fontana delle Tartarughe D7
13 Galleria Doria Pamphilj..........................F4
14 Museo Ebraico di Roma E8
15 Museo Nazionale del Palazzo Venezia..F5
16 Museo Nazionale Romano: Crypta Balbi...E6
17 Museo Nazionale Romano: Palazzo Altemps B2
18 Palazzo Chigi...F2
19 Palazzo di Montecitorio E2
20 Palazzo Farnese.....................................A6
21 Palazzo Pamphilj....................................B4
22 Palazzo Venezia.....................................F5
23 Pantheon...D3
24 Piazza Colonna......................................F2
25 Piazza Navona.......................................B3
26 Stadio di Domiziano B2
27 Teatro di Marcello..................................E8

◎ Eating

28 Antico Forno Urbani D7
29 Armando al Pantheon D3
30 Baguetteria del Fico A3
31 Campo de' Fiori......................................B5
32 Casa Bleve C4
33 Casa Coppelle D2
34 Chiostro del Bramante Caffè B2
35 Cremeria Romana D7
36 Ditirambo..B5
37 Forno di Campo de' Fiori.........................B5
38 Forno Roscioli..C6
39 Gelateria del Teatro................................A2
40 Grappolo D'Oro......................................B5
41 La Ciambella..D5
42 La Rosetta...D3
43 Nonna Betta E7

44 Osteria dell'Ingegno...............................E2
45 Pasticceria De Bellis C5
46 Piperno...D7
47 Renato e Luisa.......................................D6
48 Salumeria Roscioli C6

◎ Shopping

49 A S Roma Store......................................F2
50 Ai Monasteri..C2
51 Alberta Gloves E5
52 Aldo Fefè...D1
53 Arsenale A5
54 Bartolucci..E3
55 Borini..B7
56 Bottega Pio La Torre...............................D1
57 Confetteria Moriondo & Gariglio...............E4
58 daDADA 52...B6
59 De Sanctis E3
60 Galleria Alberto Sordi.............................F2
61 Ibiz – Artigianato in Cuoio.......................C6
62 Le Artigiane...D4
63 Le Tele di Carlotta..................................B2
64 Leone Limentani.....................................E7
65 Loco B5
66 Luna & L'Altra..B4
67 Nardecchia..B3
68 Officina Profumo Farmaceutica di Santa Maria Novella.............................C3
69 Rachele...A5
70 SBU..B4
71 Tartarughe E4
72 Tempi Moderni A4

◎ Drinking & Nightlife

73 Barnum Cafe..A4
74 Caffè Sant'Eustachio..............................C4
75 Circus...A2
76 Etablì..A3
77 Freni e Frizioni.......................................A8
78 La Casa del Caffè Tazza d'Oro D3
79 La Mescita...A8
80 L'Angolo Divino......................................B6
81 No.Au..B2
82 Open Baladin...C7
83 Salotto 42..E2

◎ Entertainment

84 Teatro Argentina....................................D5

◎ Activities, Courses & Tours

85 Roman Kitchen.......................................F4

Centro Storico

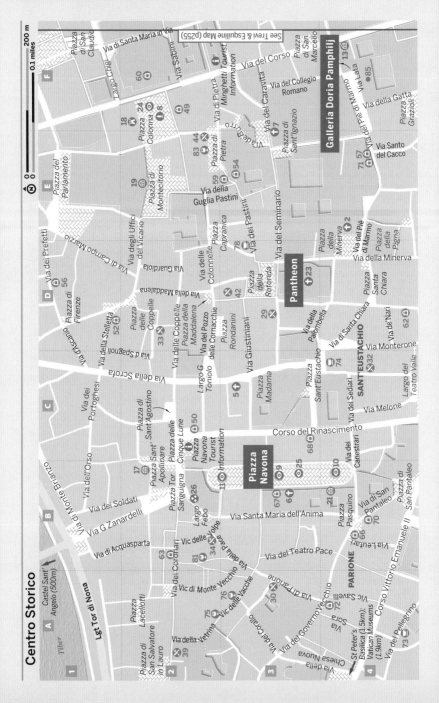

See Trevi & Esquiline Map (p255)

Galleria Doria Pamphilj

Pantheon

Piazza Navona

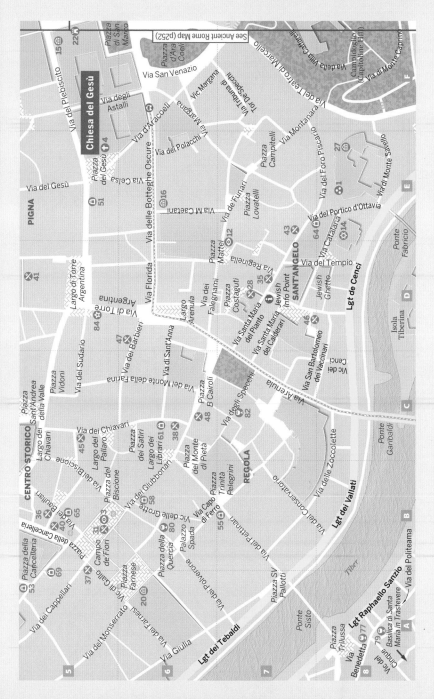

PIGNA

CENTRO STORICO

REGOLA

SANTANGELO

Chiesa del Gesù 4

(252p) paM emoR tneicnA eeS

See Ancient Rome Map (p252)

Via del Plebiscito

Piazza di San Marco

Piazza d'Ara Coeli

Via San Venazio

Via degli Astalli

Via d'Aracoeli

Via del Gesù

Via del Polacchi

Piazza del Gesù

Via Celsa

Via delle Botteghe Oscure

Via Margana

Vic Margana

Via Tribuna di Tor De'Specchi

Piazza Campitelli

Via Montanara

Via del Teatro di Marcello

Via della Villa Caffarelli

Campidoglio (Capitoline Hill)

Via di Monte Caprino

Via del Foro Piscario

Via di Monte Savello

Piazza Lovatelli

Via de Funari

Via M Caetani

Largo di Torre Argentina

Via di Torre Argentina

Largo Arenula

Via Florida

Piazza Mattei

Via Reginella

Via del Portico d'Ottavia

Via Catalana

Via del Tempio

Jewish Ghetto

Lgt de' Cenci

Ponte Fabricio

Isola Tiberina

Piazza Costaguti

Via dei Falegnami

Via Santa Maria del Pianto

Via Santa Maria dei Calderari

Jewish Info Point

Via San Bartolomeo dei Vaccinari

Vic dei Cenci

Via Arenula

Ponte Garibaldi

Via del Sudario

Via dei Barbieri

Via di Sant'Anna

Via del Monte della Farina

Piazza Vidoni

Piazza Sant'Andrea della Valle

Largo dei Chiavari

Via dei Chiavari

Via del Biscione

Largo del Pallaro

Piazza del Paradiso

Largo dei Librari

Via dei Giubbonari

Piazza del Monte di Pietà

Piazza B Cairoli

Via degli Specchi

Piazza Trinità Pellegrini

Vic Capo di Ferro

Via dei Pettinari

Via del Conservatorio

Via delle Zoccolette

Lgt dei Vallati

Ponte Sisto

Piazza della Cancelleria

Via dei Baullari

Via del Biscione

Campo de' Fiori

Piazza del Biscione

Piazza della Quercia

Palazzo Spada

Piazza Farnese

Piazza della Cancelleria

Via dei Cappellari

Vic del Gallo

Vic dei Venti

Piazza SV Pallotti

Via del Polverone

Lgt del Tebaldi

Via del Pettinari

Via Giulia

Via di Monserrato

Via dei Farnesi

Tiber

Piazza Trilussa

Via del Cinque

Via Benedetta

Basilica di Santa Maria in Trastevere

Via Raphaello Sanzio

Via del Politeama

Lgt Raphaello Sanzio

Ancient Rome

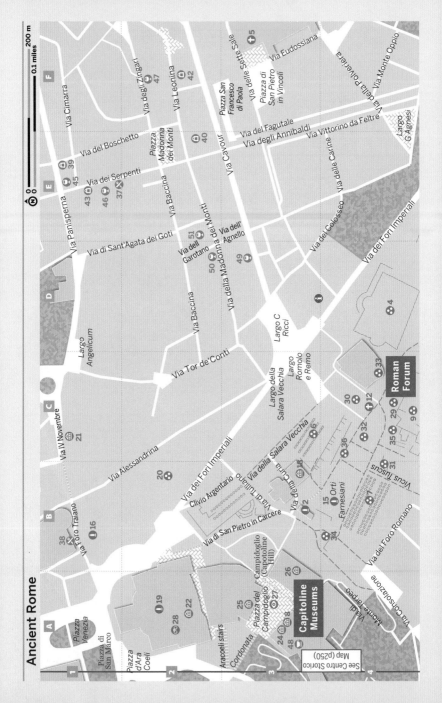

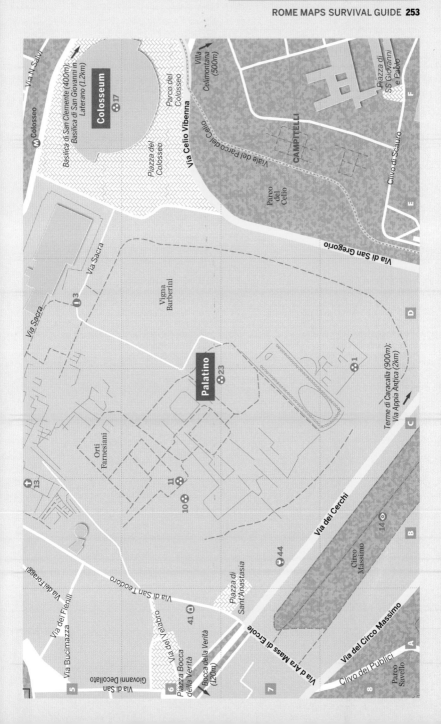

Colosseum ⊙17

Basilica di San Clemente (400m);
Basilica di San Giovanni in
Laterano (1.2km)

Ⓜ Colosseo

Via N Salvi

Parco del
Colosseo

Piazza del
Colosseo

Villa
Celimontana
(500m)

Via Celio Vibenna

Viale del Parco del Celio

Piazza di
SS Giovanni
e Paolo

CAMPITELLI

Parco
del
Celio

Clivo di Scauro

Via di San Gregorio

Vigna
Barberini

Via Sacra

🚊3

Via Sacra

Palatino ⊙23

Orti
Farnesiani

⊙1

Terme di Caracalla (900m);
Via Appia Antica (2km)

✚13

⊙11

10⊙

⊙44

Via dei Cerchi

14 ⊙

Circo
Massimo

Via del Foraggi

Via dei Fienili

Via Bucimazza

Via di San Teodoro

Via del Velabro

Piazza di
Sant'Anastasia

41 ◉

Via d Ara Mass di Ercole

Via del Circo Massimo

Clivo dei Publici

Via di San
Giovanni Decollato

Piazza Bocca
della Verità

Bocca della Verità
(120m)

Parco
Savello

Ancient Rome

Trevi & Esquiline

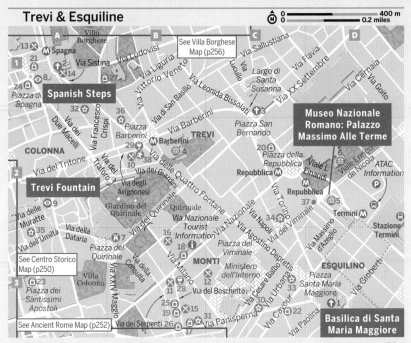

Sights
1 Basilica di Santa Maria Maggiore	D3
2 Chiesa della Trinità dei Monti	A1
3 Chiesa di Santa Maria della Vittoria	C1
4 Galleria Nazionale d'Arte Antica:	
Palazzo Barberini	B2
Keats–Shelley House	(see 8)
5 Museo Nazionale Romano: Palazzo	
Massimo alle Terme	D2
6 Museo Nazionale Romano: Terme	
di Diocleziano	D2
7 Palazzo del Quirinale	B3
8 Piazza di Spagna & the Spanish	
Steps	A1
9 Trevi Fountain	A2

Eating
10 Colline Emiliane	B2
11 Da Valentino	B3
12 Doozo	C3
13 Gina	A1
14 Imàgo	A1
15 L'Asino d'Oro	B3
16 Open Colonna	B3

Shopping
17 Abito	B3

18 Arion Esposizioni	B3
19 Creje	B3
20 Feltrinelli International	C2
21 Furla	A1
22 Giacomo Santini	C3
23 Lucia Odescalchi	A3
24 Sermoneta	A1
25 Spot	B3
26 Tina Sondergaard	B3
27 Underground	A1

Drinking & Nightlife
28 La Barrique	B3
29 Micca Club	B2

Entertainment
30 Blackmarket	C3
31 Charity Café	B3
32 Gregory's	A1
33 Orbis	C3
34 Teatro dell'Opera di Roma	C2
35 Teatro Quirino	A3
36 Teatro Sistina	B2

Activities, Courses & Tours
37 Bici & Baci	D2
38 Kami Spa	B2

Villa Borghese

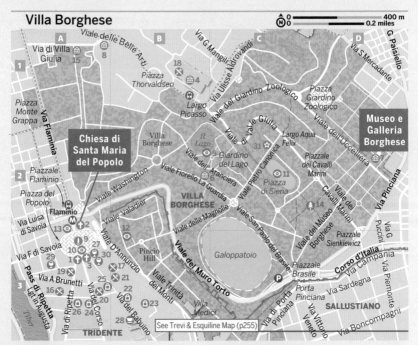

Symbols & Map Key

Look for these symbols to quickly identify listings:

Sights
Activities
Courses
Tours
Festivals & Events

- Eating
- Drinking
- Entertainment
- Shopping
- Information & Transport

These symbols and abbreviations give vital information for each listing:

Sustainable or green recommendation

FREE No payment required

- Telephone number
- Opening hours
- Parking
- Nonsmoking
- Air-conditioning
- Internet access
- Wi-fi access
- Swimming pool
- Bus
- Ferry
- Tram
- Train
- English-language menu
- Vegetarian selection
- Family-friendly

Find your best experiences with these Great For... icons.

- Budget
- Food & Drink
- Drinking
- Cycling
- Shopping
- Sport
- Art & Culture
- Events
- Photo Op
- Scenery
- Family Travel
- Short Trip
- Detour
- Walking
- Local Life
- History
- Entertainment
- Beaches
- Winter Travel
- Cafe/Coffee
- Nature & Wildlife

Sights

- Beach
- Bird Sanctuary
- Buddhist
- Castle/Palace
- Christian
- Confucian
- Hindu
- Islamic
- Jain
- Jewish
- Monument
- Museum/Gallery/Historic Building
- Ruin
- Shinto
- Sikh
- Taoist
- Winery/Vineyard
- Zoo/Wildlife Sanctuary
- Other Sight

Points of Interest

- Bodysurfing
- Camping
- Cafe
- Canoeing/Kayaking
- Course/Tour
- Diving
- Drinking & Nightlife
- Eating
- Entertainment
- Sento Hot Baths/Onsen
- Shopping
- Skiing
- Sleeping
- Snorkelling
- Surfing
- Swimming/Pool
- Walking
- Windsurfing
- Other Activity

Information

- Bank
- Embassy/Consulate
- Hospital/Medical
- Internet
- Police
- Post Office
- Telephone
- Toilet
- Tourist Information
- Other Information

Geographic

- Beach
- Gate
- Hut/Shelter
- Lighthouse
- Lookout
- Mountain/Volcano
- Oasis
- Park
- Pass
- Picnic Area
- Waterfall

Transport

- Airport
- BART station
- Border crossing
- Boston T station
- Bus
- Cable car/Funicular
- Cycling
- Ferry
- Metro/MRT station
- Monorail
- Parking
- Petrol station
- Subway/S-Bahn/Skytrain station
- Taxi
- Train station/Railway
- Tram
- Tube Station
- Underground/U-Bahn station
- Other Transport

Our Story

A beat-up old car, a few dollars in the pocket and a sense of adventure. In 1972 that's all Tony and Maureen Wheeler needed for the trip of a lifetime – across Europe and Asia overland to Australia. It took several months, and at the end – broke but inspired – they sat at their kitchen table writing and stapling together their first travel guide, *Across Asia on the Cheap*. Within a week they'd sold 1500 copies. Lonely Planet was born.

Today, Lonely Planet has offices in Dublin, Melbourne, London, Oakland, Franklin, Delhi and Beijing, with more than 600 staff and writers. We share Tony's belief that 'a great guidebook should do three things: inform, educate and amuse'.

Our Writers

Duncan Garwood

A Brit travel writer based in the Castelli Romani hills just outside Rome, Duncan moved to the Italian capital just in time to see the new millennium in at the Colosseum. He has since clocked up endless kilometres walking around his adopted hometown and exploring the far-flung reaches of the surrounding Lazio region. He has worked on the past six editions of the *Rome* city guide as well as previous editions of the *Pocket Rome* guide and a whole host of LP Italy publications. He has also written on Italy for newspapers and magazines.

Abigail Blasi

Abigail moved to Rome in 2003 and lived there for three years, got married alongside Lago Bracciano and her first son was born in Rome. Nowadays she divides her time between Rome, Puglia and London. She has worked on four editions of Lonely Planet's Italy and Rome guides, and co-wrote the first edition of *Puglia & Basilicata*. She also regularly writes on Italy for various publications, including the *Independent*, the *Guardian*, and *Lonely Planet Traveller*.

STAY IN TOUCH LONELYPLANET.COM/CONTACT

EUROPE Unit E, Digital Court, The Digital Hub, Rainsford St, Dublin 8, Ireland

AUSTRALIA Levels 2 & 3 551 Swanston St, Carlton, Victoria 3053
03 8379 8000, fax 03 8379 8111

USA 150 Linden Street, Oakland, CA 94607
510 250 6400, toll free 800 275 8555, fax 510 893 8572

UK 240 Blackfriars Road, London SE1 8NW
020 3771 5100, fax 020 3771 5101

 twitter.com/lonelyplanet   facebook.com/lonelyplanet   instagram.com/lonelyplanet   youtube.com/lonelyplanet   lonelyplanet.com/newsletter